Last of the
Ten Fighter
Boys

Last of the Ten Fighter Boys

JIMMY CORBIN

SUTTON PUBLISHING

First published in the United Kingdom in 2007 by
Sutton Publishing, an imprint of NPI Media Group Limited
Cirencester Road · Chalford · Stroud · Gloucestershire · GL6 8PE

British Library Cataloguing in Publication Data
A catalogue record for this book is available from the British Library.

Hardback ISBN 978-0-7509-4805-0
Paperback ISBN 978-0-7509-4806-7

Typeset in Photina MT.
Typesetting and origination by
NPI Media Group Limited.
Printed and bound in England.

To my darling wife Jeanne,
who has put up with me and my selfish ways,
and to my three children,
Brian, Anne and Margot

CONTENTS

LIST OF ILLUSTRATIONS

ACKNOWLEDGEMENTS

As I sit in front of my log fire reflecting on my life and nursing a glass of whisky (purely for medicinal reasons) I realise how lucky I have been. Lucky to have been born into a loving family who gave me every chance to succeed. Lucky to have survived the war and to have met so many fantastic people during my years of service. Lucky to have lived life to the full and to have made friends who have lasted a lifetime. Very lucky to have met my wife Jeanne who has been so marvellous to me over the years and together we have been lucky to raise three fantastic children. Lucky to now have five wonderful grandchildren. It is to my wife, Jeanne, my children, Brian, Anne and Margot, and my grandchildren, Megan, Thomas, Andrew, Daniel and Emma, to whom this book is dedicated, together with the memory of so many wonderful friends, many of whom are now lost to us, from my period of service during the Second World War.

I am also indebted to Tina, a young and exciting writer who has held my hand, quite literally at times, through the whole process of creating this book and to her a big heartfelt thank you. Through her patience and her tolerant and warm personality she managed to draw out long-forgotten memories.

I raise my glass to my family, whom I love, and to Tina in thanks.

What was the war to me? A period during which I was at times bloody scared and just happy to survive.

PROLOGUE –
TEN FIGHTER BOYS

In September 1939 Britain declared war on Germany. By July the following year the fighting had begun in earnest. For four long months, the
German Air Force, the Luftwaffe, sent hundreds of bombers and fighter
planes to attack Britain's shores to wipe out her air defences in preparation
for a full-scale land invasion. Day after day hordes of enemy aircraft crossed
the Channel in their quest to obliterate the RAF's airbases and render them
useless. But, it wasn't to be. Although heavily outnumbered by the Luftwaffe, the Royal Air Force fought hard to prevent the Germans taking
control of the air. By November 1940, the fighter-boys had triumphed and,
unable to penetrate Britain's air defences, the Germans shelved plans to
invade the island. The Battle of Britain was over, but the war was just
beginning.

It was against this backdrop that I was first asked to record my
experiences as a young Spitfire pilot fighting in the Battle of Britain. But my
brief dalliance with writing came about quite by chance.

It was a typically grey winter's day and the Spitfire pilots of 66 Squadron, including myself, had safely returned from a sortie and were gathered in the dispersal room at Biggin Hill aerodrome. Conversation ebbed and flowed as it always did and turned rather optimistically towards what we would all do after the war had ended and we went our separate ways.

For me the dye was cast. As a trained teacher I would exchange the battlefields for the classroom, if I survived the war. One of the other pilots, I can't recall who, spoke about his plans to take some Spitfires or 'kites' as we called them to the United States where he would stage mock dogfights for the paying public.

Squadron Leader (Sqn Ldr) Athol Forbes joined the conversation. He had always wanted to be a writer and he had decided that when the war finished he would record about his experiences of leading 66 Squadron during the Battle of Britain, just as many of the flying aces of the Great War had done twenty years previously.

Suddenly our skipper had a brainwave. Instead of waiting until war was over, he suggested that we should all write down then and there what it was like to be a Spitfire pilot living through one of the greatest aerial battles of all time. We all agreed because he was our commanding officer after all, but, in truth, I thought nothing more of it.

The following day Sqn Ldr Forbes put his ideas into action and selected a number of pilots to take part in the project. His choice included a disparate mix of pilot officers and sergeant pilots from all different backgrounds. There were dockhands, clerks, mechanics and teachers, but at that time we all shared the same profession – Spitfire pilot.

In between flying sorties against the Germans, the pilots began to scribble down their thoughts on what it was like to face the daily onslaught of the German air force in an aerial war that had possessed enough military significance for Winston Churchill to refer to it as the Battle of Britain. They wrote about what it was like to have a Messerschmitt Me109 locked onto your tail, what it was like to be shot down or to be forced to bale out. They wrote about what it felt like to shoot down your first enemy aircraft and watch it explode in front of you or spiral earthwards to its doom trailing a plume of black smoke.

The third chapter was written by me, Sergeant (Sgt) Jimmy Corbin, also known as Binder, which was RAF slang for someone who moans a lot – a charge I will counter later on in this book. I don't know why Athol Forbes chose me. Maybe he decided that as a sergeant pilot (a third of the Battle of Britain pilots were sergeants) and not an officer, my experiences of the RAF and the Battle were different from those of the others.

Whatever the reason, in November 1940 when I was asked to contribute, I was just 23 years of age, old by pilot standards, and I was based along with the rest of 66 Squadron at Biggin Hill in Kent. Despite my mature years, I was still a sprog, as we were affectionately known in RAF circles, and I struggled to know what to write. My combat experience was limited, compared to the other pilots who had seen action over Dunkirk as well as the Battle of Britain. Many of them had already been decorated with the Distinguished Flying Cross for their heroic exploits. But for me the war had yet to fully unfold.

In the end my chapter waxed lyrical on what I knew, which at that stage were my experiences at flying training school, my early encounters with the enemy and my desire to 'get up there' with the others and shoot down some Hun. In truth, despite all the brave words, I just wanted to survive. We all did. I am not a religious man, but I prayed for good fortune and held on to the hope that a healthy dose of self-preservation would carry me safely through the dogfights, the convoy patrols, the unexpected encounters with a rogue Me109, enemy flak from escorting our own bombers and even the friendly fire.

The book was published in 1942 by Collins. By then luck had already run out for five of its original contributors who were killed before it even came off the printer's press. How many copies it sold, I have no idea, but it certainly didn't win any literary prize, that was for sure.

Anyway, that is the story of how *Ten Fighter Boys* got written. It should have been my first and last venture into the literary world until my family decided that too much of my own story remained untold. Now, at the age of 89, they have coaxed and cajoled me into putting pen to paper once again. So here, in an effort to silence them, is the next instalment, so to speak, of Sgt Jimmy Corbin, Spitfire pilot.

Last of the Ten Fighter Boys is intended to be both a prequel and a sequel to the chapter I supplied for *Ten Fighter Boys*. This book charts my early life before the outbreak of war in 1939 and the decisions that I made and those that were made for me that landed me in the thick of the action in the skies over Kent in the summer and autumn of 1940. I have tried to explain as best I can how an ordinary working-class boy from Maidstone was propelled into the most extraordinary of situations.

And, of course, it also concludes the story of that naive 23-year-old fighter pilot who wrote in November 1940: 'Up to the present my flying experiences have been far from glorious, and the many hoped for victories seem far distant, but perhaps before long I shall be able to acquit myself satisfactorily.'

Whether I achieved my aim and did indeed 'acquit myself satisfactorily' is for you to decide.

W.J. Corbin
Maidstone, Kent
2007

PART ONE

THE
Battle of Britain

Chapter One

1929 – MAIDSTONE, KENT

I leaned against the deep sink and watched my mother studying thick slices of bread toasting under the grill. I wondered when would be the right time to ask.

It was early morning and a fire was already crackling in the concrete fireplace in the corner of the scullery, tasked with heating the huge copper saucepan with a wooden lid containing 5 gallons of water, suspended above it in readiness for my mother and sisters to begin washing the dirty laundry. This was the first stage of a lengthy and arduous process which as a boy I never had to endure. It took three days to complete, only for the whole tedious ritual to be repeated several days later. But I didn't skip household chores entirely. The copper was the only supply of hot water in the house and on Sundays I would be called upon to help bale the water from the pan into a bucket and lug it upstairs to my bedroom which was also the bathroom. My father had rather cleverly constructed a rectangular wooden frame with metal springs with a thin mattress on top. This was attached to the wall above a cast iron bath, complete with claw feet, by two hinges. It meant my bed could be lifted and lowered depending on whether the bath was in use or not. Hauling buckets of water up the narrow staircase and through my sisters' room into mine without spilling a drop was back-breaking work, but it was a far better arrangement than unhooking the lozenge tin bath that hung up in the back yard and dragging it into scullery like other families had to do.

Next to the copper, a row of cupboards occupied the wall of the small low-ceilinged scullery as we referred to it. One of these had a fine mesh tacked onto the front of it and acted as a meat safe where my mother would place the Sunday joint which, if we were lucky, would be 10lb of moist Argentinean sirloin steak purchased from Fletcher's, the butchers at the bottom of the road. I had no idea where Argentina was, but my dad said it took three weeks for the meat to be shipped to England and by that time it was cured to perfection. And he was right, it was delicious, which is just as well as it would have to feed us for the next four days as my mother reinvented it into various different dishes before ending up on Wednesday as beef hash. Nothing went to waste.

In another corner of the room, on the coldest of the uneven patch-work of grey flagstones, and there were many to choose from, stood a jug of creamy thick milk full to brim. Sweet with freshness, the milk had been delivered shortly after dawn.

As I slept soundly in my bed, my mother's alarm call came in the form of the clip-clopping of the horse's hooves as it pulled the milk cart up our street. Within minutes of the cart stopping, an orderly queue of women-folk wrapped tightly in their knitted shawls and clasping a range of large ceramic jugs would form behind it. Pleasantries would be exchanged as they shuffled forward until their turn came for the milkman to ladle the milk directly into the assortment of receptacles from the huge metal milk churns on the back of the cart, with not a drop split. The cold stone slab would ensure its freshness until well into the evening.

My mother removed the grill pan and turned the bread over. I waited impatiently for her response. Daisy Lizzie was her name and she was a local Kent girl from Yalding, just 8 miles from Maidstone where my family now lived. She left school at 12 and married my father in 1905 when she was 23 years old.

Dark, slightly wavy hair framed her face and bright, round eyes and she was quite tiny at just 5ft 1in. Her slight figure gave her an outward appearance of frailty, which belied an inner strength. She was a very kind and gentle lady who worked tirelessly to keep us altogether in what were difficult times for working-class families like ours.

I was always much closer to her than to my father, possibly because I was the youngest child and the only boy and so naturally spoilt for attention from her and, for that matter, my three sisters.

Twelve-year-old boys are not noted for their patience and I could wait no longer.

'Well, can I go then?' I enquired.

She looked at me and smiled.

'Ask your father,' came her reply.

I sloped off to the next room where my father and three sisters were finishing breakfast which I had already bolted down with my usual enthusiasm. I slipped back into my seat, next to my youngest sister Lily, and pondered my next move.

My father, who occupied the head of the table, was tucking into a pile of slab-like toast covered in a thick layer of shiny beef dripping much to the distaste of Daisy, my second sister, who was sitting to his left and constantly complained about her food, especially dripping which was the mainstay of our diets. It was kept in a large pot, along with two others, on the sideboard in the kitchen. The other pots contained pork and mutton dripping and we would help ourselves to whichever one took our fancy, although we didn't mix the three as they tasted quite different. It was normally accompanied by large chunks of hot fresh bread which were also in ample supply as the first of three deliveries that day had already taken place. As a family of six we consumed a lot of bread.

Elsie was already discussing her plans for the day. At 22 she was the eldest of the Corbin children and worked at the Alabaster Passmore Printing firm, but, as it was Saturday, she would only be working until lunchtime and the afternoon would be her own. She was courting John, who had joined the navy as a boy sailor at 14, and was now based at the nearby Chatham docks and often visited our house where the couple were allowed to sit in the front parlour, reserved for special occasions, under the watchful eye of my parents.

'I've invited John for tea. He'll be here at four. I finish work at twelve so I'll get back in plenty of time.'

'Just let your mother know,' my father said before turning unexpectedly to me, 'and what plans have you got today, Jimmy?'

Here was my chance. I wouldn't ask for my father's permission, less he say no, but simply tender a statement of intent. After all I was 12 and old enough to know my own mind.

'I'm going to see Sir Alan Cobham's Flying Circus today. He's meant to be coming to Maidstone today.'

Sir Alan Cobham was a hero of mine. Although I had never met him I had read all about him and his daring air displays. He put on air-shows for a living and even took his flying circus as far afield as South Africa and now he was coming to Maidstone. It was an opportunity I was not prepared to pass up. There was no reason for my father to object to my decision, unless he had already allocated my free time to help him in his workshop at the bottom of the back yard.

'Are you now?' came my father's reply and silence descended again as he ripped off a piece of bread and began to chew on it as he mulled the statement over.

It was my sister Elsie who spoke next.

'Who's Sir Alan Cobham when he's at home, Jimmy?'

Everyone called me Jimmy, although my name is William, but an Aunt of mine insisted on shortening it and calling me Willie to which I objected so strongly because of its association with a certain appendage that I began to answer only to the name Jimmy. Stubbornness was a characteristic of mine, even then.

'He's a pilot, he flies aeroplanes,' I replied. I could have gone on, but I sensed I was in the presence of a less than appreciative audience when it came to aviation.

Elsie smiled indulgently at me.

'It sounds fun, Jimmy.'

I smiled at Elsie who winked back at me. I knew she would be on my side. My sisters were much older than me and while all three of them tended to indulge me with fondness and affection, Elsie was always my favourite. We were divided by a decade, but we got on immensely well and I admired her greatly. She was smart and possessed a lively mind, and her vocabulary was formidable, but she left school at 14 and entered a role more suited to the station of a young working-class woman in the 1920s rather than one that reflected her intellectual capacity. Had she been born in a different era, I have no doubt she would have gone on to university and achieved academic success. But this was 1929 and Elsie was just grateful to have found employment. So she took up a position at the local printers where she would fetch and carry for the other employees.

But now it was Daisy's turn to chip into the conversation.

'I don't see what's so interesting about an aeroplane.'

Daisy was seven years my senior. I didn't get on quite so well with her as I did Elsie. Her fussiness over food always irked me. Dad and I often teased her about it. But Daisy was talented in her own way and such a brilliant seamstress that when she left school she was quickly apprenticed to an upmarket tailors' in Maidstone where she worked as a skilled shirt maker. Her indifference towards my schoolboy passion for aeroplanes was shared by the family.

I looked to Lily for support, but she was absorbed in her breakfast. She was just three years older than me and a nice kid. On wet days, Lily was often my table-tennis partner.

I ignored Daisy's comments and grabbed the opportunity created by Elsie to argue my case to attend the air show.

'Yes, and it won't cost anything. It's free to just go and watch.'

I directed my comment to all those present, including my mother who had now rejoined us at the opposite end of the table from my father. She kept her counsel.

'Where is it, Jimmy?' Elsie continued.

'Not far. Just off the Sutton Road. It will be starting soon.'

Still my father said nothing. At 5ft 9in, my father was also quite short, but he was broad-shouldered and thick set and what he lacked in stature he more than made up for in physical strength. He was reputed to be one of the strongest men in Maidstone, a reputation borne out of a series of wagers he and his friends devised between themselves over a pint in the pub. On one occasion, I listened in awe as he told me of the time, carrying a hundred and three-quarters weight of lead, he scaled the Style and Winch brewery in Maidstone which is 80ft high, using a series of ladders.

Although, he was the son of a butcher from Ramsgate, a seaside resort on the east coast of Kent 40 miles from Maidstone, Walter Corbin declined to enter the family butcher's business, and became a contracting plumber instead. Formal education was a privilege my father was unable to enjoy, but he was a very clever man and a truly skilled craftsman. Later in 1937, he became the only plumber to be employed to work on the new Detling aerodrome in Kent. The aerodrome needed a number of sinks in their photographic laboratories and my father was the only man around who had the skill to beat sinks individually out of one sheet of lead.

He was good at what he did which meant that although money was tight, we were better off than most. My father worked hard and played hard, so we always had money, although it never seemed to last long. He always charged what he termed 'London' rates. He would charge any-where from 1s 3d an hour to a top rate of 1s 6d an hour for his services. He was skilled enough to always be in demand and he would take on contracts for local estates as these were the most lucrative. In time he came to employ three other men.

With his strength and abilities he was an imposing presence in the household and I was more frightened of him than anyone else. He was terrifying when he was angry and, even in his calmer moments, he was a tough disciplinarian who ruled his household absolutely. Having said that, I can never recall being beaten by him, although he did chase me once and had he caught me I may well have received a thrashing, but I outran him and, thankfully, I never found out. As a result, my relationship with my father wasn't a close one when I was young. It wasn't until I was older that I grew to respect him and then to like him. But that was much later on. Right now I was a 12-year-old boy standing anxiously before him as he considered my request.

He swallowed the mouthful of bread and dripping and looked up at me and said simply, 'What d'you want to go looking at aeroplanes for?'

I shrugged and look down at my empty plate. Words deserted me.

'I just do.'

'All right Jimmy. You can go. You might be needing this, though.'

He dug into his pocket and pulled out a threepenny bit and handed it to me.

'Thanks Dad.'

And with that he returned to his meal. That summed up my father's attitude to aviation. He couldn't understand what all the fuss was about. Flying never held the same fascination for him as it did for me, but neither did he ever try and stop me from pursuing my own passion to become a pilot for which I am grateful. Back then he probably thought it was just youthful imagination, something that I would grow out of when age and reality overtook me and I came to realise that working-class boys from Maidstone didn't fly aeroplanes for a living. But for the moment I didn't care, those few words from my father were all the encouragement I needed to hear. I ran out of the dining room into the narrow hall and out through the front door before he could change his mind.

As I left my mother called out to me.

'Don't be late Jimmy, it's soup for lunch,' and with that my mother secured my prompt return with promises of her delicious marrowbone soup. She made this from the leg bones of various cattle which were stewed for hours on the gas grill my father constructed for her in his workshop at the end of the garden.

'Okay,' I shouted back at her as I stepped out into the street and walked down its sloping pavement towards the main road. Our house in Bower Street was one of a row of narrow terraced houses in Maidstone which were built at the end of the 19th century.

Few people owned their own property at that time and we were no exception. My father rented our house from Sharp's, the sweet-makers, who owned the whole street. The Sharp's toffee and sweet factory provided employment for many of those who lived in Bower Street and was situated on the bank of the River Medway in Maidstone. Every week a knock on the door announced the arrival of the rent man who would demand the sum of 9s 6d, until 1955 when I bought the house and the rent man came no more. Those who couldn't scrape together the exact amount lost the right to remain in their home.

On the corner of Bower Street and the Tonbridge Road stood two shops, Fletcher's and Ashby's, the grocers, which supplied all our needs and gave our mothers little reason to venture beyond the street's boundaries.

It was a fine morning and some doors to the houses were already standing open as neighbours wandered in and out of each other's homes with impunity. Doorsteps were already being vigorously scrubbed or were filled with mothers taking time out from their chores to chat to a friend or to the frequent delivery men.

Several young children sat on the pavements clutching their knees, immersed in their own worlds. Girls in smocks skipped up and down the tarmac road.

It was a normal everyday scene which at the time we thought would last for ever. There were thousands of Bower Streets in Britain in the 1920s and 1930s. Community spirit was a phrase that hadn't even been coined then, but it coursed through our veins.

As I tripped down the road, I looked to my left and saw a spirited game of football was already in play at the top of Bower Street. This had long since been identified as the best place for us to kick a ball around as a wall ran perpendicular to the street. It enclosed an orchard, the gates to which provided us with perfect goalposts. I glimpsed Ginger, our Manx cat, disappearing over the wall. Earlier in the week, he had turned up on our doorstep with a chicken in his mouth which we deduced must have come from the orchard. We did the decent thing and ate it.

One of the younger boys was positioned on the corner of Bower Street and Tonbridge Road with strict orders to watch out for the local copper who patrolled the area as often as four times a day. This was in the hope of catching us committing the heinous crime of playing football in the street which was illegal back then. But we were always too quick for him. When the look-out gave the signal we scattered in different directions and headed towards Cornwallis playground. He never caught us.

The boys on my street were an odd assortment. Those with fathers in employment, such as myself, were fairly well clad, but for others life was less kind and it showed. Football was played in shoes that had worn through. Their short trousers had been repaired so often they were threadbare and in some cases, boys' arses literally hung out of the back of them.

One of the Craddock boys who lived a couple of doors away, spotted me and called out to me to join in their game. Normally I would gladly have done so, especially as Elsie had just bought me my first pair of football boots, but today was different. Today I was going to watch a person flying an aeroplane.

I hurried along the street, barely able to contain my excitement and my curiosity at seeing an aeroplane for the first time in my life. Once on the main road, I jumped onto the tramway, gave the conductor my three-penny bit and climbed the stairs to the top deck. The tram made its way towards Sutton Road where it would terminate at the Mangravet estate, just a short distance from the field where Sir Alan Cobham would set his flying machine down.

Like many boys of my age, I was fed on a rich diet of books and magazines detailing the exploits of the First World War flying aces. I knew them all. I revelled in men like Albert Ball who took on the German planes single-handedly. He would get beneath the enemy so he could tilt his wing-mounted Lewis gun upwards and shoot them down. By the time he died at 20 he had been awarded the Victoria Cross (VC), Military Cross (MC) and Croix de Guerre (CdeG).

Then there was Billy Bishop, a Canadian who had an outstanding ability to see the enemy before they saw him. His magnificent eyesight, the relevance of which I was only to appreciate fully much later in my life, enabled him to shoot down twenty-five planes in just twelve days. He was awarded the Distinguished Flying Cross (DFC) for his bravery. I didn't know what a DFC was then, but it sounded impressive. In 1917, Bishop also bagged the VC when he single-handedly attacked a German aerodrome near Vimy Ridge in Northern France. Most famous of all was von Richtofen, the German pilot, otherwise known as the Red Baron or the 'ace of aces'. He shot down an incredible eighty British aircraft before he was killed himself in 1918.

These pilots were bathed in bravery and glamour. They were few in number, but special in their achievements. Stories of their heroism easily captured the young mind of a working-class boy from Maidstone and helped nurture his ambition to become a pilot one day.

I got off the tramway and ran the last half mile to the field where the display was due to take place. I arrived breathless with anticipation and, to my surprise, a large crowd had already gathered in the field to await Sir Alan's arrival. My family's indifference to flying clearly was not replicated throughout Maidstone. I took my place on the edge of the group and waited.

We heard it long before we saw it. It began as a faint low buzz in the distant sky. A voice from the back dismissed it as an insect. But the drone grew louder and more insistent and we knew it was near.

Murmurs of excitement rippled through the crowd. We looked up and scoured the clear skies, eager to claim first sight of it. It occurred to me that we must have presented a strange sight ourselves. Eighty-odd people stood in the corner of a grassy field near Maidstone squinting up at the heavens.

Suddenly, the buzzing contraption broke cover and appeared over the hedges on the far side of the field.

'There it is,' a triumphant cry went up.

'Where?' shouted someone else.

'There!' came a chorus of replies.

'That's a crow.'

'Not there, you fool, there.'

'I see it! I see it!'

And sure enough, in the distance, several hundred feet up in the air was a small dot moving doggedly towards us. It was a glorious Gloster Gamecock, otherwise known as an aeroplane. The craft flew past the crowd at the great speed of 80mph. The pilot, clad in a brown leather helmet, gloves and goggles, leaned over the side of cockpit. He grinned and waved coolly to those of us assembled below. Then he turned around and whizzed over our heads once again, completing a second circuit for good measure before attempting to land. As the aeroplane approached the field, the machine seemed to suddenly lose speed and flop gracelessly onto the ground. Its wings bounced alarmingly as it bumped along the uneven surface of the field. The long grass whipped its wheels and frame until it came to a halt just in front of a cheering crowd and the propeller stopped turning.

It was my first encounter with an aeroplane and, as a keen student of aviation, I studied every inch of the aircraft's neat, fragile wooden frame. The biplane was bright purple and about 20ft in length. It looked smaller and more strangely vulnerable on the ground than in the air. But what I really remember about the occasion, and what the books had never been able to convey, was the thick oily aroma of Castrol that emanated from the aircraft's engine. It was a pungent, but not unpleasant odour that I had never experienced before. I decided that I quite liked it, which is just as well because it was a smell that my senses would become very accustomed to.

This first plane was joined by six or seven more aeroplanes, some of which pre-dated the Gamecock which was manufactured in 1925 and had probably seen action in the First World War before retiring to the relative safety of the air circus.

When they were all in position, the air show began. It was a revelation to me. I had never witnessed anything like it.

At one point a group of clowns drove across the field in a Model-T Ford motor car. They careered and swerved over the rough ground, trying to dodge the flour bombs that were being thrown at them from one of the aeroplanes that swooped down low above their heads. I watched agog as the pilot leaned out of his cockpit and lobbed the small bags at the car below him before climbing away again.

One of the other pilots who was stunting in a Gamecock performed what I now know was a very dangerous stunt. He dived down low in front of the crowd and, to my horror, he looked like he was going to crash straight into the ground, but he pulled up just in time and the aircraft levelled out. Then one of his wings tilted slightly to one side. On the wingtip was a piece of wire which the pilot used to hook a handkerchief that had been placed on the ground. The crowd gasped and clapped their appreciation. It was a phenomenal stunt that required incredible skill.

Nothing could rival Sir Alan's show for its daring displays of aerobatics, wing-walking, diving and looping the loop. I had never seen anything like it before and it left a deep impression on me and many of my contemporaries. Years later, as pilots serving in the RAF, many of us would recall with affection the day we went to watch Sir Alan Cobham's Flying Circus. For some, it was the day they decided to become a pilot.

I watched the display in awe. Maybe one day I would learn to fly like these men. I too would be good enough to perform aerobatics. Just like them, I would effortlessly loop the loop, turn my aeroplane upside down, dive and spin at will, while waving and smiling to the crowds below – man and machine perfectly fused.

The spectators formed an orderly queue. They now decided they also wanted a slice of the aerial action. I watched as two people handed over their 5s. They clambered onto the lower wing, taking care not to hit their heads on the upper wing, and squeezed themselves into the back seat of the cockpit. The pilot strapped them in, jumped into the front seat and took off for a twenty-minute spin over Maidstone.

I looked on with envy as I knew I couldn't join them. It took my father a day of hard graft to earn 5s and he certainly couldn't waste it on joyriding in Sir Alan's flying contraptions. But that didn't dampen my desire to fly.

The display ended and the crowd dispersed. I wandered slowly homewards, back to Bower Street and back to reality. Despite my stubborn desire to fly, my family circumstances meant that the chances of fulfilling my dream were slim, even I knew that. But it was the 1920s and I also knew that flying was a wealthy man's hobby. People like me didn't become pilots, we became builders or, if we were lucky, bank clerks. Thoughts of training to become a pilot were little more than a flight of fancy, as families like mine were too pre-occupied with the business of making sure there was food on the table, clothes on our backs and shoes on our feet. But I was as good as any rich kid. Being wealthy didn't necessarily make you a good pilot. I had made up my mind. I would be a pilot whatever it took.

I sat in the RAF recruitment office in Chatham and waited patiently as the uniformed man in front of me scoured my application to join the RAF. He read out my details.

'Maidstone Technical School, eh? Impressive.'

'Thanks.'

'No previous experience of flying aircraft I see.'

'No, but I'm a fast learner.'

'And you're 17? That's very young even for a pilot.'

'I'm waiting to matriculate. If I don't get into the RAF, I'll go to teacher-training college.'

'I see, wait here.'

I knew I was in with a good chance of being accepted in the RAF. My school marks were excellent. I was a keen sportsman, better than most and not as good as some. In short, just the type the RAF was looking for, or so I thought.

It had been five years since that day in a field just off Sutton Road where the sight of Sir Alan's Cobham's incredible flying circus taught me that I wouldn't be happy being anything other than a pilot.

But that day receded and although I never lost sight of my dream to fly, the reality was that few working-class children became pilots, including bright ones like me. I knew it would be prudent to have a back plan. In my case, this was teaching.

I turned my attention to my studies. I was one of the lucky few who enjoyed school, probably because I was quite good at it. By the time I went to school at the age of five, I could already read and write, for which I have my sisters to thank and which gave me a head start over the other pupils. From infants school I went to elementary school, or big boys' school as we called it, although I wasn't that big and I was by far the youngest boy in my class. In those days progression to the next year depended on ability and not on age. So at 11 years old I was in the top class with boys of 14 which was difficult at times as there is a lot of difference between boys of 11 and 14.

As I approached my teenage years, it became clear that my parents could no longer afford for me to remain in education. School became a luxury beyond the age of 13. Ordinarily I should have left school then, like my sisters had before me. However, as a bright working-class boy, there was another option for me. A scholarship to either Maidstone Grammar or Maidstone Technical School would pay for my tuition fees and my books. The only problem was I would have to pass the entrance exam. If I failed, I too would have to leave and find employment. It was 1930, the height of the general depression. Job prospects were poor.

At the age of 13 I sat the entrance exams and won a full scholarship to stay on at school. I was given the choice of attending either Maidstone Technical School or Maidstone Grammar School. I chose to go to the Technical School because I had always been practically minded and there I would be able to develop those skills. I had had my own lathe from the age of 12 which I inherited from my father along with his practical skills, I suspect. I used to make simple bowls and small dishes that you placed under the legs of furniture to protect the flooring. Passing the entrance exam catapulted me away from the traditional working-class route of leaving school at 14 and going out to work.

On my first day at technical school, my father called me out to the back yard. My mother and my three sisters were already there waiting for me.

'Well don't you look the smart one,' Elsie eyed my red and blue uniform.

'I've never seen you looking so clean, Jimmy,' Lily teased.

My father disappeared into his workshop and re-emerged with a gleaming dark green Royal Enfield bicycle. It was brand new and cost £4 19s 6d, which was two weeks' wages. I had never owned my own bike before. It was the best present I had ever had.

'We thought this might make it easier for you to get to school and back,' my father smiled and handed me the bike.

'Good luck, Jimmy, enjoy your first day.' My mother kissed me and my sisters each hugged me in turn.

I let myself out of the back yard, jumped on the bike and cycled towards my new school. On my way I passed the Maidstone Labour Exchange, which was situated at the bottom of the hill on London Road.

As I freewheeled towards the building I saw a group of people outside its main entrance. As I got closer I realised there must have been a line of up to 400 men, in their flat caps, many of them were drawing heavily on a Woodbine amid an air of defeat and dejection as they waited for the doors to open. The Labour Exchange was meant to provide them with work, but there wasn't any, so they queued to collect their dole money instead. It was a grim reminder of the times. There was no hope of them finding employment. I passed by them every day and the queue never seemed to get any smaller. This was why my parents were so pleased that I had got myself into the technical school. It was really my only chance of avoiding joining that queue at least until things got better.

I remained at Maidstone Technical School until I was 16. It was a happy time for me. At school, I palled up with a boy called Ken Baker. I knew Ken from the Cub Scouts. He was even shorter than me, but very strong and athletic. He was a promising sportsman and we clicked straightaway. His house at 36 Tonbridge Road was a short hop from mine and became a second home, and his mum treated me like another son.

Ken was in 'b' form because his parents could afford to pay for his fees, whereas I was in 'a' form because I was a scholarship boy. This segregation, which was so much a part of pre-war life, didn't make any difference to our friendship and we became great mates.

Unaware of my desires to become a pilot, the teachers at the school encouraged me to pursue a teaching career. But by the time I reached 16, my parents could no longer support my education and I had to get a job and start earning my keep. As a way around this, the school decided to give me the important post of laboratory assistant. This job was often given to one of the brighter boys and was a means of bringing much needed money into the house while still being able to prepare for the external matriculation examination. If I passed I could attend teacher-training college. I was paid the magnificent salary of £25 per year and my duties included preparing chemicals and experiments for classes.

After a year as a laboratory assistant, I was nearly 17 and ready to matriculate. My father paid 12s 6d for me to sit the entrance examination and I set off by train and travelled to South Kensington in London where the examinations took place. In order to reach the exam hall on time, I had to stay overnight in a local hostel. I shared a room with a Japanese lad. If I had known what was coming, I should have killed him there and then!

On my return from London, I awaited my results. The school had finished for the summer and so I had more time on my hands, which my father soon noticed and recruited me to help him on the building sites. There I spent the warm days of summer 1934 fetching and carrying for my dad.

England had also changed. Officially the talk was of peace, but war was in the air and unofficially countries were developing their military capability in anticipation that the appeasement of Hitler, Germany's leader, might fail.

I had grown accustomed to aircraft flying overhead, especially in the south-east of England, which had its fair share of aerodromes by this time. Fighter planes and bombers would fly overhead with such frequency that some people no longer turned to watch in wonderment as they had in that field way back in the days of Sir Alan Cobham's Flying Circus.

At 17, even though I was firmly on course to become a teacher, my own long-held desire to fly resurfaced and I began to develop a real yen to become a pilot. One day I decided to take myself off to the RAF recruitment office in Chatham, which is not far from Maidstone. I filled out endless forms of pointless questions, but if it meant I would be accepted as a pilot, it would all be worth it.

The RAF recruitment officer returned after sometime. I don't know why, but I expected to be told there and then if I had been accepted. Instead he said briskly: 'All right Mr Corbin. Thank you for your interest. The Ministry'll be in touch.'

I left the recruitment office pondering my new career in the RAF, the fulfilment of a dream to fly aeroplanes.

Several weeks after my trip to Chatham, my father asked me to help him out on a local site where he was working with his team of men. Mum packed our lunches and we set out for the yard just as dawn broke. The morning was spent mixing cement and carrying bricks for the men employed by my father. As the day drew to a close, dad asked me to run an errand for him.

'Jimmy, I need you to go to Linton and fetch me some lead from the builder's yard. Take the cart and be as quick as you can. Your mother wants us home early tonight.'

I picked up the empty cart and headed out of the site and in the direction of Linton, a small village about 4 miles away. It was a really windy day, which made pushing the cart an arduous task. Sometime later, I arrived at the yard and loaded the cart with the lead and began the long journey back again. With the added weight, sweat started to pour down my face and progress was slow with frequent rest stops.

As I was coming down Linton hill, I heard the drone of planes overhead. It was unusually loud. I stopped the cart and looked up and waited for them to come into view. A group of Vickers Virginia bombers emerged from over a hillside and headed in my direction. As they came nearer, the noise of their engines grew louder, but the wind blew so strong they looked like they were making no headway at all. Slowly they passed over my head at little more than about 2,000ft above me. I could make out their grey undersides. It felt as if I could almost reach up and touch their underbellies. I watched them as they finally slipped out of sight.

Silence fell again, save for the wind in the trees. I picked up the heavy cart and, shifting my hands along the handles until they were comfortable, I continued on my way.

'Jimmy, you'll be up there with them some day soon,' I said to myself.

I returned to the yard where dad was just finishing up. He scolded me for my lateness and the two of us set out to walk the eight miles home.

When we arrived back at Bower Street our meal was already on the table.

I sat down to a huge plate of beef stew and large chunks of soft bread. Mum placed a steaming mug of tea in front of me.

'Oh, I almost forgot. This came for you today.' She slipped her hand into her apron and pulled out a slim official looking envelope. On the top left-hand corner was the stamp of the Air Ministry.

I tore it open immediately. As I unfolded the letter I knew that this was it, the realisation of a dream. I would become a pilot.

Chapter Two

1938 – ROCHESTER AERODROME

I scanned the letter and my heart sunk. It blandly informed me that the RAF had a policy of not recruiting young men who were still in full-time education. I knew this was not strictly true. A number of universities had RAF squadrons where students learnt to fly as part of the RAF, but these were little more than exclusive clubs dominated by public school types. Jimmy Corbin with his working-class roots didn't fit the mould of a member of a university squadron.

The letter helpfully suggested that I might like to reapply after I had completed my studies. I screwed it up and threw it away in anger and disgust. I had been thwarted this time, but the same stubbornness that forced my family to adopt the name Jimmy and had got me into the Technical School and teacher-training school would get me into the RAF – one day.

The news of my rejection left me with no choice but to take the RAF's advice and my next four years were spent, not unhappily, at Shoreditch Teacher Training College, which was part of London University. The college specialised in training students to teach woodwork and metalwork as well as all the general academic subjects. In those days, rules forbade craftwork teachers from setting foot into the classroom and their teaching was confined to the workshops. But Shoreditch and Goldsmith's colleges offered a teacher-training programme where they taught all subjects in addition to woodwork and metalwork, which made us very much sought after as it meant we could teach everything.

Everyday for three years I got up at dawn and left my house in Bower Street and took the short walk to Maidstone train station. There I paid my 1s 6d to travel to London on what was termed the workman's train.

In my last year of college, commuting into London became so tiresome that I decided to stay in digs in Tottenham. It meant I had more energy to study and, with the help of my £75 annual grant topped up by a £75 loan, I could fully avail upon myself all the traditional pleasures that accompanied student life. By day I attended lectures and the library where I poured over such illustrious volumes as Evans's *Hammered Work* and James's *Creative Woodwork for Students and Teachers*. By night I developed a passion for dancing which I indulged at every possible moment at the Hammersmith Palais and Shoreditch Dance Hall. When I wasn't out dancing, my student friends and I would dodge afternoon lectures, pay the 2d tube fare and catch the Northern Line to Brixton. There we queued at the local cinema where we were treated to two major films such as such *It Happened One Night* with Clark Gable and *Mr Deeds Goes to Town* with Gary Cooper. For me the best bit always happened after the first film had finished, because Harry Roy's Big Band would strike up from the orchestra pit in front of the screen and we would listen to live music until the second film was ready to play.

In July 1938 I graduated from college with my Teaching Diploma, granted by the Board of Education, and took up a teaching post at Collier Road Secondary Modern on the edge of Northfleet and Gravesend. The school catered for boys up to the age of 14, the school-leaving age. I started teaching in September and from day one I loved it. I taught mainly in the metal workshop, but occasionally I was called upon to go into the classroom to teach other subjects, especially maths.

As a young teacher I had to have my wits about me. Some of the boys were bloody clever and kept you on your toes. Two of them went on to become university dons, but the pupils knew a strict disciplinarian when they saw one and they were smart enough to behave themselves.

By the end of 1938, war seemed inevitable. Politicians continued to talk about peace in our time, but we all knew there was going to be trouble. The mood among young men and boys in towns across the country at that time was one of great patriotism and loyalty to the king, George VI, and to our country. When the time came we wanted to be ready to defend all that we held dear so we all joined one or other of the Reserves, as they were known. Ironically for me, the threat of impending invasion and the death of millions opened up the opportunity for me finally to fulfil my ambition to be a pilot.

One night after school, I met my old mate Ken Baker in the Star Inn pub for a drink. Ken possessed an enviable prowess for sport, but less for academia. He left school at 16 and went to work at the paper mill in Maidstone, which employed 35,000 people at that time, where he trained as a project engineer. Our friendship continued and as I walked into the pub I found him nursing a half-drunk pint of bitter. I bought a pint of the same stuff and sat down opposite him. Our conversation must have replayed itself in every pub in every part of the country.

'So, Jimmy, no point asking you which of the services you're going to go for. The RAF won't know what's hit them,' Ken grinned at me.

The RAF Volunteer Reserve had been set up in 1936. The idea was to open up the RAF to all different kinds of people and not just the upper classes who had dominated its ranks since its inception, as they were the only ones who could afford to entertain the idea of becoming a pilot and had the money to turn it into reality. Then as war approached the Air Force suddenly woke up to the idea that talented pilots could come from any social strata. Besides, if they confined themselves to recruiting from the upper classes, the pool of pilots would soon dry up. In the end it came down to logic.

Despite a desire to recruit from a wider social spectrum, the RAF's entry criteria were tough and it remained notoriously difficult to get into, although I always thought I would be accepted. In 1938 the selection process eased a little, but you still had to be near enough perfect to get in. A lot of people either failed the interview stage or medical. But I always knew that I was bright enough to be a pilot, and as such I had as good a chance as anybody of succeeding. Perhaps it was misplaced confidence and only time would tell, but my stubborn streak meant I was determined to get in and show them what I could do.

I sipped my pint.

'Just as long as they have the good sense to say yes to me this time. What about you, Ken, fancy joining me?'

'No, I've already joined the Territorial Reserves. Popped into the recruitment office today, all signed and sealed, it's a soldier's life for me. They've put me in the gunnery.'

'You are kidding?'

'Nope. Why, what's the RAF got that the army hasn't?'

'Well, for the start, the RAF pays much better than the army.'

I was referring to the fact that as a sergeant pilot under training I could expect 13s 6d a day, even more money than I got as a teacher. Soldiers got just 1s 6d a day.

'Besides, when push comes to shove, I would much rather be in the Air Force shooting at a machine than in the army sticking some poor bloke with a bayonet or worse being stuck by a bayonet,' I added.

'Well, to be honest, Jimmy, when it came down to it, there didn't seem to be much between any of them.'

'Well, there's no contest for me. When it all kicks off, I am going to make damn sure I am up in the air and not stuck in some trench drinking rain water and eating stale biscuits.'

'Perhaps we should drink to that,' said Ken. 'Hold on, I have something for you, an early birthday present. Mum asked if you'd like to come round on Saturday and celebrate your 21st at our house.'

Ken passed me a small tin. Inside were the dismantled pieces of a Rolls Razor, No1 Imperial model, no less. It was, in fact, the first razor I had ever owned.

'Thanks Ken. I'd love to come round on Saturday.'

'That's settled then,' he raised his glass, 'here's to being 21, key of the door and all that.'

We clinked our glasses, drained them and left the pub. I may have been approaching my 21st birthday, but my mother still expected me home by nine o'clock.

I spent my birthday in the company of Ken and his family. It was a sedate affair. We enjoyed a few drinks in the parlour as the gramophone played in the background. Ken and I talked about life in the Reserves while his parents expressed a forlorn hope that 'it might never come to that'.

Four months later, in December 1938, Ken learnt that he had been stationed on ack-ack, or anti-aircraft gunnery, duties in a town on the Medway and I walked into that same RAF recruitment office in Chatham to try my luck again.

I told the regular sergeant there that I wanted to have another go at joining the Reserves. He asked me the usual nonsense about my family and education and together we filled out all the forms. Several weeks later I received another letter from the RAF. This time it requested me to attend a medical at the Air Ministry in London. I had cleared the first hurdle, but I knew the medical would be stringent and often sifted out many would-be pilots.

The day came. I took the train up to London, as I had as a student teacher. The building was on Kingsway and I presented myself at reception. From there I was led into a small room, already filled with rather nervous-looking young men. I took a seat and waited to be called in.

In all, eight different doctors prodded and poked me in places I had never been prodded and poked before. It was winter time and more than a little chilly as I stood in their various offices and examination rooms, removing my shirt or dropping my trousers depending on which medical specialist I found myself in front of. I was ushered from room to room, while the doctors bombarded me with endless questions about the state of my health. I was told to do a number of tasks such as standing on one leg for ten minutes so they could check my balancing abilities. The most I could manage was two minutes.

Until then, I had always considered myself a fairly healthy specimen with little to worry about. I played football, rugby and table tennis for Kent schools throughout my youth. Now, all of a sudden, I wasn't so sure. The doctors made no comment on the short, but compact individual, standing shivering in front of them. They just frowned a lot until they had finished with me. The last white coat told me to wait in another room until the wing commander was ready with my results.

I sat with several other young men awaiting my fate. All of them appeared much younger than me. No one dared to speak. A sergeant, standing stiffly, appeared at the doorway and ran his finger down the list of names pinned to the clipboard in his hands.

'William James Corbin,' he called out.

'Yes, sir.'

'This way.'

I stood up and straightened the jacket of my made-to-measure grey pin-head suit, which I had bought especially from Burton's tailors in Maidstone for 49s 6d. The shop was situated below a billiards hall, which my father had strictly forbidden me from visiting as he believed it was frequented by men of low morals. Clutching my trilby, which I had only started to wear the year before as I felt it made me look more distinguished, I braced myself and entered the room.

'Well, this is it, Jimmy old boy, in just a few minutes you'll know if you are going to become a pilot or not,' I told myself.

The office contained a large desk, behind which sat a man in the smart blue grey uniform of the RAF. He looked to be in his mid-30s and so was not that much older than me. But his features were set in stone and he gave off a cold and remote air. The three rings on his sleeve denoted that he was a wing commander. He also wore the badge of a doctor on his lapel. More importantly he was Chairman of the Royal Air Force Medical Board and would decide if I was fit enough to join the Royal Air Force Volunteer Reserve.

The officer looked up at me briefly and then sifted through some papers lying on the desk in front of him. These contained the results of my medical. He tutted and sighed and clearly wasn't going to make this easy for me. I felt like a small child again who just been hauled up in front of my father to answer to some terrible deed I had committed.

As I stood and waited for the officer to pass judgement on my health, a wave of nerves swept over me and not without reason, for this was my second attempt at joining the RAF Reserve. I was now 22 and a fully qualified school teacher. Five years had gone by since I had first swaggered into the recruitment office in Chatham and declared that I wanted to be a pilot. And now here I was awaiting the verdict.

After what seemed an eternity, but was probably only a couple of minutes, the wing commander finally looked up from his desk. He ran a disapproving eye over me and heaved a heavy sigh.

'Well, Corbin, there's nothing right about you, but there's nothing particularly wrong with you either.'

'Thank you, sir,' I replied hesitantly. I wasn't sure whether I had just been complimented or insulted.

'Mind you, you'll have to get yourself a damn sight fitter than you are now if you're to make it as a pilot,' the officer added gravely.

'Yes, sir, I will,' I smiled and walked out of his office feeling 10ft tall. With those inglorious words I knew I had been accepted in the Royal Air Force Volunteer Reserve. I was in. I was a sergeant pilot under training. More than ten years had elapsed since that sunny day when as a boy I was mesmerised by the flimsy little Gloster Gamecock swooping and rising in the skies above me. But it had all been worth it, because I was a pilot and that was all that mattered, even if I had yet to set foot inside a cockpit.

I took the wing commander's blunt observations about my physique to heart and shortly after the RAF had accepted me, I embarked on a rigorous exercise regime. This involved getting up at the crack of dawn before school started, tugging on a tatty pair of sneakers and pounding the freezing streets of Maidstone in my quest for physical excellence.

In the New Year of 1939, I attended the RAF stores in Rochester where a store clerk eyed me up and down briefly before returning with a neatly folded bundle of clothing – my uniform was unceremoniously dumped on the counter before me with a curt 'sign here' from the store clerk as he pushed a piece of paper towards me.

Back home in Bower Street, I examined my uniform at close quarters. On the sleeve were three white strips denoting my rank of sergeant, which made me feel immensely proud, especially as poor old Ken went into the Army Reserve as a private. The coarse material of the uniform was blue-grey in colour and identical to the regular RAF uniform in every respect except one. On my shoulder was a small brass plate with the letters VR – the Royal Air Force Volunteer Reserve. This tiny shield remained on my uniform throughout the war and was there to remind me that I was never a regular member of the RAF. I was never more than a volunteer pilot.

I stood in front of the mirror in my sisters' bedroom in full uniform and set my cap to one side of my head, adjusting it until I was happy. Then I stepped back and took a long look at Sergeant Jimmy Corbin. I was on my way. It could only be a matter of days before I was in an aeroplane, flying high above the clouds. How wrong I was.

As part of the RAFVR I received fifteen days' training a year and was paid the annual sum of £35. But for the next six months my career as a pilot did not progress past the classroom. I continued to teach at Collier Road School during the day, but the evenings and weekends were taken up with attending numerous lectures at Chatham RAF Recruitment Office.

The first time I turned up, I had dashed over to Chatham straight from school, furiously peddling as I knew lateness would not be looked on kindly by the RAF.

When I arrived, the room was already full with fifteen to twenty young men who I assumed came from all over the Medway area. I found a spare seat, sat down and fell into conversation with the young man next to me. It quickly became clear his upbringing was very different from mine. His accent was rich and plummy, denoting a wealthy pedigree and an education received at a well-to-do private school. In short, he was typical RAF material – unlike me who was the antithesis of the RAF 'type'. It was the first time I had had anything to do with people from the upper classes and despite obvious differences in our accents and outlook, I quickly came to realise we were all the same.

Despite the marked social division, the rich boys never really intimidated me and I never allowed any of them to think they were better than me. I always thought I was more intelligent than many of them anyway as I had won my right to be in the RAF on merit and was not there as a result of any family connections or favours. Besides, when the war broke out, background and breeding became increasingly irrelevant. When you were 30,000ft in the air with eleven other Spitfires and approaching thirty German 109s at speeds of 350mph it didn't matter if you had been a lord or a labourer in peacetime, we were all pilots.

A uniformed instructor entered the class and our conversation fell away as he called us to order and told us what the RAF expected from us. He stood stiffly and glared at us all in turn.

'Make no mistake, gentlemen, the work has just begun and many of you won't make it. The RAF demands the highest standards and will accept nothing less. If you don't think you have what it takes to become a pilot then I suggest you go and join the TA. Right, let's get started.'

He was right. Over the long months, our lectures covered all aspects of RAF life. We learnt about Morse code and navigation and spent an inordinate amount of time learning about Air Force discipline as well as that essential life-saver – Air Force etiquette.

Then one evening, after a lecture, our instructor told me to stay behind after class. I wondered if I was in for some kind of bollocking, but I couldn't have been more wrong.

'Believe it or not Corbin, the RAF in its wisdom believes you are now ready to fly an aircraft. I want you to report to Rochester Aerodrome on Saturday at nine and don't be late. Your instructor will be Mr Arnold. Right, you can go.'

'Yes sir,' I saluted him and left the room. This was it. Months of learning everything there was to know about aeroplanes had been leading up to this point – finally I was going to fly an aircraft.

On 8 August 1939 I left 133 Bower Street in the morning and strolled towards Maidstone town centre – which was already bustling with traffic and people – feeling apprehensive. A distant fear had reared its ugly head overnight and was now taking substance in my mind. I was afraid of heights. Anything over 30ft brought on severe vertigo. I had volunteered to go up in an aircraft that was likely to reach 1,000ft. What if I panicked? What if I puked?

On Pudding Lane I caught the Maidstone and District bus and paid the conductor 1s to take me to Rochester Aerodrome, which was only 6 miles away and didn't take too long. The bus dropped me at the entrance to the airfield and I strolled through the gates.

Rochester was a comparatively small aerodrome with a grass field. Tarmac runways were still some way off for most of us. Nearest to the road, which ran alongside the aerodrome, on the right-hand side of the field, there stood a small cluster of workshops and aircraft hangars. Several Miles Magister and Tiger Moth aeroplanes were parked outside their hangars on the grass while mechanics worked on their engines in the warm summer morning. Scores of men in overalls were milling around the site. They were the aircrew and aircraft fitters, employed to work at the aerodrome by Shorts Brothers, famous for the flying boats and Stirling bombers. The officers and the instructors were all housed in a hut on the left side of the field. The flying club where we would have lunch was located on the far side of the aerodrome.

I headed for the aircrew buildings on the left, which was where the parachutes were kept, and spent the next twenty minutes being shown how to put on a parachute, although the thought of jumping out of an aeroplane attached to a piece of flimsy white silk sent chills through me. I was also issued with my leather helmet and green-grey Sidcot flying suit as well as goggles, gloves and gauntlets similar to those used by motorcycle riders.

Outside the hangar, with my parachute draped over my arm, I waited for my instructor to appear. Soon a medium built man with sharp features approached me. He was aged about 35, but was already completely bald. He shook my hand.

'Sgt Corbin, I presume. I'm Mr Arnold, your instructor. I understand that you're here for your first air experience.'

'Yes, sir,' I replied.

'Right, we'll just take her up and give you a taste of what it's like. I'll be in the back controlling the craft, you just sit in the front and get used to the feeling of flight, all right?'

We put on our goggles and helmets and climbed into the cockpit of a Miles Magister M14 aeroplane. It was a relatively new aircraft and hadn't been out long. It was a single-engined monoplane, which had been specifically designed for the RAF to use as a basic trainer. Sixteen Elementary Flying Training Schools and the Central Flying School were equipped with Magisters and many pilots cut their teeth on them. Its main drawback was that it was non aerobatic and any attempts at aerobatics were strictly forbidden because of the weight of the battery. It was a large metal box screwed into the wooden frame of the aircraft. If you did aerobatics there was the danger of it coming away from its fitting and damaging the aircraft. As a result, I received little instruction in aerobatics during my training which was to plague me throughout the war.

I placed my parachute on the seat and sat down on top of it. It was the first time I had been in a cockpit and it felt very compact.

Mr Arnold hoisted himself up onto the wing and leaned across me in the cockpit and ran through the array of dials and instruments in front of me.

'As you'll see, Sgt Corbin, the Magister is a simple aircraft so it is easy to identify the air speed indicator, the oil pressure gauge, the engine revs counter, the turn and bank indicator and the altimeter, which are all here on the left side of the instrument panel. On the right-hand side here is the compass and, of course, between your legs is the control column or joystick.'

Mr Arnold climbed into the back cockpit and issued the next set of instructions through the speaking tube into the receiver in my helmet.

'Right, Sgt Corbin, we'll just go up for a short spin, give you a chance to get used to it all. Don't touch any of the controls, just watch and listen and don't forget to strap yourself in, we don't want to lose you, do we now?' Mr Arnold said.

I pulled out the speaking tube and held it to my lips

'Yes, sir, no sir,' I shouted into it.

'Good, I am receiving you loud and clear. Let's go, shall we?'

I pulled the two straps over my shoulders and secured them in a clip in front of me. They could be adjusted as tightly as you wanted depending on whether you were performing aerobatics or not. I tugged them and made sure they were tight. I waited for the aircraft to move off.

Seated in the cockpit with no role other than to sit and observe, my stomach began to churn. I had waited so long to get into an aeroplane and learn to fly it, but this initial rush of excitement was quickly replaced by a surge of anxiety as my old fear crept into my mind. All my life I have suffered from a fear of heights. I had often helped my father out on building sites and was fine up to about 30ft, but anything beyond that and I just couldn't face it. Even today, I can't get near the edge of cliff without feeling nauseous. Now I was strapped into an aircraft about to be taken up to 1,000ft and I had no idea how my mind or body were going to react to such an alien sensation. Would I panic and scream to be taken down again or sit and shiver with cold fear until we returned to earth? I didn't know. I certainly wouldn't have been the first pilot whose career began and ended with their first flight and the discovery that they were terrified of flying.

'Right, Mr Corbin, everything all right?' Mr Arnold's voice filtered through as if he had read my mind.

'Er, yes sir.'

'Let's go then.'

Mr Arnold pushed the two magneto switches down, leaned over the side of the aircraft and shouted 'Contact' to an airman standing in front of the Magister. He flipped the propeller, which sucked petrol into the engine, causing the little craft to spark into life until the propeller began to turn on its own and whirred around happily. Mr Arnold switched off one of the magnetos and opened the throttle, which was a small lever on the right hand side of the cockpit. This was to check the revs, which I could see remained constant. He then checked the second magneto.

'Chocks away,' Mr Arnold shouted down to the airman who tugged on a string attached to two blocks of wood wedged under the wheels and the aeroplane rolled steadily forward.

We taxied slowly along the 'drome and then paused before turning into the wind for take-off. The plane then began to gather speed as it bobbed along the uneven ground towards a hedge at the far side of the field. I braced myself. Then just as it looked as if we would plough into the thick bushes, the little craft seemed to magically lift itself from the ground and we began to climb skywards. My heart was pounding. I was flying and I was terrified. Would I end my first flying experience a simpering shell of fear?

The altimeter told me we had levelled out at around 1,000ft. My heart rate eased and I realised that flying and I were going to get along. Relief washed over me and I began to feel what could only be described as exhilaration. This was the start of my love affair with flying.

It was a beautiful day with very little cloud cover. Confident I wasn't going to panic, I ventured to peer over the side of the cockpit. Below, a great spectacle was laid before me.

Rochester, Maidstone and the whole of the River Medway stretched out as far as the eye could see, snaking its way towards the English Channel. I could see the concrete slipway of the Shorts Brothers factory, where they made the flying boats, and barges shipping coal and supplies along the river. The spire of Rochester Cathedral rose above the tiny matchbox town and villages and hamlets huddled in the corners of the patchwork of green fields. I could see the paper mill in New Hythe where Ken worked and, of course, somewhere down there is 133 Bower Street, I thought to myself.

Air experience was everything that I had hoped it would be and more. The years of doubt, rejection and then anticipation of this moment melted away. This is what I had waited for. Jimmy Corbin, son of a plumber from Maidstone, was flying.

We circled the area at about 2,000ft for about forty-five minutes as Mr Arnold pointed out various landmarks that, when the time came, would help me to navigate my way back to the aerodrome.

Through the speaking tube he drew my attention to the main railway lines and roadways and told me to memorise as much as possible.

'It might save your life one day, Sgt Corbin.'

How prophetic those words were to become. At that time we had no other means of navigating our passage. We had maps, of course, but none of us bothered much with them and so they tended to remain permanently tucked into our air boots while we were flying. Instead, most of us preferred the tried and tested but frequently unreliable method of leaning out of the cockpit to try and spot familiar landmarks. Fortunately this was easier for me than some of my compatriots. Kent was my home county. Maidstone, Rochester Chatham, Ashford and the coastal towns were as familiar to me as my own back garden. I didn't know then that this intimacy with my surroundings would stand me in such good stead, not just in training, but also during combat. The Battle of Britain was destined to be fought above the very towns and countryside I had explored as a child. I wasn't just defending Britain. I was defending my home-town.

Finally the Miles Magister banked slightly and turned for home. The grass of Rochester airfield came into view and Mr Arnold deposited the craft expertly on to the ground. We taxied to a halt.

'Well, Sgt Corbin, how was that for your first time?'

'Very interesting, Mr Arnold.'

Mr Arnold took me up in the Miles for the next four flying sessions. As an ex-RAF flight sergeant with twelve years flying experience, he had the well-deserved reputation for being a brilliant pilot, but for me he was an equally talented instructor. Many people can fly, but teaching others is a skill that few can master well. As he was my instructor I kept a respectful distance from him and always addressed him as Mr Arnold, but, despite our formal relationship, Mr Arnold was such a friendly person that I instantly warmed to him. His approach to teaching was based on encouragement and praise, which I responded to as I was determined to perform well for him because I liked him and not because I was frightened of him. He never shouted at me. Instead he would just quietly tease the best out of me.

Slowly I grew more used to the controls and a week later Mr Arnold met me by the Miles Magister and climbed into the front of the cockpit instead of the back.

'Right, Sgt Corbin, your turn. In you get. Just relax. Remember, take-off into the wind, throttle open, stick forward and as soon as the tail's up, you're off.'

I obeyed his instructions and got into the aeroplane. We taxied towards the end of the field where I lined up the Magister into the wind. You always had to take off into wind because if you had a 20mph headwind you had to take that into account when you were taking off. If you took off and you were travelling at 60mph, your air speed would be 60, but the ground speed would be 40mph, 20mph slower. If you got it wrong you wouldn't have enough speed to take off, and were likely to go ploughing into a hedge. It was a simple as that.

I checked over my shoulder and made certain there were no aircraft coming into land behind, which was also very important, of course, as I heard the stories of young pilots who remembered all the necessary manoeuvres only to smash into another aircraft because they had neglected to look over their shoulder as they took off.

The coast was clear so I eased slowly forward to full throttle. The aircraft gradually gained speed as I held the column firmly to keep the machine moving in a straight line. When I reached 45mph, I kicked the rudder peddle and felt the aeroplane shift beneath me. She was eager to get airborne so I eased back the column and she rose off the ground. I knew I could now either hold her low and build up speed and then climb slowly, which looked impressive and was often the mark of an accomplished pilot, or I could climb as quickly as I could. I opted for the latter. In fact, I always chose to get up to a decent height as soon as possible. It always worried me that holding the aircraft low for the sake of appearances merely increased your chances of hitting a hitherto unseen obstacle. Airfields didn't benefit from miles of perimeter fences. They were often little more than a field that had been deemed flat enough to land an aeroplane on. As a result, you never knew when a hedge or some overhead power lines would unexpectedly appear, usually when it was too late to do anything about them. The 'drome at Rochester was a respectable length, but some airstrips weren't and they ended rather abruptly. Gravesend was a particularly unpleasant set up. Here you had no choice. If you didn't take off and climb quickly enough you were in serious danger of colliding with the 6ft hedge at the end of the airfield.

As the aeroplane responded to my touch and we nosed up to 1,000ft, I felt a strong sense of relief mixed with pride at what I had achieved. Not everyone could fly an aeroplane. I eased back on the throttle and we levelled out. With the take-off successfully completed, Mr Arnold told me to make a couple of circuits of the airfield and, then when I felt ready, I could tackle my second test of the day – landing.

My smugness over my successful take-off disappeared smartly. As every pilot knows landing an aeroplane is much harder than taking off. I had got the thing up without damaging either myself, the aircraft or Mr Arnold and now I had to get the damn thing down again.

I put the Magister downwind and selected my height of 800ft. As I approached the field, I cut the engine and turned across the wind. I used the wind to help land the plane and so had to take extra care not to undershoot or overshoot the landing field. This gliding-in approach was mandatory and we were fined if we didn't do it as it was considered shoddy flying to use the power of the engines to deposit the aircraft onto the ground. We even did it in the early Spitfires. It wasn't until later that the pilots adopted the powered or engine approach to landing.

The Miles Magister touched down, did a little bounce and then put itself firmly on the ground. We trundled along the grass for some yards. I held the column steady and applied the brakes until we slowed to gentle pace. The aircrew directed us to our parking space and we ground to a halt.

'That was excellent, Sgt Corbin. You see, there's nothing to it.'

His words left me with a feeling of great satisfaction at landing the Miles Magister successfully. With the basic principles of taking off and landing now fully mastered, it seemed to me that I just had to add the fine detail.

Keen as I was to progress to more complicated manoeuvres, I hadn't anticipated that the day would arrive quite so soon. Two days after I flew an aeroplane for the very first time in my life, I arrived at Rochester for my lesson as usual. However, there was no sign of Mr Arnold. Instead, the Chief Flying Instructor, a Mr Holt, who was an ex-RAF officer, made my acquaintance. He was a completely different kind of instructor from Mr Arnold. As the Chief Instructor, Mr Holt was a hard taskmaster who expected much from his pupils and offered little praise in return. He was a difficult man to please and I knew I would have my work cut out with him.

'Right, Corbin. I'll be taking you up today. We're going to try a couple of spins, so keep your finger out.'

'Yes sir.'

The thought of putting the Miles Magister into a deliberate spin causing it to plunge earthwards while rotating all the way until Mr Holt instructed me to pull the aircraft up didn't fill me with a great deal of cheer.

There were two types of spin, an intentional one and an accidental one, which can happen through bad flying and carelessness. Neither is particularly pleasant, but it was a necessary part of training. I learnt later that sometimes the only way to evade being shot down was to put the aircraft into a spin. The bottom line is no one is actually taught how to spin an aircraft as such. It is the recovery that is the most important part of the manoeuvre because that is the part that saves your life.

We took off and climbed to a height of 5,000ft to allow plenty of room to pull out of the spin. Accidents did happen where pilots failed to pull up in time and slammed their aeroplanes into the ground. This was less likely with a basic aircraft like the Miles Magister, but Spitfires were a different matter. They reached speeds of more than 300mph. There was no room for mistakes.

Mr Holt did a practice spin to show me how it was done. It was a perfect spin, of course. He recovered the aeroplane effortlessly and took her back up to about 4,000ft. He barked his instructions down the speaking tube: 'Your turn, Corbin. Right spinning. Pull left rudder. Don't pull up until I say. Got that?'

The Magister had dual controls so Mr Holt could take over the aircraft at any time, but that wasn't the point. If he had to step in every time I made a mess of a maneouvre, I would never make it as a pilot. I had to get it right first time.

I checked the speed dial. It read 45mph. I took a deep breath and put the aircraft into what was called the stalling position where I pulled the throttle right back until the roar of the Magister's engine fell away to be replaced by the unwelcome sound of wind whistling past my helmet. Suddenly I was thousands of feet up in a tin machine with no power. If I didn't put it into the spin now, we would drop from the sky like a stone. I kicked the rudder bar over and she turned to her right, her nose dipped down and she slid gracefully into the spin. The plane plunged 500ft turning all the while and gaining speed as the aircraft fell out of the sky. Its engine screamed in protest and the earth rushed towards me at a terrifying speed. My stomach lurched up into my throat. Racing towards certain death was a terrifying feeling. Come on, Mr Holt, that's enough, tell me to pull up. After a few agonisingly long seconds, Mr Holt's voice came over the speaking tube: 'Pull up, Corbin.'

At last, I eased up the control column. The Magister levelled out and I returned to the aerodrome.

When I got out of the aircraft, Mr Holt simply said: 'Well, that was OK then,' and disappeared. High praise, indeed.

I was just relieved to have come out of it alive. I had a feeling that I had done something that wasn't necessarily that easy and although I then went on to spin two or three times during combat, I never got used to the sensation. It remained an uncomfortable and frightening experience.

After I had mastered the basic tenets of flying, life became more complicated with every passing day. Some of the training offered a sobering insight into what we could expect and reminded us that this wasn't a game. We were taught what action we should take if we found ourselves in a burning aircraft at 20,000ft. In truth, the answer was very little, but we went through the motions anyway.

'Any fire is most likely to come from the engine,' the instructor told us. 'You could carry out a side slipping or diving manoeuvre to try and put flames out. This involves turning the aircraft, using the top rudder to encourage the direction of the flames away from the cockpit. But be careful, if you overdo the turn, the aircraft could stall and you could kill yourself anyway. The only other alternative is to bale out of the aircraft and take your chances on the end of a parachute.'

In short, if your aircraft caught fire, things didn't look good. Nobody wanted to burn. Some pilots made a habit of baling out quite successfully, but it never appealed to me. Perhaps it had something to do with my fear of heights. Whatever it was, the few times when my aircraft became defunct, I opted to crash-land it instead of trusting my life to a flimsy piece of material.

Blind flying was another skill we had to acquire and for me it ranked almost as high as spinning for sheer unpleasantness and occasional fear. Blind flying was more difficult for me than anything else. Flying is a simple process, if the nose of your aircraft is above the horizon you know you are going up and if it is below the horizon then you know you are going down. With blind flying there is no horizon. The exercise involved putting a crude canopy over the cockpit so you couldn't see out and so had to fly by your instruments. The idea was to simulate night-time flying. You just had to trust and obey your instruments and fight the urge to follow your own instincts.

Over the weeks I began to develop into a reasonable pilot. I was not a natural, but I believe I was what I would call a good average. And, after fifteen hours of flying with an instructor, it was decided that I was ready to fly solo. Fifteen hours was about average for a pilot to go it alone. Some of the young men did it in eight hours, some took much longer and some never made it all.

Flying solo is a pivotal moment in all pilots' lives and quite a few failed to clear this hurdle. The truth is not everyone can fly. Sometimes they just didn't have the feel for it. I always believed that if you followed the instructions you were given you would get through, but some of them had to battle their nerves and that was one fight they couldn't win. A lot of young pilots got into trouble because they froze at the controls through panic and fear. This happened in training and in combat when they forgot everything they had ever been taught. And it cost them their lives.

On the morning of my solo flight, I caught the bus to the aerodrome and spent the journey reasoning with myself that I was more than capable of flying an aeroplane alone. I had reservations in my mind over whether I was going to make a decent job of it, especially the landing because that bit was seen by the instructor on the ground. But, it wasn't complicated, I told myself. They wouldn't send you up solo if they didn't think you could make it. They didn't let you go up on your own unless they were fairly sure you were going to bring their aeroplane back in one piece.

It was 30 August and I peered up at the sky from my seat in the bus. Visibility wasn't great. To make matters worse, I didn't have the kindly Mr Arnold to coax me to success. First solos could only be performed in front of the Chief Instructor, Mr Holt. I didn't expect any words of encouragement from him.

Mr Holt met me on the airfield. He came up with me on the first flight and made me do one or two landings to get a feel for conditions.

After we had finished, he said: 'Right, Corbin, you're on your own.' With that Mr Holt got out of the aeroplane. He tied up the straps of his seat and made sure they were secure. Loose straps in the back passenger seat could get tangled up with the controls of the aircraft, which could land you in a lot of trouble.

'I want you to do two circuits of the aerodrome. And let's not have a repeat of what happened last week Sgt Corbin. One idiot is quite enough,' warned Mr Holt.

The Chief Instructor was referring to the spectacular failure of the first 'solo' effort of our group. I remember him as a bright young man who had too much to say for himself. He was what we called the 'line-shooting' type, that is, he was rather conceited and a little arrogant. Anyway, he was the star pupil and the first to go solo, which made him particularly intolerable.

Visibility for his solo was quite poor, but not bad enough to suspend flying. The young pilot took off in a burst of confidence and disappeared into some low cloud. After a pre-determined length of time, we began to scour the skyways in anticipation of his return. We waited and then waited some more, but he failed to materialise. Eventually the airfield received a phone call from a rather sheepish pilot saying that he had parked his aeroplane some 54 miles away in a field in the middle of no-where after getting hopelessly lost in what he thought was Norfolk. Oh, and could someone come and get him? Sometimes, there is justice in this world.

But now it was my turn. It was a nerve-racking experience and I began to feel some sympathy for my fellow student. Alone for the first time in the cockpit, I taxied down to the bottom end of the airfield. I checked the wind-sock for the direction of the wind and taxied to take-off position, scanning the skies to make sure there was nothing coming. Then I turned the aircraft left into the wind and opened the throttle to let the speed increase until the dial tipped 65mph. The aeroplane bumped along the grass until I gently eased her up by pulling the control column back.

After take-off, I climbed to a pre-determined height of 1,200ft and because I was going away from the aerodrome I turned left and completed a turn. I knew I had to do it exactly right and I decided not to stray too far from the aerodrome. I completed a couple of circuits, as instructed by Mr Holt.

I could see Mr Holt watching me from the ground. I was nervous and tense. I had only had fifteen hours flying time.

It was time to come down so I came across the bottom of the aerodrome and put the aircraft downwind. When I reached the correct position, I put the Magister into gliding mode so the engine was just ticking over. Then I turned crosswind and then into the wind and landed at the aerodrome. I taxied towards the instructor and came to a standstill.

Mr Holt looked at me.

'Well done, Corbin,' he said. That was the first and last time I ever heard him say that to me.

'Now you're ready to begin to learn to fly, do it again,' he continued and then marched off.

I was elated at having flown an aeroplane on my own, but now the real business of learning to fly was about to begin. Without the eagle eye of the instructor on me, I was more relaxed at the controls. I took off and swooped and soared above the aerodrome. I was a pilot, at last.

My solo flight was cause for celebration, of course. I didn't need many excuses to celebrate. Some friends and I headed for a local restaurant in Maidstone and then on to the Star Hotel in the town. It had a lovely dance hall with a sprung floor that attracted all the big bands. I was quite a good dancer because I had learnt to dance as a student at Shoreditch Town Hall and Hammersmith Palais, which gave me an advantage with the women. These were merciless times. If you couldn't dance to the required standard, it wasn't unusual for your female partner to walk off mid-song and leave you stranded in the middle of the floor. That night, like many nights, we drank and danced as if we didn't care.

On 3 September 1939 Britain declared war on Germany. I had an idea it was coming as the RAF had tipped me off several weeks earlier when they mobilised me. This meant I was now a full-time Reserve member in the RAF and required to wear the uniform at all times. I had flown an aircraft for the first time on my own two days before I was called up. I had completed just seventeen hours of flying time and now I was at war.

Chapter Three

1939 – Burnaston, Derbyshire

The official declaration of war proved to be an anti-climax for most if us. It was Sunday and I was at home in Bower Street when Neville Chamberlain's voice filled our living room with his famous announcement that we were at war. But Mr Chamberlain's address merely confirmed what we had known for sometime – that war was imminent, if not today, then sometime soon and, as if to give us a taste of what to expect, the Prime Minister's speech ended in air-raid sirens that sounded across the county.

The country braced itself, even though it would be many months before any bombs fell on our shores. I could also afford to be a little more relaxed. The announcement of war meant that I was no longer a part-time Reserve, but a bona fide member of the RAF. However, I had only just learnt to fly and still had to clear the considerable obstacles of elementary and advanced training school before I could take my place in fighter command or whatever command the RAF had lined up for me. And it seemed the RAF was in no hurry to have me.

A period of inertia gripped the service in the days immediately following Chamberlain's speech. It seemed that they just didn't know what to do with us all. It was a complete shambles in those early days of war and one could only guess what conversations were taking place in Whitehall.

'Right, sir, we have called up all the RAF Reserves.'

'Excellent, send them to Flying Training School immediately and let's get out there and stop Jerry.'

'Yes, sir. Ah, just one problem, we don't seem to have any aeroplanes for them to train in.'

'Oh, I see.'

'And, we're bit short of airfields, too, sir.'

'Ah, well what shall we do with them all while we get the planes built?'

'Not, sure sir. What about trying the old pin in the map technique? It's helped us before, sir when we've been in a tight spot.'

'Right, good thinking.'

'Here goes . . . ah Cambridge, good choice, very nice at this time of year. Shouldn't have too many complaints from them about being sent there, should we?'

And so it was that I was sent, along with eighty other young men, for a seven-week sojourn to Selwyn College, part of Cambridge University. It was an incongruous setting in which to train soldiers. The college was surrounded by acres of landscaped gardens on the edge of the city. Its distinctive red-brick building was steeped in history and built round a quadrangle. A Master's lodge, chapel and dining hall were part of its estate.

Selwyn was famed for its religious connections, having been founded by the first Bishop of New Zealand and it felt vaguely sacrilegious to billet scores of young men there who were hell bent on having a good time.

It was early September when we arrived and the university term had not yet resumed so there were no students around and we had the place to ourselves. We had a room each in the old college digs and the food served up in the dining hall was as good as any restaurant. All in all we had little to complain about.

The days were marked by one or two lectures in subjects like Morse code which was always tricky to pick up, unless you were a Naval officer like my brother-in-law, who was in the Signals and brilliant at deciphering all those pips. Outside the classroom our flight sergeant taught us drill which, for some reason, the RAF considered a necessary part of pilot training. The flight sergeant was an amiable enough chap and was not at all the bullying type like some of them. I think he realised we were all a lot brighter than he was and so left us mainly to our own devices.

As the days wore on, we slipped into a routine of marching four miles out of Cambridge to a local country pub where we indulged in a few pints of Bass and made sure we bought the sergeant enough beer to keep him happy before marching the four miles back to the college, singing vulgar limericks to pass the time.

As I sat in my ivory tower in Cambridge, the prospect of fighting the enemy seemed a long way off. This was my very own 'phoney war' and it was all rather dull.

Finally, autumn drew to a close and so did my time at Cambridge. In November 1939 I received notice that my elementary flying training was about to begin. As part of No.1 War Course, I was told to report to RAF Burnaston in Derbyshire. It would be their job to turn raw recruits, some of whom had done little flying but were rather good at marching, into pilots fit for combat.

I returned home to Bower Street for a couple of weeks' leave. My visits home followed a pattern. I appeared briefly in the kitchen where my father greeted me and my mother enquired after my diet. I never discussed my training or, later, my experiences of combat with my family. It was something you just didn't do back then. After a quick bite to eat, I would slip on my sports jacket and head into Maidstone for some fun.

At the end of my leave, my travel permit arrived telling me to take the train to Derby. I boarded at St Pancras and headed towards the Midlands. As the locomotive neared the city, I could see hundreds of barrage balloons floating high above the buildings. They were there to protect people from the anticipated onslaught of enemy bombers which at that stage had yet to materialise. Derby was, and still is, the home of Rolls-Royce, makers of the Merlin engine that powered the Spitfire. This made the city a target. It was only a matter of time before Hitler came calling. It was the first real evidence I had come across that the people of Britain were taking the threat of fascism seriously.

I stepped off the train. A biting wind swept across the platform.

'Sgt Corbin?' a voice enquired.

I turned around to face a young woman in RAF uniform. She was a member of the WAAF, the Women's Auxiliary Air Force, and they were often employed as drivers. It took me a moment to register that she was talking to me. As an RAF regular, I was now referred to by my rank. It felt a very special privilege to hold the rank of sergeant, not least because I had neatly sidestepped the ranks of private and corporal.

'Yes.'

'This way, sir, the van is waiting outside the station.'

The RAF service van took me to the airfield, about five miles outside the city. RAF Burnaston was bigger than Rochester, which was a peace-time aerodrome. Burnaston was noticeably geared up for war preparation with all the paraphernalia of military equipment such as anti-aircraft guns and petrol tankers or bowsers, as they were called, much in evidence.

A young man in RAF uniform showed me to a large hut which was to be my home for the next few months.

'You'll be bunking down at The Dorchester with us,' the young man grinned and nodded at a door with a small sign scrawled with 'The Dorchester – Abandon hope all ye who enter here'.

'By the way, I'm Goughie.'

'I'm Jimmy. The Dorchester? Sounds all right.'

'Well, Jimmy, you can decide for yourself,' he smirked as he pushed the door open onto a large dormitory tightly packed with twenty to thirty beds, one of which was mine. It was a far cry from The Dorchester or any other hotel for that matter. It was clean, but sparse and was certainly a comedown after the comparative comfort of Selwyn College.

Goughie directed me to an empty bed.

'That's yours Jimmy, next to me and Geoffreys, another renegade.'

A young man with fair, chiselled good looks was stretched out on his bed smoking and reading. He looked up, waved and grinned at Goughie's description of him. I noticed when Goughie spoke his breath hung in the air and despite the presence of a small coal burner in the centre of the room, it was clear the temperature inside was the same as outside. I dropped my kit on my bed and sat down rubbing my hands.

'Right Jimmy, don't make yourself too comfortable, we're going out. Geoffreys, you coming?'

'Certainly am.' He leapt up and pulled on his overcoat.

I had the sense they both knew where we were going, even if I didn't. The three of us left The Dorchester and ambled towards the perimeter fence.

'So, Jimmy, how old are you?' Goughie enquired as we wandered along a country lane away from the airfield.

'I'm 23.'

'Really? A man of the world then. Bet you've been out with a few women then in your time?'

'One or two,' I replied warily.

'Careful, Jimmy, Goughie's love life or rather lack of it is an ongoing saga,' Geoffreys nudged Goughie.

'It's all right for you, mate, women can't get enough of you. Anyway, I'm only 19, I've got plenty of time.'

'Well, you have either got it or you haven't.'

Goughie ignored him.

'So, Jimmy, got a girlfriend?'

'No, not at the moment.'

'That won't last, there's a massive WAAF unit nearby. Enough to go round for all of us, even you Goughie,' Geoffreys laughed.

The banter continued until we came across a group of houses, shops and pubs clustered around a small village green.

'This is Mickleover,' announced Goughie.

'How d'you know about this place?' I asked.

'I'm from just down the road at Nottingham. Right there's three pubs, the best of which is the Nag's Head. Good beer and a gorgeous barmaid, what else could a man ask for?'

'Possibly for the barmaid to take some notice of you,' teased Geoffreys.

We entered the pub and were instantly greeted by the landlord. Geoffreys did the honours.

'Jimmy, this is Stuart, our landlord. Stuart used to play football for Scotland.'

Stuart greeted me, 'Right, gents, what can I get you?'

'We'll have three pints of Burtons, Stuart.'

Geoffreys and I chatted to Stuart while he pulled our pints. Goughie was busy watching a young girl who was absorbed in cleaning the table tops. I presumed this was Stuart's daughter who was indeed strikingly attractive. Geoffreys also noticed Goughie. He nudged me and rolled his eyes.

'Unrequited love, it's a terrible thing,' he grinned, 'anyway, cheers Jimmy. Here's to No.1 War Course.'

The next couple of days were spent adjusting to my new surroundings and sorting out my equipment such as parachutes and flying gear. Two days after my arrival, I was ready to fly. I reported to the airfield and was pleased to find a familiar looking Miles Magister waiting for me outside the instructors' hut.

Once again I was blessed with a lovely instructor by the name of Mr Watson. He was short, shorter than me and I'm not tall, but a good-looking man with a black moustache. He was smart and dapper and I enjoyed his tuition throughout my initial training.

'Right, Sgt Corbin, are we ready?

'Yes, Mr Watson.'

'When was the last time you flew young man?'

'I haven't been up since August, Sir.'

'Let's hope you've not forgotten what to do then.'

I climbed into the compact cockpit of the Maggie and went through the cockpit drill. When we were ready I took off. In the distance, the barrage balloons swayed over Derby. To the north the green fields fell away. It was good to be airborne again, although, in truth, I hadn't completed enough flying time to say that I had missed it greatly. Once I was aloft, the cold began to bite even though I had two pairs of gloves underneath my gauntlets. It was November and the hoodless cockpit was draughty and ice-cold. The windscreen frosted over making it impossible to see where I was going. I judged my position and navigated my way back to Burnaston by leaning out of the cockpit. The airfield came into view and as I touched down and came to a standstill, Geoffreys and Goughie were stood waiting for us.

'You survived then, Jimmy,' said Goughie.

'Just,' I replied.

'I think that's cause enough for celebration. Get your glad rags on, we are going into town. Even Goughie's feeling lucky,' said Geoffreys, and we headed for The Dorchester.

We changed quickly to stave off the biting cold and climbed into the back of the service truck which would drop us off in Derby town centre.

We felt well-off for those times. My salary was 13s 6d a day and with a pint costing just 7d, I got a lot of beer for my money.

The truck deposited us in the town. As it left, the driver leant out of the window and scowled,

'Pick you up here, 10 o'clock sharp. Don't be late, or you'll have to walk back.'

Goughie, with his local knowledge, took the lead.

'Right, I reckon a couple of pints in the Bell and then on to the Assembly Rooms. It's got a great band and there'll be loads of WAAFs there for the taking.'

'Sounds good to me,' I replied and we headed down the dark streets. Emboldened by a few pints of beer, we decided it was time to treat the ladies at the Assembly Rooms to our presence.

The Assembly Rooms was a big venue with a huge dance floor and by the time we arrived the excellent dance band was in full swing.

We ordered our drinks at the bar and soon enough our uniforms attracted interest from the ladies and a group of local girls approached us and we fell into conversation.

'You're pilots, aren't you?' one of them asked coyly.

'Yes, that's right. We are based up at Burnaston,' said Goughie.

Another of the girls pointed to the three chevrons on my sleeve.

'Here, don't those stripes mean you're an officer, one of them wing commanders?'

The other girls 'oohed' in appreciation. I winked at Goughie.

'That's right. Wing Commander Corbin at your service,' I grinned.

After all, who was I to correct them and admit I was in fact a just lowly sergeant and under training to boot?

I continued to enjoy my pint of Burtons and looked around the hall. On the far side, I spotted a beautiful young girl. She was tall, about 5ft 7in, and very fair. She held herself with such grace as she stood with her friends by the dance floor. I decided to go up and introduce myself.

The slow foxtrot, my favourite dance, came on.

'My name is Jimmy Corbin. Would you care to dance?'

She said yes and we took to the floor. Her name was Audrey and she was a WAAF who helped to maintain the balloon stations.

After the dance had finished, I noticed that it was five to ten already.

'Look, I have to go, but can we meet again?'

'I would love to,' she smiled.

After that night Audrey and I enjoyed many an hour in each other's company on and off the dance floor.

War may have raged in France, but No.1 War Course was making the most of its time in the Midlands. Our pressure came in the form of flying tests and exams, which I always felt that if you did as you were told you would pass and get through.

Our evenings were spent either at the Nag's Head or I would meet Audrey for a night of dancing or a trip to the flicks. Apart from the cold, life was good.

As winter wore on the freezing weather continued unabated, putting our training in doubt as flying could be suspended in extreme weather conditions.

One morning we woke up and the room was even colder than usual. Thick ice had formed on the inside of the windows. We got dressed hurriedly and emerged from The Dorchester to find that a thick layer of snow had fallen during the night. We knew there would be no flying that day.

'Anybody fancy a spot of ice-skating?' grinned Goughie.

'Top idea.'

We collected our skates and made our way to a pond near the airfield. Sure enough, it had completely frozen over so we slipped on our skates and took to the ice. We must have looked quite a sight. Twenty or so young pilots in RAF uniform pushing each other, laughing and sliding all over the place.

As the day wore on someone suggested that we all decant to the Nag's Head. Darkness fell as a group of about ten of us, wrapped up in our flying jackets and scarves disappeared in the direction of Mickleover in search of liquid refreshment. Fresh snow began to fall.

We arrived at the Nag's Head, but not before enjoying many snowball fights on the way.

'The usual, is it boys?'

'Line them up, Stuart.'

My tipple was Bristol Cream Sherry, although I was very partial to the local beer and there was certainly plenty to choose from. Derby was blessed with numerous breweries. The evening wore on and conversation flowed with the normal high-spirited exchange of jokes and banter.

At 10.30 p.m., Stuart rang the bell and called time.

'Right, c'mon lads, let's be having you. Time to go.'

Reluctantly we drained our glasses and, still in high spirits, we slipped on our overcoats and headed for the exit.

'Night lads.'

'Cheers Stuart, see you soon.'

Goughie opened the pub door and a wall of snow tumbled into the pub.

'Hey, Jimmy, look at this.' He called me over.

We gathered round to inspect the white stuff on the floor and then realised that the windows were also completely obscured by drifting snow.

'Well,' said Stuart philosophically, 'There's no chance of you boys going anywhere tonight.'

It has to be said that we all took the news in our stride and were philosophical about being marooned in a pub with excellent beer, a generous landlord and a pretty barmaid. We retired to the bar for another pint and the Nag's Head became our home for the next six days. It beat The Dorchester, that was for sure.

When we finally emerged and made our way back to the airfield, no-one seemed overly perturbed by our absence. It was clear that no flying was going to take place for sometime. The snow had drifted as high as the hangars. The RAF service vans were completely covered in snow and the aircraft remained inside for another three weeks, so further delaying my training and, by default, entry into the war. There was little for us to do other than build snowmen and wait for the thaw.

In February, the cold eased a little, the snow melted and we were flying once more. The aim of the EFTS was to make sure that we had grasped the basics and to propel us towards more technical flying. We spent long days perfecting our take-offs and landings. We had to master making steep turns, stalling, climbing and, of course, spinning. It was also the first time I flew cross country. Until then I had only practised flying within a relatively safe distance of the aerodrome. Now the instructors had to be sure that we could follow a pre-determined course and navigate our air-craft safely back to Burnaston. I had already done thirty hours flying by this time. The instructors set our courses west and south of Derby town to steer us clear of the barrage balloons.

I met Mr Watson in the morning, as usual.

'Right Sgt Corbin, I want to you to travel to Ashbourne and back again, of course. Here are the co-ordinates. Keep a sharp look out. If you go wrong keep an eye on your fuel gauge. OK, good luck.'

I climbed into the Miles Magister, did my checks and taxied to the end of the runway. My take-off was smooth as I turned the aircraft and climbed to a height of about 2,000ft. It was cloudy in places which didn't hinder me as I kept well below the cloud line. What I remember most was the biting cold that seeped through my gloves and flying jacket.

As soon as I gained height I could make out the spires of Derby Cathedral jutting up in the distance surrounded by the barrage balloons. Soon I had left the aerodrome and was heading south away from the city. Then I turned north, as instructed. I picked up the River Derwent and followed it as far as I thought was necessary before banking away in search of the town of Ashbourne which was somewhere in the Derbyshire Peak District. I scoured the green terrain which was rough and hilly. Patches of snow still covered the high ground. The odd hamlet appeared, but there was nothing as substantial as a town to be seen anywhere.

Slowly it dawned on me that I didn't know where I was. I wasn't even sure if I was still heading north. I twisted around in the cockpit. It didn't matter which direction I looked, all I could see were hills and more hills. There were no rivers, no railway lines, no church spires. In fact, there was nothing to help me work out where the hell I was. I wished I was back in Maidstone where I could just peer over and there would be the trusty Medway River to guide me home. Derbyshire was unfamiliar territory to me. I didn't know what to do. I didn't know which direction to head in: south, north, east or west. I was angry with myself as I hadn't be paying sufficient attention to landmarks.

As time wore on, I knew I couldn't stay in the air just flying around forever. I checked my fuel gauge. At least there was something still left in the tank, but for how long? There was nothing for it, but to try and put the aeroplane down somewhere.

I looked over and spied a farmer's field. It looked relatively flat, well, flat enough. I circled it a couple of times to make sure there was room enough for me to land and then on my third approach I eased back on the throttle and brought her down as gently as I could. Some high electricity pylons appeared suddenly out of the corner of my eye. I cursed myself for not noticing them before, but it was too late for me to do anything other than just hope someone up there liked me. I missed them by what felt like a fraction of an inch.

Thankfully everything else went according to plan and, all in all, it was a good false landing. I brought the Magister to a standstill and got out of the cockpit.

A farmer who must have watched the whole scene from his farmhouse window was walking towards me.

'You'll be wanting to use the phone, then,' he said and turned to head back in the direction of the farm buildings.

I followed him, feeling rather foolish. I phoned the aerodrome and my instructor flew over and landed in the same field. I flew back with him. It transpired that I was a good 30–40 miles away from Burnaston, but to this day I have no idea where I was.

Mr Watson guided me back to Burnaston. There was no question of being punished that time round. Getting lost was an occupational hazard for the inexperienced pilot. Thankfully it was my first and last time. My second attempt and subsequent cross-country flights ended more successfully, but despite this there was always a nagging element of doubt about it. You couldn't be sure you had got it right until the welcoming sight of the airfield and the aircraft hangars came into view. It was a great sight. In fact, seeing any airfield hove into view always brought with it a rush of relief that you had made it back in one piece.

Inevitably the others ribbed me mercilessly for my mistake.

'Jimmy, fancy a pint at the Nag's Head, that's if you can find your way there,' Geoffreys teased.

'I will draw you a map, if you like,' Goughie chipped in.

'Very funny. It's all right for you, you live round here. I would like to see you find your way around Kent. You wouldn't know your arse from elbow. Anyway, I'm off to see Audrey, at least she'll give me some sympathy.'

'I'm sure she will, Jimmy,' winked Geoffreys.

During the day, our training also began to progress at a pace. Low level flying was a skill that I had to acquire before I could pass EFTS. I found this type of flying a real pleasure and low flying was easily the most thrilling aspect of any of my training.

On 20 March 1940 I took the Maggie up for my first low-flying experience. We flew out towards a designated low-flying area which was in a relatively isolated part of Derbyshire. Low flying was a vital part of our training, but it was considered a pest by the local people as the noise worried the cattle and the sheep. This meant we could only practise in certain places. When I reached the correct area, I reduced my height from 4,000ft to less than 1,000ft and opened the throttle. The craft tipped 120mph. The combination of speed and proximity to the earth was an amazing sensation. This was real flying. This was why I wanted to be a pilot.

The aircraft moved in tandem with the undulations of the ground. It followed every curve and contour of the land. It was truly thrilling. For the first time I could really feel the speed of the aircraft. High-level flying offered no appreciation of speed, but low down it was a different story altogether. I was on a high as I experienced the exhilaration of flying a machine that travelled faster than anything else. I was so close to the ground I could almost lean out and touch it as it raced away and disappeared beneath my wings. I went as low as I could get away with and even had to pull up to avoid tall trees and hills. If I hit anything at that height I didn't have a hope. It was possibly the most exciting experience of my life, but it paid not to be over-confident or foolish. Death could come quickly for the cocky young pilot.

After an hour I decided I had better return to the airfield. Reluctantly, I climbed back up to 4,000ft and flew back to Burnaston. When I landed I was still buzzing from my first low-flying experience. I could only imagine what it was like in a Spitfire which was three times as fast as the Miles Magister.

The last time I flew at RAF Burnaston was on 8 April 1940. My EFTS should have lasted no more than seven weeks, but bad weather had delayed the completion of the course by another five weeks.

During EFTS there had always been the threat hanging over our heads of being told, very politely, that you would never make a successful pilot and, in point of fact, you should never have been born. In which case, you were cut from the course. Many pilots did not make it through this stage.

Fortunately, Goughie, Geoffreys and I all passed the course and so were able to move on to the next stage, which for me was 14 Flying Training School (FTS) at Kinloss in Scotland.

I was ready to move on, but I would miss Derby, the Nag's Head and all the other places we had made our own during our stay there.

One evening shortly before I left for Scotland, I met Audrey for what was to be the last time.

We were in a café just off the main high street, near the cathedral.

'Audrey, my posting has come through.'

'That's great, Jimmy.'

'Not really, it's Kinloss in Scotland. They couldn't have sent me further away if they'd tried,' I said.

'It won't be forever. Besides we can always write to each other,' she smiled at me.

'Well, that's just it, Audrey. I don't think we should continue.'

Her face fell and she stared into her coffee cup.

'Why not? I thought you really liked me.'

'I do. It's not that. It's just that if I get through Kinloss then it's on to advanced training. I could be in combat in just a few months.'

'I know that. But we can deal with that when the time comes.'

'Look Audrey, you're a great girl and if things had been different, who knows, but I don't want to make a widow out of you. It's best if we say our goodbyes now.'

With such uncertainty ahead, I didn't think it was fair to prolong our affair. Unlike some of the pilots, I wasn't interested in marriage. I was still only 23 and enjoying the bachelor life too much to want to get tied down. But there was another reason. The war was getting closer for me. The news from France wasn't promising. It was only a matter of time before the country fell to the Germans. Next it would be us. I had come to realise even then that the chances of my survival were fairly remote. Audrey was too young to grieve over me.

Her eyes welled up.

'All right, Jimmy, if that's the way you want it.'

She got up and left and that was the last time I saw her.

Chapter Four

JUNE 1940 – CRANFIELD, BEDFORDSHIRE

Goughie, Geoffreys and I said our goodbyes at RAF Burnaston in April and went our separate ways. Regrettably, I never heard from either of them ever again and I have no idea whether they survived the war. Life was like that then. You were thrown together with people for short periods of time only to be split up. Some people you stumbled across again later, but mostly you were so caught up with the business of war that you had no idea where those who had once been your closest friends and confidantes ended up. But we left with good memories of each other's company during those brief few months in Derbyshire and now it was time to move on. There was nothing left to do but wish each other luck.

Kinloss was a desolate place and full of foreboding. Although it was April, it was bitterly cold in Scotland and the draughty Nissen huts where we were billeted were heated by a stove that belched noxious fumes from the centre of the room. Ice on the inside of the windows revealed that other than slowly poisoning us, the stove had little impact on the temperature. The only upside was that I would have to endure just two weeks of this before I would be moved on again – assuming I mastered how to fly the North American Harvard.

For some the Harvard was an unwieldy beast of an aircraft, but there was little time to worry about it now. On the first day, the instructor stood on the aircraft's wing and launched himself into a well-rehearsed speech on how to treat the Harvard. I realised just how daunting the task ahead would be.

'Right gentlemen, there are several differences you'll notice about the Harvard. Firstly, this is an oxygen tube which means you're going to be flying higher than you could even imagine. Your first task will be to take her up to 15,000ft and stay up for half an hour so you know how a lack of oxygen affects you. Once you start feeling unsteady don't hang around, get the oxygen mask on. Keep an eye on your altitude at all times, it could save your life. Pass out at 15,000ft and the next thing you'll see is St Peter at the Pearly Gates.'

I turned to one of the others in my group.

'Christ, I've never been higher than 10,000ft before.'

'Me, neither.'

'Got something to say Mr Corbin?'

'No, sir.'

'Good, then you can go first. In you get.'

I climbed into the two-seater and the instructor got in behind me. It was surprisingly roomy and comfortable, which I put down to the fact it was American-made and the Yanks always designed their aircraft with one eye on comfort.

The instrument panel in the cockpit displayed a bewildering array of dials, switches and levers. Even for a confident young pilot who thought he knew how to fly aeroplanes, it was a humbling sight. At first glance I thought to myself 'How could anyone learn all that?' The prospect of getting my wings seemed a dim and distant one.

The other notable difference with the Harvard was the control column or joy stick. On it was a small gun button, or a tit as we liked to call it. Its presence made me realise that combat duty was drawing nearer with each passing day.

I composed myself and went through my cockpit checks, which were daunting to say the least: Hydraulics – Trim – Mixture – Pitch – Flaps – Fuel – Gills – Switches. I checked the lot. If I forgot any part of the drill, it would be me who would pay the price.

Checks completed, as far as I knew, I was ready for the off. I switched on the ignition, pumped 5lb of pressure in the fuel line with my left hand, using the wobble pump on the left-hand side of the cockpit. With my right hand I primed the Ki-gass pump. My thighs clutched the joystick back and my right foot nudged the inertia starter switch down. The starter suddenly screamed into life. I estimated when it had reached the right pitch and nudged it back up with the same foot. The engine rotated and fired, but I had to keep pumping pressure and priming the pump to keep it going. Soon the aircraft was ticking over happily and we were able to set off.

Take-off was smooth, although I could feel she was a heavy plane to handle. My only real cause for concern was that I knew the levers that controlled the flaps and the undercarriage were positioned immediately next to each other and there was the ever present danger of selecting the wrong one. The only way round this was always to move the undercarriage lever with a clenched fist, but actually to grasp the flaps lever so as not to confuse the two. Not everybody got it right.

Once in the air we picked up our speed and hit an effortless 160mph, still half of what a Spitfire was capable of, but for the moment it was fast enough for me.

We started to climb. The altimeter went through 10,000ft and then 12,000ft before hitting 15,000ft. I levelled out and waited for my body to react to the dwindling supply of oxygen it was now receiving.

Oxygen starvation affected people differently. From time to time pilots misjudged the correct oxygen level and passed out. If they didn't regain consciousness in time, they killed themselves. In truth, I always thought it was a bit like drinking alcohol, you quickly understood how much you could take before you needed to resort to oxygen. But there were always those who misjudged their limits and paid the price. I didn't have a great deal of sympathy. You had to be bloody stupid not to realise that you were feeling unsteady.

In fact, as the Harvard reached 15,000ft, I felt fine and I later found that I could cope at 20,000ft before I needed to release oxygen through my mask to stop myself passing out. It was a huge relief. I had passed the height test.

After circling the base a couple of times to ensure I had got the hang of the controls, I brought her into land. There were several rumours doing the rounds that if you relaxed too much on landing, the Harvard could swing wildly and had a tendency to ground loop or flip over on its nose. I was not going to let that happen to me. I accorded the aircraft the respect she deserved and we touched down safely and came to a halt.

The instructor and I eased ourselves out of the cockpit. He turned to me and I could tell he was impressed.

'Well done, Sgt Corbin. I think we can safely say you have mastered the Harvard.'

My next move was to RAF Cranfield, the RAF's central training school in Bedfordshire. It was a flat and featureless aerodrome, but a marked improvement on Kinloss as it was considerably warmer.

At Cranfield I was due to complete the Advanced Flying Training course as part of 14 Advanced Flying Training School (AFTS). Cranfield had just upgraded to three tarmac runways and the smooth take-offs and landings were a joy in comparison to the lumpy grass runways that we had been used to.

It was June 1940 when we started at Cranfield. By now we were aware that the RAF had become heavily embroiled in the fighting just across the channel. France had fallen to the Germans and the War Cabinet's priority was to evacuate the hundreds of thousands of British soldiers who had become stranded on the beaches of Dunkirk in Northern France as they retreated from the Germans. Many were saved in a heroic effort by the Navy and hundreds of merchant ships, but news of the dead and wounded filled the newspapers. I had met a couple of Army boys at Kinloss who had survived Dunkirk and they seemed to have a low opinion of the RAF and the role they had played in trying to protect them as they waited to be evacuated from the beaches of Northern France. But the RAF was losing pilots. Suddenly the war did not seem so far away any more. The Battle of France was over. The Battle of Britain was about to begin.

Despite events going on around me, I tried to concentrate on the job in hand which was to fly well enough to please the instructors and finally get my wings.

I graduated from the Harvard to the Miles Master Mk I. They were fast, sleek and aggressive animals. Their all-wood construction meant they were much lighter than the Harvard and as they were powered by a Rolls-Royce Kestrel inline engine they could reach speeds of up to 243mph with ease. The Master could fly to heights of 28,000ft which was 18,000ft higher than the Magister could muster. I would be flying 5 miles up in the sky. Surely you couldn't fight at those heights? How naïve I was. This latest leap to a faster more powerful machine was a reminder that I was inching ever closer to combat aircraft.

Another quirk of the Master was a side-hinged hood which on my first flight my instructor had in the clearest terms possible been keen to remind me of.

'Make sure it's locked, or it will blow off when you open the throttle and knock the bloody tail off,' he growled at me and I sensed his comments were the result of bitter experience of young pilots who failed to heed his word.

Take-off in a Miles Master was an adrenalin pumping experience. Everything seemed to happen at once. I opened the throttle and then lifted the tail. The high power-weight ratio meant that the Master had exceptional acceleration and, as it rushed down the runway, I had to apply full-left rudder to prevent it veering off course. Once airborne it climbed rapidly and within five minutes we had reached 10,000ft. The high-pitched whine of the Kestrel engine was audible for miles around.

All in all, the Miles Master was a lovely aircraft, but something told me that it still wouldn't be a patch on the Spitfire.

My flying training proceeded at pace and with few obvious hitches. One day, about half-way through the course, I ambled into the mess and came across a group of pilots crowded around a noticeboard. One of them spotted me and shouted, 'Jimmy, you're down here.'

I jostled my way to the front and scanned a list of names that had been posted. There it was in neat type: William James Corbin.

'Well I'll be blowed,' a grin spread across my face, 'they've only gone and given me my wings.'

'There's hope for us all then,' some wag replied.

The RAF had decided in their wisdom that I was finally competent enough to be awarded my wings and to call myself a fully-fledged pilot.

The news that I had been given my wings was significant for another reason. It meant I was no longer just a sergeant any more, I was a sergeant pilot.

I had made it. I had fulfilled an ambition I had clung onto since childhood. Jimmy Corbin, son of a plumber from Maidstone, was an RAF pilot. It was a proud moment for me. That first flight at Rochester, when I stepped into a cockpit for the first time and fretted that the experience might terrify the life out of me, now felt like a lifetime ago. Then we had climbed to dizzy 2,000ft and travelled at 60mph. Now I flew at speeds of 200mph and at 10,000ft without so much as a second thought. My log book showed that I had completed 150 hours of flying.

Later that day, those who had received their wings were invited to attend the usual formality of a bullshit parade where the wing commander officially presented us with this tiny piece of material in the shape of two wings. I took it directly to the tailors who sewed it on to my tunic for me.

As we dispersed, I turned to one of the other pilots.

'Well, there's only thing left to do now.'

'What's that?'

'Have a party, of course.'

After the parade, a group of us headed to a local pub to show off our wings and celebrate our achievement. Parties were a large feature of my life back then and this one was ranked among the best. The booze flowed well into the night. The following day I awoke with the mother and father of all hangovers. I knew I wasn't fit to fly when I reported for duty that morning, but I didn't dare tell them I was still drunk as I would have been court-martialled.

Just to add insult to injury, the CO instructed me to carry out some air-to-ground firing practice. With my head pounding and my stomach lurching wildly, I obeyed the order and took the Master up. We headed towards a pre-determined area where there were targets positioned on the ground. I put the Master into a steep dive towards the targets and as I grew close I let off a round of ammunition vaguely in their general direction. If I hit anything it was more by luck than judgement as I was in no fit state to shoot anything with any degree of accuracy. Finally I completed the task and broke away from the target area and headed gratefully towards home.

As I descended towards the airfield, thoughts of returning to my bed filled my mind, still badly fogged by alcohol and a lack of sleep. The excesses of the night before began to overwhelm me and I battled to concentrate on the landing strip ahead of me. The pounding in my head had now been replaced by a low buzzing tone. I shook my head in an effort to rid myself of this irritating drone, but it didn't seem to matter what I did, the noise persisted.

Just as I was about to touch down, I realised to my horror that the buzzing noise wasn't coming from my head, but from the cockpit. It was the alarm warning me that I had failed to release the undercarriage and I was about to land with no wheels.

'Shit,' I exclaimed. It seemed the most appropriate word to describe that terrible feeling that I had no control over what was going to happen next.

The plane hit the runway with a horrendous crunch and skidded forwards, lurching and screeching violently all the way down the aero-drome. I clenched the control column and fought to keep the craft straight as it seared the tarmac at 60mph on its belly. I switched the engines off. Suddenly my hangover disappeared, but there was nothing I could do other than brace myself until the machine came to a standstill.

After an age, the Master finally stopped and everything fell silent. I checked myself over and could see no obvious damage so I hauled myself out and stood shaking next to my machine.

As the ground crew approached, I stood and winced at the sorry scene in front of me. The propeller had been mangled on impact, but the shell of the aircraft appeared relatively intact. Once the erks had ascertained that I was intact, their sympathy rapidly dissipated.

'I just forgot,' I shrugged.

They regarded me with utter disdain, sighed and turned their attention to their precious charge to inspect the damage. I stumbled off towards the mess and a certain dressing down. It may even cost me my wings. I would go down in RAF history as the person who managed to be stripped of his wings just twenty-four hours after gaining them. At that moment, I didn't feel I deserved those wings anyway.

I waited to hear the worst, but my CO never called for me. Miraculously no one realised my accident was the direct result of a boozy session with the lads the night before. In fact, it transpired that so many pilots forgot to lower the undercarriage on landing, even when they hadn't been drinking, that it wasn't worth causing a fuss over, let alone taking their wings off them.

To my amazement and relief, I wasn't even reprimanded for my appalling mistake and the wings that had been sown onto my tunic the day before remained firmly in place – just.

From then on I ensured that I put plenty of distance between partying and flying and life proceeded without further mishap. In early August my time at 14 AFTS ended. Another notice appeared on the board requesting us to attend a large room at the station later that day. We all knew what this meant. This would be the day when I would find out which RAF command was going to have the pleasure of my company.

The RAF home commands were Bomber, Fighter, Coastal and Balloon Commands. The chaps and I had spent some time mulling over the merits of each of the different commands, although, in truth, we knew little about them or what to expect. Undeterred by this dearth of knowledge, many of us had already decided where we wanted to go.

We filed into the room and took our seats. One of the chaps leaned over my shoulder and whispered,

'Well, Jimmy, old boy, what's it to be?'

'No contest. It's got to be Coastal Command.'

'Why's that?'

'Well, on Coastal Command you get to fly those lovely Sunderlands and you have twelve crew members on board with you. So it would be a bit like being the captain of your own ship. Besides, if I get hit, I have decided it's easier to die in company,' I grinned.

'Good point,' my companion laughed and sat back into his seat to hear what the wing commander had to say to us.

'Now you have completed your advanced flying, you will move on to the operational training units. You will be allocated to the separate commands where you will continue your training on dedicated aircraft of those commands.' The wing commander droned on a bit longer about what was expected of us and then the moment came to put us into the different commands.

Unusually for the RAF, we actually had some say in which command we wanted to be posted to. First up was Coastal Command. Those of us interested stood up and made ourselves known. I scanned the room, it was a popular choice and there were more volunteers than were required. The wing commander picked a select few from the group. Much to my disappointment, I wasn't chosen so I sat down again. That only left Fighter, Bomber and Balloon Commands. I didn't know much about Balloon Command, but I knew I didn't want to go to Bomber Command which struck me as particularly dangerous. Bombers were heavy and unwieldy aircraft, good at dropping bombs, but not that good at defending themselves from enemy aircraft or ground attack. At least in a fighter plane you had a chance to hit back. But, saying that, some of the boys were itching to get on to Bomber Command. Each to their own, I suppose.

Volunteers for Fighter Command were called and I jumped up smartly. This time I was in luck. The wing commander nodded in my direction. I was selected. I was now a member of RAF Fighter Command. In one brief moment the odds on my survival, as far as I was concerned, had suddenly lengthened.

At that stage, I still didn't know what aircraft I would be flying, but my suspense didn't last long. A couple of days later I was told that I was being posted to No. 7 Operational Training Unit (OTU), based at RAF Hawarden in Cheshire, for my conversion course to learn to fly fighter planes. I didn't know much about Hawarden, but I did know it only trained fighter pilots to fly one type of aircraft – the Spitfire.

Of course, we had a party to celebrate the end of 14 AFTS. A group of us headed for the local pub where we spent the evening knocking back the sherries and recounting the past months at Cranfield. Towards the end of the evening, one of the other pilots called the unruly gaggle of young men to order.

'Just before we all go our separate ways, I want to make a few awards.'

I put my glass down and listened with interest, wondering where this was going.

'Now, we all like to see what our machines can do, but perhaps trying to land without wheels may not be the best idea a person could have. Anyway, I'd like to present Jimmy with a little memento to remind him what happens when he doesn't lower the undercarriage.' With that he pulled out a smooth triangular block of dark wood. A small brass plate had the legend '14 AFTS' etched on it. I knew instantly it was the tip of a propeller that had once belonged to the Master that I, while suffering a fearful hangover, had damaged when I tried to land it with no wheels. I have kept it ever since.

Chapter Five

AUGUST 1940 – HAWARDEN, CHESHIRE

hortly after leaving 14 AFTS, I travelled to Hawarden aerodrome, just outside Chester. By either a strange coincidence or appalling planning, Hawarden was also right next to another airfield named Sealand. It was so close that when we took off we had to fly a right-handed circuit otherwise there was a real danger of colliding with aeroplanes taking off from Sealand.

Hawarden was a strange choice for an acrodrome, because when it rained the grass runways often became waterlogged. Work was going on to build a new runway, but in a rather desultory fashion as the workmen spent much of their time dodging the incoming planes.

A maintenance unit was also established at Hawarden and so the whole area, on and off the aerodrome, was liberally sprinkled with all types of aircraft. On the east side of the airfield was a large factory producing Wellington bombers.

No. 7 OTU was imaginatively housed in a large crate which had originally been home to a Lockheed Hudson aircraft. It was dark and dingy and had a tarpaulin sheet for a door. I was grateful to be there in the summer.

The crate was used by the instructors who were ex-Hurricane pilots of 73 Squadron and veterans of the Battle of France. Poor as it was, the instructors' accommodation was infinitely more salubrious than our own. Next to their 'office' stood a camouflaged bell tent where the student pilots could be found.

On the soggy grass were parked two gawky Miles Master Mk I trainers and half a dozen Spitfire Mk Is with yellow propeller spinners. The Spits' upper surfaces were camouflaged in their battle colours of dark earth and green. RAF roundels were painted on the wings and fuselage sides, and large white capital letters either side of the fuselage roundels denoted the squadron the aircraft had served and the aircraft's individual identity.

The Battle of Britain was now at its height and was mainly being fought in the skies over south-east England. As such, the Spitfires donated to Hawarden for our use were the RAF's cast-offs. They were in various states of decrepitude. But despite their tired exteriors they still looked as if they could pack a punch.

Set apart from the pilots' Spitfires was a brand new machine with a red and white spinner, the property of the chief flying instructor. It was on permanent standby for the chief instructor to take up, should an enemy aircraft decide to take a pot shot at the aerodrome.

It was 11 August 1940 when I flew a Spitfire for the first time. The day had started unspectacularly enough as I ambled over to the tent to join the other pilots. Nick Carter, a tall, blond, good-looking boy, who became a good friend, was already there, hunched around the crate with two others, shuffling a deck of cards.

'Ah, Jimmy, just in time, fancy joining us?'

I had become an enthusiastic member of the card school and enjoyed a game of poker when the opportunity arose which, in the RAF, was frequently.

'I certainly will.'

I found a spare crate and joined the group. I lit a cigarette and settled into the game as there was no telling how long we would have to wait before it was our turn for practice.

Nick dealt the cards. Something caught his eye and he stopped and then nodded in the direction of the officers' mess.

'This looks like trouble,' he said.

I looked up and saw Joe Pegge marching purposefully towards us. Joe wasn't a trained instructor, but a very experienced pilot who was taking a 'rest' from the frontline action. He had become 'tour expired' as it was called and was posted to Hawarden to give us young, up-and-coming pilots an insight into what to expect.

I had already met him the previous day when we took a Master II aircraft up. What Joe wanted me to do was a routine take-off, several landings and a few turns, just to prove that I could handle the aircraft and therefore could be trusted with one of the more precious Spitfires.

As he approached his eyes locked onto mine.

'Put the cards down, Mr Corbin. I have got a treat for you.'

He looked across at a tatty Spitfire standing alone on the airfield.

'Think you're ready to handle her?'

'I certainly am, Sir.'

'Good, collect your gear and meet me by the kite.'

I stacked my cards and left the tent.

It was a bright sunny afternoon – perfect conditions for flying – as I collected my parachute, put on my helmet and walked towards the little Spitfire. Joe emerged from the crate shortly after.

'Right, in you get.'

I fastened my parachute, got onto the wing, lowered the side-flap in the perspex hood that covered the cockpit and climbed in. There was the strong smell of glycol in the cockpit and the floor was covered in mud left by the previous occupant.

Joe climbed onto the wing. He leaned across and ran through the instruments for me. I sat and studied the dials and knobs which were more advanced than any previous aircraft I had flown, but were reasonably familiar as I had been given all the manuals to study in advance of my first flight.

I was keen to take her up and see how she handled, but I waited patiently until Joe had finished his well-rehearsed lecture.

'Don't forget to pump up the undercarriage using this large handle on the right. After take-off, give it a few pumps on the large lever there and then select "Up" on this small lever below it. Got that?'

I checked the levers on my right-hand side.

'Yes sir.'

'Good. Now pump the large lever until the red light comes on and the wing indicators drop out of sight. Don't pump the control stick at the same time, or your take-off will look like a bloody switch back. And what ever you do, don't forget to lower the bloody things down again when you come back in otherwise you'll fall flat on your face. Got that?'

'Yes, Sir.'

'Right, taxi slowly and zig-zag, so that you can see where you're going.'

This was a quirk of the Spitfire. Its long nose obscured the view out of the front of the aircraft so you had swing it from side to side slightly to see where you were going.

'I understand, Sir.'

'Good. Now if you have a taxing accident, you will have to pay a fine of 5s. Get off the deck as soon as possible otherwise the glycol engine coolant will boil and that will cost you another 5s. If you get stuck in the mud, don't use too much throttle, or you will tip up on your nose and damage the propeller which. . . .'

'I know, which will cost me 5s, Sir.'

'Right. Good. Now remember what I said. Take it easy. Don't try anything fancy and off you go.'

He jumped off the wing and moved a short distance away from the aeroplane and stood with folded arms watching me intently.

I fastened the Sutton harness, shut the side flap to the cockpit and plugged in my radio transmitter (R/T) lead. The petrol cocks were already in the 'on' position, but it needed a few strokes on the primer knob to prime the Merlin engine. One of the ground staff then opened the flap on the side of the Spit's nose and plugged in the end of the mobile starter cable. He pressed the button on the battery top and held up his thumb. I switched on and pressed the starter button, and the airscrew began to turn the propeller slowly. There was a slight cough, a cloud of blue smoke and the Merlin engine roared into life.

Joe's words played over in my head. What was it he said about the glycol? I knew that if I made any mistakes it could cost me a small fortune in fines and I wasn't going to let that happen. The money collected as a result of shoddy airmanship were shared out among the ground crew or 'erks' as they were known. They did particularly well out of some of the courses. Well, I thought, not me, they don't. That was it. He said there was no need to wait until the engine warmed up. The radiator was under wing and partly masked by an undercarriage leg and the engine would boil if the aircraft didn't get off the ground quickly enough. Right, in that case, here we go.

I shouted 'contact' and the fitter unplugged the battery, closed the flap on the side of the engine and gave me another 'thumbs up', signalling that I was ready for the off. He then removed the chocks wedged in front of my wheels. The propeller began to turn. This was it, my first flight in a Spitfire Mk I.

I moved off along the airfield. I kicked the rudder bar from side to side so I could zig-zag down the field and get a better view of what was ahead of me. The craft trundled the 200yd or so to take-off point. There I paused and went through the cockpit drill – RAFTS, as it was known.

The 'R' referred to the retractable undercarriage. Yes, the green light was on and the wing pegs were showing. I noticed that part of one of them had been broken off where someone had used it as a convenient hand hold for getting on to the wing. Next was 'A' which meant I had to make sure the airscrew was in fine pitch for take-off. Those pilots who left it in coarse pitch paid dearly with their lives, because in coarse pitch, the aircraft could not gather enough speed for take-off. 'F' meant I had to make sure the flaps were up and wing indicators were flush. 'T' was trim. That was just a little behind the mid-point on the cockpit wheel and 'S' was the 'Sperry gyro' in the instrument panel which was caged or locked so that it did not spin unnecessarily.

I scanned the skyways in all directions to make sure there was no other aircraft in sight. No, it was all clear. I turned the Spit into the wind and opened the throttle as far as it would go. A great roar followed. The aircraft churned across the ground, bumping along its uneven surface, and gathering speed all the time. I pushed the stick forward, taking care not to let it go too far forward otherwise the propeller could just dig into the ground. I checked my speed and as the needle glanced 65mph the aircraft lifted from the ground and began to climb with ease.

But my work wasn't over yet. Far from it. I turned my attentions to the undercarriage.

'Right, what did Joe say I had to do? Oh yes, I remember now.'

I grabbed the big lever and pumped it three times. Then I moved the smaller lever into the 'up' position and then pumped for all I was worth.

'Bloody hell, I thought he said it took just a couple of pumps? It was more like twenty!'

I broke into a sweat. The real problem was trying to hold the control stick steady while I pumped up the undercarriage. It reminded me of that party trick where you have simultaneously to pat your head while rubbing your stomach. In other words, it was a bloody tricky thing to do. Finally the red light came on which meant the undercarriage was firmly up and the undercarriage indicators on the wing were out of sight. Now, I could relax.

I made the right turn away from the airfield to avoid anything that might be coming from Sealand aerodrome. When I reached a height of 25,000ft I throttled back into a cruising speed and really began to enjoy the machine.

The power of the engine was fantastic, the like of which I had never experienced before. It was 1,275hp which sounds like a meaningless statistic until you were seated in the cockpit and only then could you appreciate the sheer power of the Spitfire's engine.

As far as I was concerned, the machine was practically viceless. In addition to the enormous surge of power you felt beneath you, it handled smoothly, could turn in a small radius and could be manoeuvred with relative ease. Later, when I practised spinning, I discovered, along with every other Spitfire pilot, a very welcome quirk. The aircraft would judder slightly just before reaching stalling point, giving me ample time to react and prepare myself for the plunge downwards.

The aircraft reacted with ease to my every request and together we swooped and soared high over the North Wales landscape, above the clouds even. It was a magical beginning to a friendship that was to last five years. A feeling of total elation washed over me. I cannot describe it in any other way. It was a combination of the power, the speed, the height and the feel that made the Spitfire such a special aircraft. It felt as if she was on your side. I didn't want it to end, but of course it had to. I checked my watch. I had been up for an hour and fifty-five minutes. The fuel gauge told me it was time to return to base.

As I came in for my landing, Hawarden was on my right. Joe's words came to the forefront of my mind once again. I made sure I was downwind. I was still travelling at about 180mph. I moved the airscrew from coarse to fine pitch and pumped the wheels down. Then I moved across wind and the flaps came down.

I pressed a little metal tab on the instrument panel and there was a hiss of compressed air and the nose dropped. I eased back the trimming wheel, brought the tail down level, then, opening the hood, I slid it back and turned gradually into the wind on a curved approach so I could still keep sight of the airfield. If I had flown straight, the Spitfire's nose would have restricted my view.

There was a large patch of rough grass not too far from B Flight which I aimed for. I levelled off. My airspeed was now in the region of 90mph as the edge of the field shot past me. I throttled back and the wheels touched down quite gently. The Spitfire bowled along the grass. As it slowed, the tail wheel dropped and the aircraft was firmly down. As it rolled to a halt, I braked carefully, remembering to put the flaps up so as to avoid being slapped with a 5s fine for taxying with the flaps up.

After applying the brake, I pulled the slow-running cut-out ring. The airscrew flipped around a few more times before finally stopping. The Spitfire was still. It suddenly seemed very quiet. I climbed out stiffly and unfastened my parachute.

An aircrew member met me as I jumped off the wing.

'Was everything all right with her, Sgt Corbin?'

'Yes, not bad, not bad at all.'

Joe emerged from the 'crate'

'Ah, Sgt Corbin, I was beginning to think you had decided not to bother coming back.'

'Sorry, sir, got a bit carried away.'

And with that I swaggered off in the direction of the sergeant's mess. It had been a good day. I understood why Spitfires were a pilot's dream. Surely, in one of those, I would be safe from anything the Germans might have?

The finishing touches were put to our training, including getting to grips with the R/T, which was still in its primitive stages then. R/T training consisted of being vectored, which meant we were given a set course to fly in various different directions.

I also had my first taste of formation flying where the instructor would take up two pupils at a time and lead them around in a large 'V' or 'Vic' formation as it was called. It was a difficult skill to master.

'Right, keep it tight, try and stay about 50yd apart. Keep an eye on who's on your wing. Don't get too close. We can't afford to lose any of you at this stage,' the instructor told us.

I turned to one of my fellow pilots and grumbled,

'This is a load of bollocks. I am going to spend all my time just trying not to fly into you while the Germans pick us off one by one.'

Even then the flaws to formation flying in combat were obvious. There were twelve planes in a Vic formation in total, but the only person who could look out for the Germans was the commanding officer up front. If he missed them, the rest of us were sitting ducks.

But the other pilot just tutted, 'Do you ever stop binding, Jimmy? I think the RAF knows what they are doing.'

We were also taught how to attack, which at that time was through a simple approach from the stern or behind the target aircraft. Our instructors, having benefited from first hand experience of shooting the enemy, were clear on their tactics.

'Get up close behind, put the red dot of the sight just above the fuselage of the 109 or whatever it is and press the button.'

It sounded simple enough in theory, but the difficulty was getting yourself into position behind an enemy aircraft in the first place, especially, as they employed the same tactics and were equally resolved to get behind you.

The course highlight was air-to-ground firing. In turn, we were despatched to the mouth of the River Dee in north Cheshire. When we got there we were allowed to shoot eight guns into a sandbank. The Spitfire carried eight Browning guns, four of which were encased in each of its wings. When fired they made an impressive purring noise. Orange streaks shot out from my wings and hit the water in a neat line. It took about eleven seconds to deplete the Spitfire's ammunition stocks and we were warned to fire in only two and three-second bursts or risk running out of bullets while surrounded by enemy aircraft.

The 22 August 1940 marked my last flight at OTU, although I didn't know it.

My instructor told me to carry out some aerobatics in the Spit. This filled me with dread. I had never been taught properly how to do aerobatics. We were banned from trying them in the Magister and I never seemed to get round to it when I flew the Master. Now my first proper attempt would be in a Spitfire which meant the odds of success were stacked against me. Aerobatics in an aeroplane with a maximum speed of 140mph is a somewhat different experience from that of an aircraft travelling in excess of 300mph.

I took her up and braced myself. As I climbed to a roomy 20,000ft, I decided the best option would be to avoid anything fancy and stick to a slow roll which, as far as I was concerned, was complicated enough.

I pulled the nose slightly above the horizon and then started to apply the bank. When I got into that position, the nose started to drop so I had to apply top rudder and forward pressure in order to roll over and come out the other side. As I tentatively carried out the procedure, the aeroplane swung wildly from side to side and felt as if it was going all over the bloody place. Finally I managed to correct her until we were travelling in a straight line once again. It was the best I could manage, given my inexperience, but I cursed the fact that I hadn't got to grips with aerobatics earlier in my training.

I reported to the ground operators that I was returning to base and I headed for Hawarden. My instructions to the radio operator were met with silence. Instead the sound of heavenly choirs began to filter through my headset and I found myself listening to a rather pleasant rendition of *The Lord is My Shepherd*. I tapped the headset, but the divine music continued to fill my ears. Perhaps I had botched the roll after all and I had in fact crashed and died and this was the fanfare that had been laid on to greet me at the pearly gates. It took me some seconds to realise that it was the BBC choir. The TR9 sets we used had a reputation for being slightly unreliable and as it was Sunday I had picked up the BBC church choirs that played most of the morning. It was quite a relief to find an earthly explanation.

I landed to the accompaniment of *Dear Lord and Father of Mankind* and brought my Spit to a halt. The instructor was waiting for me. He seemed content enough with my efforts, but I vowed to myself that if I ever survived the war I would bloody well learn how to do aerobatics properly.

I got out of the cockpit and ambled over to the bell tent with every intention of picking up from where I left off at the card table, but as I approached, one of the other pilots looked up from the table and told me that the CO wanted to see me.

'Ah, Sgt Corbin,' the wing commander greeted me as I entered his office. 'Your posting has just come through.'

So this was it. The war had finally come to Jimmy Corbin.

'You are going to 66 Squadron,' the officer continued. 'They are currently at Coltishall in Norfolk, so I think you can expect to be kept busy. Good luck, Sgt Corbin.'

'Thank you, Sir.'

I wandered back to the mess where I found Nick Carter deep in thought.

'I've just been posted,' I offered.

He turned to me.

'So have I.'

'Where to?'

'Sixty-six.'

'Me, too. Looks like we're stuck with each other a bit longer then.'

Nick smiled. 'It should be a good show. They have had it a bit rough recently by all accounts.'

That night as I packed my kit bag the Luftwaffe strayed over north-west England and bombed Liverpool and Manchester. Twenty civilians were killed and nearly 400 were injured. It rounded off a good day for the enemy. During the day, they had twice raided the coast of Kent. In the ensuing dogfights, nine RAF planes were shot down and two pilots were listed as killed or missing. The Luftwaffe outnumbered the RAF two to one.

I picked up my flying log which all pilots kept and flicked through its pages to the latest entry. My instructor had signed me off as 'ready for combat'. In addition to his signature, he recorded that I was an 'average' pilot who was 'inclined to be careless' which was, no doubt, a reference to my escapade at Cranfield. But, despite my apparent mediocrity, the RAF deemed me ready for operational duty. Finally, a year after I had joined the RAF, it was my turn to join the war. I had been at Hawarden for just twelve days. Two years later, when the RAF had plenty of pilots, OTU training took three months to complete. But, for the moment, the RAF was losing men as well as machines and couldn't afford to let us train at our leisure. We were despatched to the squadrons with almost indecent haste.

And so it was with just twenty-nine hours of flying Spitfires that I joined 66 Squadron. It was soon to move from Norfolk to Kenley aerodrome, Surrey, just 20 miles south of London. I didn't know a great deal about the place. But I knew one thing – not many people survived at Kenley. Things were going to get hectic.

Chapter Six

AUGUST 1940 – KENLEY, SURREY

If I had any lingering doubts about how real the war was up until that point, they were dispelled for good on my first day at Kenley aerodrome. It was Saturday 28 August 1940. The squadron were detailed to fly their Spitfires onto Kenley after they had completed their last sortie of the day. The new boys, which included me, had to make their own way there. Four of us, including myself and Nick, from Hawarden had been posted to 66. We didn't give it much thought at the time, but, in retrospect, the squadron must have suffered considerable losses if it needed four new young pilots to fill the gaps.

One of the other lads, I can't remember who, had a Rover car and so early that morning we piled in to it and set out for Kenley. For reasons which escape me now, we decided to take in the bright lights of London and drive through the centre of the city. It was a Saturday so there would be lots going on and we could stop for a jar or two at a pub in the West End before continuing south to Kenley.

We arrived in Oxford Street in the early afternoon expecting to find the pavements thronging with shoppers, most of whom would hopefully be young women, but the streets of London were deserted. Instead the sound of an air-raid alarm filled the air and people had already taken refuge in the underground stations. Nothing could be heard above the high pitch whine of the siren so we stopped the car and got out to search the skies ourselves for evidence of an impending air attack that had triggered the alarm.

In the distance we could just make out about twenty silvery specks darting around the sky. They circled and swooped in what looked like some bizarre mating ritual, but it quickly became evident that there was no love lost here. This was a lethal fight between the RAF's Spitfires and the Luftwaffe's Messerschmitt Me109s. Shielding the sun from our eyes, we watched in awe as the pilots dipped and turned and twisted their aircraft in all directions leaving curly white contrails in their wake. The fight drew closer and the noise of the aeroplanes got louder until we could hear screams of protest from the engines as they were pushed to their limits. The aircraft dived to avoid each other only to climb back up again in a bid to gain some height advantage from which they could fire at the enemy. The high pitch squeal was overlaid with occasional bursts of machine gun fire. Suddenly one of the aeroplanes burst into flames and disintegrated. Debris floated down to the earth. It was a far cry from shooting at the sandbanks on the River Dee.

The four of us stood, mesmerised by the scene. Thoughts tumbled through my mind. Where were the tight flying formations and the systematic attacks that we had spent weeks trying to learn? This was just a jumble of aircraft with no order whatsoever. You couldn't even tell who was on which side. Surely those pilots knew who they were shooting at. Then my mind cleared and left me with just one thought. That would be me in a matter of days, maybe even tomorrow.

Beyond the aerial fighting there came the distant crump of bombs which signalled that despite the efforts of the RAF the German bombers had succeeded in reaching their targets. Scores of Heinkel He111s had broken through our air defences and had released their load somewhere over London. We later found out that this raid caused enormous damage as bombs scored a direct hit on the oil tanks at Tilbury docks in East London. Fire crews fought for days to extinguish the flames which provided a beacon to guide the German bombers to London. It was said that at night the raging fires at Tilbury were so intense that you could read a paper by their glow as far away as Piccadilly Circus.

The air-raid siren finally signalled that the attack had ended and the four of us got back into the car and continued our journey, each of us lost in our own thoughts. What we hadn't realised at that time was that we had been watching 66 Squadron in action – the very same squadron that we had all been posted to.

Our posting to 66 meant we were joining illustrious company. The squadron had a proud history as the first squadron to record a kill in the Battle of Britain. We had all heard of the story of Sgt Robertson, who was a sergeant pilot as I was.

One morning in June, he took off at 04.40hrs with two other Spitfires. They climbed to 15,000ft where they intercepted a lone German Dornier Do17 bomber in the skies over Winterton. A gunner from the enemy aircraft successfully hit one of the Spitfires forcing him to return to base, but the remaining pair, including Sgt Robertson, continued the attack. Finally, Robertson scored a direct hit and the Dornier crashed into the sea. Robertson survived the confrontation and earned himself the accolade of being the first pilot to shoot down an enemy aircraft over Britain. I never met Sgt Robertson. He was killed later that summer, just before I joined the squadron.

We arrived at Kenley aerodrome where a sergeant called Claude Parsons from 66 met us. He shook my hand and gave us a tour of the base. It transpired that before he joined the RAF to train as a pilot he worked with Supermarine, the makers of the Spitfire.

'So if there is anything you want to ask me about the Mark I, go ahead. Always happy to help. I'll show you around the mess and then take you over to the dispersal hut.'

The sergeants' mess was, of course, separate from the officer's mess and a fairly basic affair. It didn't bother me greatly that we were in separate mess rooms. The officers also had their own batmen to tend to their needs whereas we were left to fend largely for ourselves. Still there were some advantages to being a lowly sergeant. The officers had to foot their own hefty mess bills whereas we didn't. In any case, as the war went on this division between the various ranks became less and less pronounced and, unlike the other military services, pilots were always on first name terms with each other, regardless of their rank. Respect for experience was always greater than respect for rank.

Outside the mess hall a distant hum of Spitfires signalled their return to the airfield. Members of 66 Squadron's 'A' Flight were coming back in dribs and drabs, until the last of the stragglers finally touched down. Since the dogfight we had witnessed earlier that day in London, the squadron had been scrambled again. It was from this sortie that they now returned.

Claude led the way to the dispersal hut which was on the edge of the airfield. 'B' Flight was now at readiness and was about to take over from 'A' Flight who would be stood down. The crew room was full of pilots, playing cards and chatting quietly. All of them were wearing variations of RAF regulation flying gear which were topped by their yellow-doped Mae West life jackets. At a table in one corner sat the flight commanders and next to them was the duty telephone operator. On the table in front of them was a large black telephone.

Claude briefly introduced us to a few of the pilots who showed a mild interest in our arrival.

'Right, that's Bobby, or Oxo as he is affectionately known. That's Durex, don't ask,' Claude added quickly, referring the officer's unusual name. 'Pretending to read a book is Pickles. That's Johnny and believe it or not that scruffy beggar over there is a pilot and he's called Bogle.' Claude pointed at a young man in a fraying RAF issue sweater and dishevelled hair.

Some of the pilots introduced to us nodded in our direction while others made the odd facetious remark.

'Ah, more sprogs, just what we needed.'

'Welcome to the show, boys, front seats available daily.'

Claude then introduced us to the flight commander, Flt Lt Hubert Allen, or 'Dizzy' Allen as he was more popularly known. He had unruly red hair and freckles. He looked tough, even menacing, and took his job seriously, but off duty he proved to have a limitless capacity for fun.

He looked us over.

'So, are you boys operational?'

'No, Sir, but we have had a good few hours on Spits already,' one of us replied.

'Well, that's something I suppose. Don't worry, we will have you operational in no time. We have allocated you your flights anyway. Corbin, you will be on 'B' Flight.'

'Bad luck,' someone shouted and the others laughed.

All squadrons were divided into two Flights: A and B. Each Flight was made up of approximately twelve pilots who were then divided into Sections. Each Section had three pilots in it and was identified by a colour such as red, blue, yellow or green. The Flights remained the same, but you found out which Section you were on by checking the noticeboard in the crew room.

The flight lieutenant ignored the comments and continued. 'You can spend the rest of the day getting to know your way around. Any questions about Spits, ask Claude, he's the expert. You need to pick up your life jackets and get them painted pronto.'

'Yes, Sir.'

We left the dispersal hut and collected our own inflatable life jackets. These were primitive affairs worn over the chest. They were covered in stout canvas and blown up by mouth and we spent the rest of the day painting them with yellow dope to make us more conspicuous should we bale out and end up in the sea. Unbeknown to us the yellow dope made them highly inflammable.

When I had finished I strolled out onto the airfield and watched the squadron, or what was left of them, returning from the fray. Some of the Spits were badly shot up, their tails and wings peppered with bullet holes.

The planes trundled into their parking bays and rolled to a stop. I watched the pilots descend from their cockpits. They eased themselves carefully out of their aircraft and jumped to the ground where they exchanged a brief conversation with the ground crew who, like anxious parents, had searched the skies awaiting their return. Then they ambled off towards the dispersal hut. I had lost count how many times 66 Squadron had been up that day. Maybe three times, but it could have been four. Some of them were still sporting bandages from previous skirmishes and they all looked rather unkempt.

One pilot whose name I don't recall pulled back the perspex hood of his Spitfire and emerged from his plane. He got out onto the wing and pulled off his helmet. A member of the ground crew met him and he gave him a grim smile and spoke a few words to him. The erk looked at the Spit and nodded gravely. I noticed that the pilot's face was smeared with oil and I presumed that he must have sprung a leak at some point. The thick dark liquid was clearly irritating his face as he kept picking at it and rubbing it. He walked towards me and as he drew nearer I realised that it wasn't oil at all, it was blood. His face was covered in tiny cuts from which blood now oozed.

A group of pilots who were seated on the grass outside the dispersal hut enquired after him.

'What happened to you?'

'I got hit in the reflector sight, the bloody thing exploded and a load of glass shot into my face,' came the pilot's irritated reply.

'Get yourself patched up. We'll take you for a drink.'

'You're on.'

And with that he wandered off towards the dispersal hut to get cleaned up and be debriefed by the intelligence officer. I watched him go. Welcome to 66 Squadron, I thought.

As the day came to an end, the aircraft were put in their dispersal pens for the night. At that time, there was little night flying so our time was our own. The pilots who were on readiness the next day tended to rest quietly in their respective messes, but those on standby or rest days filled their evenings with trips to the nearest pubs for a few pints.

It had been a long day and Nick and I decided that we also deserved a drink which would give us an opportunity to familiarise ourselves with the local hostelries. We set out for a pub in nearby Purley that was a favourite haunt of pilots. It was Saturday night and when we got there the place was already packed with local lads and young girls all enjoying a few drinks. We ordered a couple of pints of Bass at the bar and chatted about our first impressions of Kenley.

Half way through the evening, the air-raid siren went off. This was directly followed by the ack-ack from our boys, signalling that the German bombers were somewhere overhead. Soon we could hear the crump of bombs landing in the distance. A couple of people debated the possible target.

'Sounds like Tilbury again, to me.'

'Nah, I reckon, it's more likely to be the city itself this time.'

Without warning, the thuds got louder until the distinctive sound of explosions could be heard. The bombs were getting nearer. Too near, and it was too late to try and find an air-raid shelter. All we could do was hope.

Suddenly there was a terrific crash and the pub door flew open. The walls shook and dust sifted down from the rafters. I leapt at the noise, but when I turned around everyone had disappeared. I looked down at the floor and it was a carpet of bodies lying face down with their hands covering their ears. My friend and I were the only two people left standing by the bar still clutching our pints. We both threw ourselves on the floor and joined the others until the raid had passed.

It was my first encounter with air-raid etiquette and although it was a thoroughly unpleasant experience it did have its upside. Lying on your stomach with the bombs raining down seemed to make it easier to strike up a conversation with some of the local young ladies.

The following morning we met our commanding officer, Sqn Ldr Rupert Leigh. He was a kind and charming man and popular among his men. The four of us stood to attention in front of his desk. He looked at us for a moment before he spoke. This is it, I thought. From today I would be a fully operational fighter pilot.

'You've had a little time now to get used to the way we do things round here. What are your thoughts?' the officer asked.

'It's certainly a busy place, Sir,' Nick offered a tentative reply.

Sqn Ldr Leigh smiled at the understatement.

'You can say that again. Well, we certainly need more pilots, but we need you alive. I know you've all flown Spits, but you still have a long way to go which is why I've decided that you won't be put on operational duty just yet. You need just a little more experience before you face the Hun. Get in as much practice as you can. You're going to need it.'

'Yes, Sir.'

We filed out. 'Just our luck to miss out on all the fun,' one of others said and we all agreed. Privately, yes, I wanted to be up there doing my bit, but a small part of me felt relieved that it wouldn't be today.

While the other pilots flew sortie after sortie, we filled the hours watching the ensuing dogfights which often occurred close to Kenley. We versed ourselves in squadron procedure and continued to practise our formation flying. It was a surreal situation to be in. I felt like a member of a cinema audience watching the latest action film. Only I didn't want to be seated in the stalls munching popcorn, I wanted to be one of the cast, preferably the hero who survived at the end.

The other pilots were polite and friendly. They would often share with us their stories of flying into gaggles of Messerschmitt 109s as they swarmed across the Channel. We would listen to their tales of watching a Messerschmitt 109 as it flashed vertically downwards right in front of them. Sometimes they were so close that the pilots said they could see the rivets and the streaks of oil on the fuselage. They impressed us immensely, but something set them apart from us. We were still sprogs whereas they were highly experienced combat pilots. They were in a different league from us. They had met the enemy.

From the mess hut we watched the squadron as they raced across the aerodrome to their planes. We would be transfixed as they took off and within minutes they were nothing more than black specks in the distance. We always hoped for their safe return, but the realities of war meant that some days they all came back and would be buzzing because they had survived the fight and so had their friends. As memories of the battle were exchanged and verified, the mood would be buoyant and jocular. But other times the air was thick with defeat as the squadron fresh from the fight reassembled in the dispersal hut and it slowly became clear that the young pilot who had shared a laugh and a joke with them that morning was not coming back. But there was never any time to mourn their loss.

By early September it had become clear the squadron was taking a hammering. Two days previously Peter King, one of the squadron's pilots, but not someone I had known well, had been killed. He had successfully baled out of his Spitfire only to find that his parachute wouldn't open and he plummeted to his death. It was stories like these that led me to promise myself that I would never bale out even if it meant going down with the plane. Two days after Peter had bought it, Flt Lt Dizzy Allen, Plt Off Johnny Mather and another chap called Christie crash-landed. Thankfully they were unhurt, but their Spits had all been written off. All we could do was continue our roles as partial observers.

On the morning of 7 September, the squadron was scrambled just before dawn at 4.45 a.m. with orders to intercept a raid by German bombers. No one knew how many would return. Mid-morning we were called into the CO's office.

'One of ours has crash-landed in a field near Sevenoaks.'

'I want you to go and fetch him.'

'Of course, Sir.'

'And one other thing. We don't know yet if the pilot survived or not.'

We jumped into the CO's staff car and headed off in the direction of where the aeroplane had last been seen. Thoughts that we might find a dead pilot strapped into his plane were pushed to one side and instead we discussed those pilots who had baled out or crash-landed and returned to the airfield in one piece.

As we turned into a country lane, we spotted a Spitfire lying on its belly in the middle of a small field. Clustered around it were a number of people. In among them I spotted the distinctive yellow of a Mae West life jacket. It belonged to Flg Off Crelin Bodie, a 19-year-old pilot who was also known as 'Bogle'.

Bogle was a scruffy-looking individual who liked to wear a pullover full of holes and snags. He had a big smile and boundless energy and he constantly whistled some catchy number like the *Bugle Call Rag*, which was one of his favourite tunes.

Through the crowd of interested locals, Bogle saw us approaching him and broke away from the group.

'What kept you?' he grinned.

As we travelled back to Kenley, Bogle talked us through his experience. He was a superb pilot and, as such, he was often used as a weaver. There were usually two weavers on an operation. It was a hazardous role and involved the pilots taking their Spitfires a few thousand feet higher than the rest of the squadron in order to search out the enemy. When they spotted a German aeroplane they would relay their position to the rest of the squadron. The problem was if the enemy sighted them first, because without the protection of the rest of the squadron they were highly vulnerable to attack. I was allocated as the weaver on a couple of occasions. I did it, of course, but it was a role that took its toll on my nerves, that was for sure. You never knew from which direction the bastards were going to come at you.

This particular morning Bogle had been on an interception patrol with the rest of the squadron when they were 'bounced' unexpectedly and set upon by scores of Me109s.

'I heard the bullets strike the side of the kite, but when I opened the throttle to try and escape the machine didn't respond. Then suddenly she seized up altogether. The propeller stopped dead with me 15,000ft in the air. I knew then I had no choice but to try and land the plane quickly.'

'Why didn't you bale out?'

'Not really my style, besides the kite was still intact and I fancied my chances. Trouble was there was no time to get back to Kenley so I scouted around for a field to land in. By this time the visibility was pretty poor so I dipped down below the low cloud to see if I could find a good landing site.'

'As soon as I came through the cloud I saw a large field and decided to land the Spit there. It wasn't until I got lower that I saw the farmer had littered the place with cement blocks, old cars and trip wires which is all very good if you are the enemy, but not if we are on the same side.'

'How high were you?'

'That was the problem, I couldn't do a thing about it, I was already down to 1,000ft. There was no time to find anywhere else, so I just banked steeply and made for the small stubble field next door. But it was really tight. I was still going at 50mph and I knew I was headed for the woods. I whipped up the undercarriage to try and slow her down.'

Bogle demonstrated the incident using his hand as the aircraft.

'As the plane hit the ground it slid along the grass and all I could do was pray. Then it suddenly tipped forward onto its nose and then crashed back and stopped. Smoke filled the cockpit and I thought 'bloody hell, if I stay here I'm going to get roasted' so I tore off my helmet and straps and jumped out of the aeroplane with my parachute still flapping around my legs and ran as fast as I could.

'When I thought it was safe, I turned back expecting to see my little Spit blazing away. Instead it was lying perfectly still and completely intact apart from a large cloud of earth which was just settling around it.'

We returned Bogle to Kenley where his appearance was warmly received by the others. The next day he was flying again as if nothing had ever happened. I couldn't help asking myself that when the time came for me to crash-land my aeroplane would I be as cool and expert as Bogle had been? Only time would tell.

Chapter Seven

SEPTEMBER 1940 – ACKLINGTON, NORTHUMBERLAND

The next day I rose early and followed my usual routine of taking breakfast in the sergeant's mess. I was detailed to spend the day practising formation flying which filled me with irritation and I vented it at the breakfast table.

'It's ridiculous. What use is it for us to waste hours learning to fly in pretty patterns?'

Nick, who was sat next to me, sighed, 'Jimmy, give it a rest. It suited the chaps in the Great War.'

'Well that was then and this is now.'

At that point, Claude appeared at the table and grinned at us.

'Don't tell me, Jimmy is still binding on about formation-flying. Well, you may be saved the effort today boys, because the CO wants to see you both in his office in half an hour.'

'What about?' asked Nick.

'No idea, perhaps you're going to join the rest of squadron.'

'Well, it has to be better than formation-flying,' I grumbled.

'I wouldn't count on it,' Claude replied grimly and silence fell on the table as we finished our breakfast lost in our own thoughts.

After we had eaten we made our way to Sqn Ldr Leigh's office and mulled over what was in store for us.

'I reckon this is it, Jimmy. No more rehearsing. He's going to tell us we're ready for the real thing.'

'I don't feel ready, but all this practising seems pointless when the others are under the kosh.'

We reached Sqn Ldr Leigh's office and were shown in. The officer looked up at us and smiled.

'The Air Ministry has decided to post you two to 610 Squadron, which is currently based in Acklington. It's just for a short while.'

'Where, sir?' Nick and I exchanged glances.

'Acklington. It's in the north. Don't worry I'm sure you will see plenty of action up there. Good luck, Sgt Corbin and Sgt Carter. I'm sure we will see you again soon.'

We left the office slightly stunned at the news. We had been at Kenley just a few weeks. It was chaos, the squadron desperately needed more pilots and now we were being sent away again. It didn't make sense.

'I can't believe it,' said Nick, 'What are we going to do up there? All the action is here.'

'I know, a bloody stupid decision, if you ask me.'

Back at the mess, we bumped into Pickles.

'Blimey, what's got you two?'

'The CO is sending us to the north-east, to 610.'

'Bad luck, chaps,' he commiserated with us.

We continued to moan about not wanting to go to Acklington and complained bitterly about what a 'bind' it was going to be. Later, in *Ten Fighter Boys*, I wrote of how we felt 'very depressed' about this posting because there was 'no action up north'.

Looking back now, I believe that whoever took that decision probably saved my life. Kenley aerodrome, and 66 Squadron in particular, were on a losing streak. They were getting hammered by the Luftwaffe. We had lost five pilots in just two days. Many of those killed were sprogs just like me. Some of them were killed on their very first mission without ever firing a shot. Why should I believe it would be any different for me? At least by heading north for a few weeks my entry into the air battle might be postponed long enough for me to gain some experience that might give me a chance of surviving for more than just a couple of days. Despite my outward annoyance at my posting, secretly I was rather relieved.

On 10 September Carter and I travelled north to 610 Squadron. On our arrival we were swiftly introduced to the rest of the squadron. They had the same weariness about them as the 66 boys. We knew we were in hallowed company. This squadron had done remarkably well during the early days of the Battle of Britain and nearly all the pilots who were left had been decorated for their efforts with the Distinguished Flying Cross or Distinguished Flying Medal.

The CO did the honours, with each pilot responding to his name with a slight smile or wave of the hand.

'That's Clarke, he's from Belfast, but don't hold it against him. And this is Sgt Hamlyn, you may have heard of him.'

The pilot looked up from his magazine. He struck me as a quiet, but dapper young man with his neat, tiny moustache and shy smile.

The CO continued. 'Hamlyn here only went and shot down five Hun in one day.'

'Just lucky, I suppose,' replied Hamlyn.

'Wish some of it would rub off on me then,' replied Clarke.

I was put into 'B' Flight and spent the first few days with my new squadron perfecting our formation-flying which still persisted as the preferred method of attack.

It is quite ludicrous to think that as we went into battle, uppermost in our minds wasn't the enemy but holding our correct position in the formation so we didn't crash into one of our own. Even then it had begun to dawn on me and others that tight formation flying had no place in the battlefield and should be consigned to air shows.

Four days after my arrival I finally had a taste of what was to come. It was 5.10 a.m. and I was on readiness. I had dragged myself from my bed and made my way to the dispersal hut where I had every intention of continuing my sleep. There was nothing else to do. I sank into one of the armchairs and made myself comfortable. It was too early for banter or pranks. Most of us were still coming to after being rudely awoken, especially as some of us had travelled into Newcastle the night before for a boozy session at the Turk's Head.

By the time I reached the dispersal hut the other pilots were already assembled. Each pilot had his method of coping with the tension and tedium of spending hours in the dispersal huts. That day I found myself fiddling with a champagne cork that had got into my pocket after a particularly memorable night out in Newcastle. I noticed that Nick, who was also suffering as a result of the previous night's exploits, simply sat and stared into space. Hamlyn seemed absorbed in a novel, although the pages were rarely turned, and Clarke, who was more restless, strolled around the room, pausing every now and again to look out of the window.

The boredom was mind numbing until the telephone rang, causing a couple of us to start. We all stopped what we were doing and listened in. The operator nodded solemnly into the receiver and then put the phone down. He spoke to the flight commander who shouted: 'Scramble Blue Section. Bandits. Angels 20.'

That was me. I was Blue Three. We were already on our feet and racing out of the dispersal hut, leaving behind half-drunk mugs of tea and open magazines on the table where we had been sitting just seconds earlier.

The Spits were in their dispersal pens ready to go. Their propellers were already turning and engines were roaring in anticipation as the fitters and riggers made sure the aircraft were ready for combat.

I jumped into the cockpit. Adrenalin coursed through me. My breathing began to quicken. Months of rehearsals had gone into this moment. It was time to see if I had learnt any lessons from Rochester, Burnaston, Kinloss, Cranfield and Hawarden. It was time to see if my training would keep me alive.

Without a second thought as to what I was flying into, I plugged in my R/T lead and oxygen mask and released the brakes. The chocks were removed. The CO glanced across from his Spitfire and we gave each other the thumbs up. I opened the throttle and moved off with the other two aircraft.

The CO took off first, closely followed by Blue Two and then me, Blue Three. Once we were airborne we reformed into our familiar V-shape formation. By now dawn was beginning to break and the half-light cast an unwelcome haze that would hamper our ability to spot any enemy aircraft.

We climbed to 20,000ft as directed and flew flat out towards the shipyards where we would head off the German bombers that, according to Ops, were also making their way towards their intended target. There was a lot riding on us. A decent strike on the ships being built on Tyneside could set the war at sea back by months. We all knew that. Flying through the morning mist, my nerves were in a heightened state as I battled with myself not to think about what lay ahead.

'This is it Jimmy, old boy, your turn to join the fight,' I told myself. I felt a faint flutter deep in the pit of my stomach, and I knew then what fear felt like. I looked across at the other two pilots. Were they feeling the same as me? Were they scared too? But they had been scrambled 100 times before. Surely, it was easier for them. In time I came to realise that it didn't matter how often you were scrambled, the fear never left you.

We reached the skies around the shipyards without mishap. Through the patchy grey cloud I could make out the neat rows of terraced streets far below me that led down towards the yards where gantries lined the docks like giant steel horses standing guard over the half-built ships. It was a scene of industrial calm. The area clearly hadn't been attacked recently and life continued thousands of feet below us unhindered by bombs.

Our cautious CO ordered us to circle overhead to check that there were no enemy aircraft lurking in the clouds waiting to pounce. We followed his instructions, but it was difficult to make anything out through the columns of cumulus clouds. The tension began to tighten its grip on my chest. Ops had said there were bandits in the area, so where were they? I scoured the horizon and squinted at every possible speck that I imagined

I'd seen in the distance. There was nothing. I was sure of it. Or maybe there was something and I just couldn't see it, but it could see me. The clouds cleared momentarily and I squinted towards the sun until my eyeballs ached. They would almost certainly be planning to attack with the sun behind them, so we wouldn't sight them until they were right on top of us. The bastards. Still, you couldn't blame them, I suppose. We used the same tactics whenever we could. This wasn't about fighting fair, this was about surviving. If you had the upper hand, you had a chance of getting out alive. That was all I was interested in.

I twisted around in the cockpit. No, there was still nothing in the great expanse of blue sky that surrounded my little craft. Below me stretched a vast carpet of the bright white cotton wool cloud. It was a beautiful sight which could easily lull you into forgetting that enemy aircraft lurked in the folds of the clouds just waiting to attack.

The pressure of flying an aeroplane while trying to spot the enemy was taking its toll. My body was racked with nervous tension which had reached an almost unbearable pitch.

'Come on, you bastards, if you're out there, show yourselves.'

We flew out towards the North Sea and the CO ordered us over the R/T to reduce our height to take us below the cloud line. I nervously followed his instructions. Flying through cloud was dangerous. Scores of 109s could be lying in wait for me on the other side. Pilots often disappeared into a mass of cloud and were never seen again. It was presumed the enemy had simply picked them off as they emerged from the cotton wool.

As the Spitfire slid through the banks of grey, my vision was as restricted as I had feared it would be and I was relieved when the view from my cockpit finally cleared and I found myself above the unusually calm waters of the North Sea. The R/T crackled into life once again and the CO's voice came through the headset.

'Boys, I think we have got ourselves a bandit. Take a look on the ground. I reckon he might have a spot of engine trouble.'

My false sense of security dissipated in an instance. My nerves were taut once again. The ground? It hadn't occurred to me to look downwards as there was nothing below me other than the sea. I turned the aircraft and my starboard wing dipped slightly enabling me to get a better view of what was happening below. Sure enough an aircraft emblazoned with the black iron cross of the Luftwaffe stared straight back up at me. It was a Heinkel 115 seaplane. These were used by the Germans for reconnaissance duties and for laying mines. I watched it taxi slowly along a small land mass in the Farne Islands, just off the Northumbrian coast. The aircraft looked undamaged and I suspected that he had probably developed engine trouble and been forced to land.

'Blue Two and Blue Three circle above at 1,000ft. Let's make sure he doesn't get any ideas of getting off the ground until the Navy boys arrive.'

I followed the CO's orders and three of us swooped and circled menacingly above the German. He took the hint and aborted his take-off. The aeroplane came to a standstill. We remained in our positions until a Naval warship appeared to take the crew prisoner and then we headed back to Acklington.

I touched down on the aerodrome and felt a rush of euphoria. It was good to be back. It was good to be alive. The ground crew met me and enquired after my trip.

'Nothing much doing. Just a Heinkel that won't be doing us anymore damage,' I replied casually.

I removed my helmet and as I strolled towards the dispersal hut I became aware of a hard lump in my trouser pocket, pressing against my leg. I reached down and pulled out the champagne cork I had been idly playing with just before we'd been scrambled. I must have slipped it into my pocket without realising it. I'm not a superstitious man, but I decided then I would keep hold of that champagne cork.

My first encounter with the enemy had undoubtedly been a gentle one, for which I was grateful. The enemy hadn't even been airborne, let alone in a position to shoot me down. I couldn't even dare hope to be so lucky next time around. Gentle or not, the mission to prevent the Heinkel from taking off was deemed a success and so cause enough to celebrate. Nick Carter, myself and a few others decided to make a night of it in nearby Newcastle. Those who enjoyed a good knees-up which, it has to be said was most of us, were known as the booze-wine boys. I and my fellow party-goers squeezed ourselves into Nick's old Rover car and drove away from RAF Acklington. Thoughts of the German Luftwaffe receded rapidly as we headed off in search of fun.

We ended up at the Eldon Grill, a superb restaurant in the city. There we dined on their excellent mixed grill which set us back 36s each, but it was well worth it. Afterwards we made our way to our old favourite, the Turk's Head pub. As we crowded around the bar in our usual high spirits, the barmaid homed in on me.

'Right, love, what's it to be?'

'This lot will have pints and I'll start with a vodka.'

'Anything with it?'

'OK, how about a bit of rum?' I grinned.

'And some sherry,' Nick chipped in. The barmaid frowned at me.

'Better do as he says,' I said and shrugged.

'You've got to have some gin in there,' someone else offered.

Finally the barmaid presented me with a cloudy concoction. I looked at it for a while, before picking it up and knocking it back in one fell swoop and slamming the empty glass on the table. The drink seared the back of my throat and caused me to gasp out aloud much to the amusement to the assembled company.

'Wow, that's got quite a kick,' I blinked back the tears.

'So, Jimmy, what's this drink of yours called?'

'A Spitfire, of course.'

And so the Spitfire cocktail was born. This cloudy brew contained just about any alcoholic liquid you could get your hands on it. It was a lethal and foul-tasting concoction. Its only virtue was that it got you drunk. I returned to the Turk's Head later on in the war and, out of curiosity, I asked for a Spitfire. Without a second glance, the barmaid duly threw together a terrifying mixture of spirits and presented it to me to which I said, 'You're not still serving that disgusting stuff, are you?'

We staggered back to camp several Spitfires later. Clarke led the singing and we all joined in. We looked for all the world what we were – a group of young men having a good time. You wouldn't have known there was a war at all.

Our days were spent patrolling the Tyneside shipyards protecting them from the German bombers while they built warships for the Navy. It was an undemanding time and readiness consisted of us hanging around the dispersal hut for hours on end waiting to be scrambled. Occasionally the call came through that there were bandits in the area and we were hastily sent up in our Spitfires. But these sorties never amounted to anything much and life at Acklington was a stark contrast to the intense fighting that was happening a few hundred miles south of us. As a result, long periods of time were spent sat in the dispersal hut idling away the time as best we could waiting for night time to come so we could decamp to the pub.

Occasionally I thought about the boys at 66 Squadron who faced the enemy two or three times a day. I thought about Claude, Pickles, Bobby Oxspring, Bogle and the rest. Were they still alive? I didn't know.

One particularly unremarkable day, the CO came in to address us all.

'Right lads, in the absence of the real thing, I have decided you can spend the day doing combat practice.'

'Right Blue Section, we will have you and Red Section go up first. Keep your distance from each other.'

I was Blue Section along with Nick and Clarke. We climbed into our Spits and took off. When we reached 30,000ft, we took up our positions for the staged dogfight. The idea was that we would dive down after each other and then climb back up again. We would then swoop past each other and turn to repeat the performance just to give ourselves a mild taste of what a real dogfight was all about.

We engaged in our pretend battle. I dived down after Nick and followed him as he banked and swooped upwards to gain height on me. We then turned away from each other before turning back to face each other. We flew towards each other before peeling off in plenty of time to avoid a collision. It was controlled, measured and planned and, in fact, nothing like the real thing.

Next it was Clarke's turn. He repeated a similar manoeuvre with a pilot from the other section. All was proceeding well with the planes chasing each other across the skies as Nick and I flew around them and watched from a safe distance.

Then quite suddenly one of the planes misjudged its distance from the other and instead of careering past each other in style, they collided in mid-air. There was a loud bang followed by a bright yellow flash. Debris shot out from the core of the explosion.

From my cockpit, I watched with total horror as both planes dropped like stones, trailing black smoke before smashing into the ground near the airfield. I knew that both pilots must have been killed instantly. Clarke was dead.

I decided to return to the airfield. As I touched down and came to a halt, the erks met me.

'Did you see what happened?' one of them enquired.

'Yes, they had no chance, the poor bastards,' I replied.

I returned to the dispersal hut where there was commotion. Nick was already there.

'They think Clarke baled out,' he said.

'That's impossible. It was a complete wipe out.'

'Well, one of the ground crew thinks they saw a parachute after the collision.'

'The only problem is, it didn't seem to open properly.'

'Poor bastard. Let's hope he was unconscious and knew nothing about.'

It was always the way. If death came calling, we all hoped it would be quick and we would know little about it. I didn't dare dwell on the thought of either men being alive as they fell through the air to a death they knew was unavoidable. When and if the time came, I promised myself I wouldn't bale out. I would go down with my aircraft. I couldn't contemplate the cruel injustice of successfully baling out and surviving only to land in the sea and drown or for my parachute to fail and to have merely postponed death by several minutes. I hoped that when it came it would be quick.

Then the CO appeared.

'They have found Clarke. He's bit smashed up, but they think he's going to be all right. They're taking him to hospital now.'

Later that evening Nick and I paid Clarke a visit. He was a mass of bandages, but he managed a smile as he saw us approaching.

'How are you, mate?'

'Surprised I'm here.'

'What happened up there?'

Nick and I sat by his bedside and listened enthralled to Clarke's heavily-accented account of the accident.

'There was a huge bang and I seemed to be sailing through the air. I must have passed out because the next thing I came round just above the cloud. I looked down and was amazed to see my parachute just below me.'

'I also realised I was hanging by one strap with the other one wrapped around my leg. I pulled myself up and held on to the remainder of the harness, and that's the last thing I remember. I must have passed out just before I hit the deck.'

The following day Nick and I examined his parachute. Two white silk panels had been completely ripped out. The pack was ripped to threads and the quick release box was missing altogether. Clarke swore he did not pull the parachute's rip cord and so when he collided with the other plane, the force of the impact must have thrown him out of the cockpit. His chute pack must have caught on some part of the aeroplane, ripping it open. By rights, looking at the shreds of material that had once been a parachute, he shouldn't have survived.

It was a remarkable escape. His only injuries were several minor bruises and a deep cut on his chin which was probably caused when his helmet was wrenched off as he was thrown from the cockpit. He was, of course, in shock.

Flying accidents during training were not widely publicised by the RAF despite their frequency. It was unbelievable to think that more pilots were killed in training than they were in combat.

Clarke recovered and returned to duty, but on 24 October Nick and I got the call to leave Acklington. I was told to rejoin my old squadron, 66, which was now operating from Gravesend in Kent. Nick was posted to 32 Squadron, based in Southend in Essex.

We said our goodbyes at Acklington train station and wished each other good luck. It was quite a moment. We had trained at Hawarden together and survived the early days at Kenley and Acklington. Now, in the same way I had said goodbye to Goughie and Geoffreys in what seemed like another life, I was saying goodbye to another good friend. Despite assurances that we would stay in touch, we both knew we would probably never see each again as separate chapters in our lives were beginning.

As I travelled south on the train, I wondered what lay in wait for me at Gravesend. A month had gone by – a long time in warfare. By mid-September the politicians had begun to tell us that the RAF had won that particular battle and Hitler would not be mounting an invasion of our island just yet. The Battle of Britain may officially have been drawing to an end, but the war as far as the pilots were concerned rumbled on relentlessly. Calls to scramble were as urgent as ever and our friends were still getting shot down at an alarming rate.

After a short leave I presented myself at Gravesend aerodrome and went in search of my old squadron. Things had changed at 66, but some of the old stalwarts still remained. As I walked into the mess, it was a relief to see the familiar face of Bogle who had brilliantly crash-landed in a field the size of postage stamp. He was just as scruffy and, I swear, was still wearing that same pullover.

I also found Claude who was as cheery as ever. He shook my hand.

'It's good to see you Jimmy.'

'And you, nothing much has changed, I see.'

'No, the Spitfires have done us proud these last few weeks.'

'Good, well I'd better let Sqn Ldr Leigh know I'm back.'

'Ah, that's one change that's happened. He's been moved to a job in London. We've got a new chap. Athol Forbes. He's tough, but he's good.'

The new CO, Sqn Ldr Athol Forbes, was the old boy of the squadron, being all of 30 years of age. When I presented myself at his office,

I found a tall slim man with slanting deep-set green eyes, a large beak nose and hair that curled up over each ear. He had come fresh from 303 (Kosciusco) Squadron where he had been a flight commander. The squadron was made up largely of Polish pilots who had fled from Europe earlier in the summer.

'Ah, Sgt Corbin, good to see you've returned safely from Acklington. We'll give you a couple of days to settle back into things and then get you up with the others. In the meantime, Bobby Oxspring shot a 109 down today so we're holding a little celebration tonight, if you'd like to join us. Give you a chance to get to know everyone.'

'Excellent, Sir, thank you.'

I loafed around until the evening and then joined those who were off duty. We went to the Star Hotel in Maidstone, which was familiar territory to me. Sqn Ldr Forbes joined us with his wife who was quite stunning. He introduced us to a couple of Polish pilots from his old squadron who were also off duty and enjoying a drink.

'This is Jimmy Corbin, just rejoined us from 610 Squadron. And this gentleman here shot down a 109 today, quite something it was,' Athol informed them. The Polish pilots turned with admiration to Bobby.

'Really, tell us what happened?' one them asked.

Bobby recounted the incident briefly and when he had finished, one of the pilots took a sip from his beer and added, 'Well done, but I want to ask you something.'

'Yes, what is it?' asked Bobby, slightly confused.

'Did the bugger burn?' he asked eagerly.

I looked at him and realised he was serious. His friend nodded and Bobby was clearly thrown by the question.

'Well, I'm not sure, I suppose so.'

I realised while this was a job that I was given to do, for the Polish pilots, it was personal and 303 in particular had a reputation for being bloodthirsty and showing little mercy towards the enemy.

On my return to 66, I began to feel less of a sprog and more of a valued member of the squadron. I was put on B Flight and my name appeared on the blackboard telling me whether I was flying as part of

Red, Blue, Yellow or Green Section. I was on readiness, standby and rest, just like the other pilots. This time it was no longer the case that I sat in the wings waiting for my turn. I had joined the cast of 66 Squadron. I was a fully operational fighter pilot.

A few days after my return, I was asked if I would like to go up. The squadron was ordered to scramble, but we saw nothing which wasn't unusual. The next day I watched a ferocious dogfight some 10,000ft below me. Close up I could see why it was called a dogfight. Fighters on both sides just kept going back in for more. It was relentless and the tenacity shown by both sides was awesome. I circled above the angry roar of the aeroplanes, waiting for the skipper to order me to join in. Instead my instructions were to stay at 30,000ft and wait to intercept another raid that we had been told was on its way. It never materialised. By then the fight below me had petered out and I returned to base. I had survived again. I didn't dare start to think that I was lucky. When you began to think you were invincible, that was when you got killed.

Several days later I finally had a taste, or rather a gutful, of what my fellow pilots had endured for months. As a fighter pilot, I would be properly blooded, so to speak, although the day began just like any other.

I rose just before dawn at 5.30 a.m. and headed to the mess where I dozed until breakfast and then enjoyed a good fry-up of bacon and eggs. From there I made my way to the dispersal hut. I was part of B Flight. It was a miserable day with low grey cloud and a cold irritating drizzle. I waited with the others at the dispersal hut. So much of our time was spent waiting. In my pocket was the champagne cork that I had picked up at a party in Newcastle. It had now assumed its rightful status as my lucky mascot and accompanied me on all operational flights. I often found myself turning it over in my pocket as I waited to be scrambled.

I cast an eye around the dispersal hut. Pilots who I'd barely known when I was first posted to Kenley were now friends of mine. There was Pickles who had been in the squadron when I joined in August. He was short, thin and 20. His hair was all over the place and he seemed to walk twice as fast as everyone else and he couldn't handle his beer. Next to him Plt Off John Kendal, or 'Durex' as he was known because of his stamina, paced noisily around the room. He had come up through the RAFVR just as I had. He was boisterous and good fun with an unusual talent for mimicking every noise known to man.

The telephone rang and everyone paused to listen. The operator called out across the room.

'Johnnie, it's for you. Some little WAAF says you were supposed to meet her last night.'

The officer blushed as we all laughed. A couple of pilots threw objects at the smirking officer. We were grateful for the diversion, small as it was, from the tension that always hung in the air first thing in the morning.

'Tell her, I'll call her when I get back,' the officer replied and silence resumed.

As always, we passed the time in our own individual way. Some sat quietly and read a book, but they were few in number. For most of us the quiet was oppressive and made the waiting far worse.

Suddenly, Durex threw a cup at Pickles and several seconds later shouted 'catch'. Inevitably it smashed to the floor as a hapless Pickles tried to grab it.

'Butter fingers,' Durex grinned.

Pickles scowled at him. Durex was unrepentant.

'Don't look at me like that. It's too quiet in here. It's good to have some noise about the place, takes everybody's mind off things.'

Pickles rolled his eyes and returned to his pastime of playing with some paper clips on the table as time wore slowly on.

Maybe Durex had a point. The silence could be oppressive as we slipped into our own private worlds. I chatted quietly with Bobby Oxspring over a game of chess. Bobby, or Oxo as he was sometimes called, was an outstanding pilot. His father had served in the same squadron during the First World War. He was tall, blond and good looking, but quite shy until you got to know him. He was an excellent flight commander and was awarded the DFC in October 1940.

Eventually, the silence was broken once again by the telephone. This time it wasn't some lovelorn girlfriend. We stopped and listened.

The commander shouted: 'Scramble base, angels one-six.'

Chairs scraped along the bare floor. We leapt up as one. Outside the Spitfires belched blue clouds of smoke and roared into life as the fitters started them up.

I sprinted out with the others to my plane and grabbed the parachute resting on the wing. I climbed into the cockpit as the aircrew who had prepared the aircraft stood on the wing to one side. Once I was in, he fastened my straps and closed the cockpit flap.

'Good luck,' the erk shouted above the roar before jumping down from the aircraft.

I smiled and gave him the thumbs up. My hands pulled on my helmet, clipped the oxygen-mask-cum-microphone across my mouth and pushed home the R/T plug.

The other erk disconnected the battery plug and slammed the flap on the aircraft's nose shut. We exchanged the thumbs-up signal and I was ready for the off.

Once again, just as it had been in Acklington, all thoughts of what might lay ahead were suspended. My reactions were automatic, almost instinctive. I couldn't even tell you how I managed to get the aeroplane airborne. I just did. I had done it so often before that the procedure was little more than a reflex action. Hesitation was a combat pilot's greatest enemy and had no part to play in our lives.

I looked across at the rest of my section in the half light of dawn. Red One and Three were already moving along the grass, gathering speed. As Red Two, I hurriedly waved the chocks away and then released the handbrake. The aircraft bumped off after them and I took up my position to the right of Red One. Red One, who was always the flight commander, gave the thumbs-up and we opened the throttles and took off. Behind us came Yellow, Green and Blue Section. The whole process was completed within two minutes. If it took longer than four minutes, the wing commander would be waiting for us on our return demanding to know why.

The radio fizzed and buzzed. It was noisy with atmospherics, but suddenly the squadron leader's voice came through loud and clear over the interference.

'Are you in position, Green, Red and Yellow leaders?'

One by one the replies were fed back to him. Our section leader obligingly responded.

'Red One calling, Red Section now airborne, sir.'

'Don't forget to use a weak mixture to conserve fuel and be sparing with the oxygen,' came back the voice. 'Stand by for pip-squeak zero in fifteen seconds.'

At the right of the cockpit was a small pointer and dial marked in four fifteen-second sections. When switched on, a high-pitched fifteen-second transmission was sent out to the ground station. On the dial, the transmitting section was coloured red; when the pointer passed through this section the 'squeak' drowned all R/T conversation, and in theory the section leader was supposed to avoid giving orders at that time.

'FIVE, four, three, two, one, zero, pip in, Red One, pip in.'

'Hello . . . Red One calling, pip in, pip in, listening out.'

At last the response came from ground control with our instructions.

'Hello Red Section, vector one six zero.'

We turned to follow the new course we'd been given, spreading out slightly to search the skies for the enemy.

At 15,000ft the cold began to seep through my clothing and I shivered. I pulled down my oxygen tube from its clips and fitted it to my mask. I turned the oxygen on. I knew I could cope with no oxygen at heights of 20,000ft, but I was taking no chances. I needed a clear head.

Our operational orders took me towards the familiar territory of Maidstone and Dover where we were to intercept the bombers before they crossed our shores. But the German bombers would be protected as usual by scores of Messerschmitt 109s. It was these that would cause us the real problems.

The R/T was quiet, until a steady voice filtered through my headphones.

'Bandits! At two o'clock!'

I swivelled around as far as I could, but I couldn't see a thing. The pale pink sky was empty. What was he talking about? I strained to see in the far distance. My eye trained on the horizon and then I saw them. Several miles away a line of black specks like a swarm of flies were sprinkled out loosely across the sky. They were heading away from us. Someone else had spotted them too, as another voice came over the airways which echoed my own thoughts more closely than the CO's had.

'I see them. There are hundreds of the bastards.'

The squadron leader had no time to admonish the pilot for his pointless remark. The R/T even in combat was meant for essential traffic only.

The dots became clearer until the definition of their aircraft came into sharp focus. They were enemy aircraft all right – Me109s. The CO ordered us to break and take up our attack formation. From now on I was on my own. I peeled away from the rest of the section and tried to get some height from which I could then dive in and attack one of the aircraft. That was the theory anyway.

In truth, what happened next would be little more than guesswork on my part, maddening as that may sound. But the ensuing engagement was just a hazy memory of aircraft shooting all directions across the sky, firing at every opportunity.

I can only assume that months of automatic training took over which allowed me to keep the Spit airborne, because I have no recollection of making any conscious decision to fly my aircraft in any particular way.

At one point, a Me109 shot past overhead, closely followed by one of ours, I think. Another 109 dived down past my starboard wing. Was it being chased or was he chasing someone? I couldn't see. Overhead several planes swooped and then climbed. I couldn't even tell which side they were on. What the hell was going on? And what the hell was I meant to be doing? It was like taking part in a complicated dance routine when I didn't even know the basic steps.

The R/T provided a clipped commentary to the scene being played out around me, but it didn't appear to tally with the action and I was no nearer understanding what was happening. The controlled voice of the CO was now replaced by random and disconnected shouts of 'He's on you Blue Two' and 'I've got him', which were then followed by long eerie silences.

My training, such as it was, kicked in. I knew that my main priority was to get above the enemy and behind them. Only when I had the height advantage could I have any hope of hitting one of them or indeed of not getting hit myself. Whatever happened, I couldn't let one of them get onto my tail. If they did it would probably be a case of 'good night nurse' for me.

I checked my rear mirror. It was all clear. I searched for a potential target, but couldn't make any out as they were either too far away or in the wrong position to get into my sights.

I checked my mirror again and froze with fear. Was it? Yes, by Christ, it was. I had a Messerschmitt 109 locked onto my tail and I was now almost certainly in his sights. Silver bullets streamed from his wing. My God, the bastard is firing at me.

I pulled the Spitfire into a tight evasive turn and rolled it into a dive to avoid the burst of gunfire coming from the 109. The Spitfire had a carburettor and relied on positive G for the petrol to flow, so if you pushed the stick or control column forward quickly the engine would cut out and the aircraft would go into a half roll and automatically dive downwards. But the positive G had other effects which I was now about to experience. As the aircraft plummeted, I felt a huge pressure on my backside and the blood seemed to drain from my head. Before I knew what was happening I had blacked out. When I came too I had dropped several thousand feet and was close to the coast of Calais.

I checked my mirror; it was clear. I looked all around me and there wasn't a soul, enemy or otherwise, about. The skies were empty. The battle might be continuing elsewhere, but for me it was over. For now.

The fight had lasted no more than a couple of minutes. I had no idea what the outcome had been. But I had survived. A huge surge of relief, more like elation, surged through me. My nerves had been through the mill. Tension, terror and now a terrific feeling of just being alive left me feeling utterly exhausted.

I stooged around for a few more minutes in case the fight was still going, in which case it was my duty to re-join it, but there was no one around. I turned for home. I was completely alone and free. In peacetime this would have been an exhilarating thought, but in wartime a lone aircraft was the equivalent to the wounded animal that becomes separated from the rest of the herd and inevitably falls prey to the nearest predator. I was a sitting target for the Luftwaffe. So without wanting to tempt fate any further than I had already done that day, I gave up trying to locate my squadron and flew back at full speed to Gravesend.

I opened the throttle and hit 400mph, tilting the Spitfire slightly to starboard to improve my vision from the cockpit and searching the landscape until Gravesend aerodrome finally came into view. It was always a relief to return to the relative safety of the airfield after a sortie, but none more so than on this occasion.

I came into land and pulled the throttle back to fine pitch. My speed slowed to a still impressive 180mph. I selected 'wheels down' and pumped the handle. A green light lit up clearly on the instrument panel to show that the wheels were now down and locked. I turned in for my final approach at 140mph and put the flaps down. The nose came up as I applied the throttle. My speed dropped down to 80mph and the aircraft sank closer to the ground. I held her steady until she touched down. Then with the throttle right off, I kept her straight and eased the brakes on. We bumped across the uneven surface and taxied towards the dispersal hut and the aircraft's allocated resting position and finally we rolled to a stop. As I came in to land I noticed I wasn't the first back. Several Spitfires, some with visible bullet holes in their tails, were already parked up and being worked on by the riggers and fitters. I hoped I wasn't to be the last either.

The ground crew greeted me as they always did after each sortie.

'Good to see you, Sir. Was everything all right with her?'

'Yes, thanks, went through the gates no problem, but otherwise fine,' I replied, referring to the fact I had needed extra boost during combat and so had to push through the gate, as it was known. This then tripped a wire which gave the Spit a useful surge of power that got me out of numerous scrapes. But it was vital to tell the ground crew you had gone through the gates, so they could check to see if the valves had been scorched and needed replacing before you were scrambled again.

I trudged towards the dispersal hut. An intelligence officer, or penguin as we called them because they couldn't fly, approached me and quizzed me gently on what had happened.

'Right, Sgt Corbin, just talk me through what happened.'

'I can't remember much. One minute there were aircraft all over the skies, the next, I was on my own. I don't even think I fired my guns. I think I must have blacked out. Sorry, I can't remember much more than that.' Undeterred, the officer made some cursory notes and left me sipping a welcome hot mug of sweet tea and munching some toast. My heart no longer raced. The adrenalin began to seep away. I felt calm again.

The other pilots also began to drift back. Bobby Oxspring, Bogle and Claude all made it home safely. They had their own stories to tell. None of their versions seemed to tally with mine or with each other and no one was really sure what the outcome had been. Clearly every pilot's experience of the battle was unique. I relayed my tale to Bobby who reassured me that my experience mirrored that of just about every other combat pilot.

Slowly the pilots of 66 Squadron made there way back to the 'drome. But there was one person missing. As the hours passed Plt Off Johnny Mather failed to materialise. Like anxious parents, his erks paced around in the dispersal area for him, awaiting his return.

We replayed the battle among ourselves, but none of us could remember seeing him during the combat or afterwards. Neither had the airfield received any information that he had been picked up somewhere over the Kent or the Channel. But it was early days still. Some pilots didn't return for several days depending on how far away they crash-landed or where they baled out.

'He'll be fine. He has probably forced lobbed somewhere,' Bogle said confidently.

'He baled out last month and survived that in one piece. He's probably done the same today,' agreed Claude.

'He'll turn up,' added Durex, 'he always does.'

We nodded in hope and clung on to the fact that Johnny had been lucky once before and perhaps his winning streak had held again.

The remainder of B Flight assembled once again in the dispersal room. We were still on readiness. It was now mid-day. I wondered if that would be it or if, God forbid, I would have to go up again. The telephone remained silent. The minutes ticked by. In another hour A Flight would arrive to relieve us. I picked up an out-of-date *Strand* magazine and idly flicked through it. Claude and Bob played chess. Outside the dispersal hut an army of fitters and riggers fussed around their aircraft in a bid to get them airworthy as soon as possible.

Five minutes to go and we would be off duty. Thank God. The phone rang again. The CO shouted: 'Scramble base.'

I jumped up and ran for the door with the others, leaving behind the remaining dregs of my tea and a slice of toast. We flew towards Dover once more on the direction of Ops who warned us of enemy aircraft in the area. This time there were no bandits and we returned safely, but empty-handed. By the time we had touched down A Flight had arrived to take over and we stood down.

I returned to the sergeant's mess where I lay down on my bed and briefly pondered the day's events until thankfully one of the other pilots suggested we all go for a drink which then became several drinks.

Just as we were leaving, Claude came in.

'Jimmy, there's a call for you.'

'Thanks Claude. You lot go ahead, I'll catch you up.'

I went out to the hall where the receiver lay next to the phone and picked it up.

'Sgt Corbin speaking.'

'Sgt Corbin, I'm sorry to have to tell you this, but I thought you'd like to know, seeing you were a friend of his. Nick Carter was killed today.'

I put the receiver down. Durex came by.

'What's up Jimmy?

'I just heard a friend of mine went down today. He was a good chap.'

'I'm sorry Jimmy. What d'you say I buy you a drink and we can say a toast for him?'

'I say, that sounds like a good idea.'

That night we honoured Nick Carter in the same way that we honoured all our friends who were killed. We drank to his memory and privately thanked God or whoever that we were still alive.

Chapter Eight

NOVEMBER 1940 –
BIGGIN HILL, KENT

The squadron's stay at Gravesend was brief and from there we were moved to West Malling aerodrome, also in Kent, which had been the home of Maidstone Flying Club in peacetime. Again our stay was short, but was not without its mishaps which began the moment I touched down on the airstrip.

I had taken off from Gravesend in the morning to carry out a patrol and instead of returning to base as usual I was instructed to fly onwards to West Malling. Somehow I became separated from the rest of squadron and by the time I reached West Malling the landing field was shrouded in darkness. I touched down as normal, but unbeknown to me the airfield had been attacked previously and small bomb craters pock-marked the field. I eased the brakes of the Spitfire only for one of the oleo legs to get stuck in a bomb hole that had been poorly filled. The leg wedged itself in the mud and acted as the axis while the rest of the plane with me inside spun round on it in fast tight circles. I remember thinking that I had survived fierce dogfights only to die swirling around on the aerodrome in my Spit like a fairground attraction. The plane finally came to a standstill leaving me shaken, but unhurt. What was far worse was the weeks of ribbing from the others and references to Corbin's merry-go-round which I had to endure from the rest of the squadron who had witnessed my accident.

Despite my altercation with the West Malling airfield, I was flying the following day. The intensity of the Battle of Britain had begun to wane. Don't get me wrong. We still encountered enemy aircraft, but not in the numbers or the frequency that we had in the summer and early autumn of 1940. It meant that when were scrambled we didn't always come across German aircraft and would return to the 'drome empty-handed. Personally, I never complained. It increased my chances of survival.

Towards the end of our stay at West Malling, we had been on just one of those patrols. The squadron was returning from a sortie over the Channel and had failed to sight any enemy aircraft. Feeling in rather a good mood I called up Dizzy Allen, who was leading the squadron that day, to ask if I could 'beat up' Maidstone. Beating up is a common practice among most pilots and involved flying as low as possible over an area in order to frighten the inhabitants. It was nothing more than harmless fun, but, of course, it was frowned upon by the Air Ministry, not least because it could be rather dangerous, although this didn't stop us. Pilots often would beat up their own homes or those of some girl they were hoping to impress. I had flown over my hometown of Maidstone many, many times before, but on that particularly day I suddenly felt the urge to beat it up just for the sheer hell of it. To my surprise Dizzy was happy to oblige and decided that the entire squadron of eighteen Spitfires would join in with the jape.

Flying in our usual V formation we reduced our height from thousands of feet to just a couple of hundred and approached the unsuspecting Kent town where I had grown up. We neared the outskirts and then the Spitfire Mk IIs opened their throttles and proceeded to thunder over the chimney stacks and rooftops of Maidstone at 300mph. Somewhere down there was Bower Street. I grinned at the thought. We must have scared the hell out of the residents. The roar of the aeroplanes would have been deafening. Not to mention the fright of not knowing if we were British or German. What I didn't know was the town had been bombed heavily that morning, so to have a bunch of fighter aircraft suddenly swooped down on from the skies was truly terrifying. They probably thought they were being attacked again. But we thought it was all jolly good fun. Word later reached us that the townspeople were not impressed and I never told my parents about the incident.

Six days later we were on the move again. This time we were sent to the spiritual home of RAF fighter pilots – Biggin Hill in Kent. 'Biggin on the Bump', as it was known, was a rather untidy agglomeration of hangars and huts, offices, barrack blocks and messes positioned next to an airfield. It was a favourite among pilots and was famous within RAF circles. Unfortunately, it was equally famous among Luftwaffe circles too. By the time the Battle of Britain was well under way, the aerodrome had become a Spitfire station operating with such squadrons as Nos 92, 72, 74 and 610. And now it was to become our base station too.

Biggin Hill's strategic importance meant the Luftwaffe frequently came calling. Between 18 August 1940 and 7 January 1941 the aerodrome was attacked twelve times. On 18 August KG76, a Luftwaffe bomber unit, sent in high-level and low-level attacks with Dornier Do17s and Junkers Ju88s. The main damage was caused by the bombs which left craters in the landing area. In the second of two attacks on 30 August a small formation of less than a dozen bombers at low level reduced Biggin Hill to a shambles with bombs of up to 1,000lbs in weight. Workshops, stores, barracks, WAAF quarters and a hangar were wrecked, and thirty-nine people were killed. The next day a high-level attack did further extensive damage to the airfield, including a direct hit on the Operations block. Just weeks before our arrival the Luftwaffe had attacked the airfield twice. The second time, Dornier Do17s hit runways and the Sector Operations Room. The defence teleprinter network was wrecked by a 500lb bomb. Three members of the WAAF who worked on until the last moment each received the Military Medal for bravery.

Despite the attacks, Biggin Hill remained operational throughout the course of the Battle. For one week, however, the damage was so severe that only one squadron could operate from it.

From a pilot's point of view, Biggin Hill was a good posting. We were billeted in bungalows just outside the aerodrome and we had a good time. The dispersal huts were warm and comfortable with deep leather seats. On the mantelpiece, above the log fire, was an iron cross which had been presented to the base by the local constabulary who had cut it from a Me109 that had been shot down in the area.

Biggin Hill was also perfectly placed. It was surrounded by country pubs, including the famous White Hart at Brasted. But the more adventurous among us could easily jump into the squadron car and go dancing in Bromley or into London to enjoy its more sophisticated pleasures.

It was now October 1940 and the final month of the Battle of Britain. In the first few days of our arrival we continued to take off for real panics as wave upon wave of enemy bombers continued to try and penetrate our air defences, but by the end of that month it was all over. The Battle of Britain had finished and the German's invasion plans were abandoned. Nevertheless they kept up the ante and for me, 14 November, six days after the squadron arrived at Biggin Hill, marked the last real scrap of the Blitz.

It was an hour before dawn when we crawled out of bed. It was cold and miserable outside with a freezing damp mist lying low over the airfield. The previous night I had been to the White Hart and had had a couple of pints, but not too many as I knew I was on readiness the next day. I had a slight headache from too little sleep which I tried to dispel with some tea and toast in the sergeant's mess. The dispersal huts were located next to the airfield, some distance from the sergeant's mess, so we all piled into an open-topped truck which transported us across the aerodrome to the huts. I sat shivering from cold and lack of sleep in the back of the van. Even the sight of a pretty WAAF at the wheel couldn't rouse me from my semi-comatose state. The others winked and grinned knowingly at me.

The rocky suspension and uneven ground made my head pound. This was further compounded when we arrived at the dispersal to the cacophony of Merlin engines being warmed as the fitters tested them to make sure they were airworthy. Many of the men had been up all night trying to rectify faults with the rigging or the engines and to repair tails that had been shot up during a dogfight.

I checked the board in the dispersal hut to find out which section I had been allocated. I was on Red Section today and I was Red Two. From there I collected my Mae West and put it on. I picked up my parachute and helmet and trudged out to my aircraft.

I carefully arranged the safety harness and parachute straps and plugged in the helmet leads to the radio and oxygen. I checked to make sure the oxygen was flowing through the mask and the gun sight was working with spare bulb in place. The rigger was cleaning the condensation off the cockpit hood. After I had completed all the pre-checks I sloped off back to the crew room.

Most of the other pilots had already gathered in the hut. We lounged around the dispersal room talking, playing cards or just sitting. A whiff of alcohol hung about the place. Durex and Bob teased me about my antics the night before. I sat and nursed a coffee, trying to keep my head still so it would stop pounding. The lump in my tunic pocket told me that, tired as I might be, I hadn't forgotten my champagne cork which was now my constant companion. My mood was low and I grumbled about the amount of time we wasted hanging around the base when we were on standby.

'I don't see why we have to stay here sitting around on our arses doing nothing all day. Why shouldn't we be allowed to go on leave?' This was one of my pet moans. We spent hours hanging around the camp when we were on standby and I could see no reason why we had to be there.

'Jimmy, do you ever stop binding?' asked Bob.

'That's it. I think we should call you Binder from now on because of all the moaning you do,' Durex grinned at me. And that is how my nickname of Binder came about. Personally I didn't think I moaned any more than anyone else, although I did have a tendency to speak my mind. Anyway, the name stuck with me throughout my time with 66 Squadron and I took it in good spirits.

The conversation moved on and Claude and Pickles Pickering, another 66 veteran, began discussing formations. Normally this was a debate that I heartily enjoyed. Along with many Spitfire pilots, I had long felt that flying in tight formations was an outmoded method of flying. Its place belonged where it had first been developed – in the First World War.

Now with planes flying at 300mph and more, formation flying was obsolete. The Germans had realised this already and used much looser formations with more room to manoeuvre. Despite my interest in the topic, my bad mood precluded me from joining in and I decided to sit it out.

The phone rang. We all stopped and turned.

'Squadron scramble, Dover, angels two zero,' the CO shouted across the room.

We rose instantly as one and sprinted to our Spitfires. My sluggishness was pushed to one side by the adrenalin coursing through me. The fitters fired the starter cartridges and the propellers turned the engines, which burst into life once more. I leapt into the cockpit, fitted my straps and pulled them tight. The chocks were removed and I joined the rest of the team.

When the aircraft were in position, Sqn Ldr Forbes's raised hand came down and twelve pilots gunned their throttles and sped away up into the air. It was an incredible sight.

As we headed out to Dover, our information was that there were a number of Ju87s which had just bombed Dover and were returning to France, flying in formation. It wasn't the bombers that concerned us so much as the 109s that would be protecting them. We were un-sure how many we would encounter. We were up with another squadron from Biggin Hill, so we numbered twenty-four planes in total. It wouldn't be the first time we were outnumbered by the Germans. But we had faith in our Spitfires and always believed they were far superior to the 109s.

No. 66 Squadron, under Forbes, took the lead. We were about 1,000yd in front and 1,500ft below the other squadron. We flew over the channel and turned back towards the coast of Dover.

'Bandits at 3 o'clock. Looks like Ju87s. Look out for the 109s covering. About fifty of them.'

Sqn Ldr Forbes's voice filled the cockpit, but the information wasn't necessary. We all saw them as they raced towards us for a full headlong attack. The skies were full of them. A large bomber formation, carrying thousands of pounds of bombs, was approaching at full throttle, surrounded by scores of Messerschmitts. They meant business.

We maintained our own course and the Ju87s scattered in response to our head-on approach. As the bombers peeled away to avoid us, the other squadron which had also been scrambled from Biggin Hill began its job of singling them out one by one for an attack. As they did this, we concentrated on trying to engage the 109s to distract them from what was happening to their precious bombers.

Ninety aircraft filled the sky above Dover. Engines roared and screamed as Spits and 109s hurtled in to the attack, or a Ju87 dived away to escape. Machine guns burst across the sky. One of the bombers exploded in a huge ball of fire. A 109 coughed out a stream of black smoke before plunging towards the sea.

I chose my 109. He was below and slightly in front of me. I dived down to come up behind him. He was unaware of my presence as I moved him into my sights. A thrilled went through me. I was in control. I was on top. Where I had experienced gut-wrenching terror when I had had a 109 on my tail, it was now his turn to feel the cold fear of death whispering in his ear. I flicked the gun button open on my control column and pressed the tit. A short burst of fire shot out from my wings and passed a shade above his starboard wing. Damn. He must have spotted me seconds before I fired, he quickly turned into a steep dive. The tracer bullets missed him by a fraction. Then he was gone, along with the rest of them.

The battle was over. I had survived once again and this time I had even managed to get a squirt at one of them. The same elation that I had experienced many times before now returned. I was alive. The only evidence of the short fierce battle that had taken place seconds before was the swirl of contrails in the sky and eight white parachutes that now descended gracefully down from the sky into the channel waters below. The navy would pick them up later and they would sit out the rest of the war in a PoW camp somewhere in England. Their war was over.

In total the squadrons shot down twelve 87s. No. 66 Squadron took out three Ju87s and two 109s. The best news was that casualties on the British side were nil, although one pilot crash-landed at RAF Hawkinge.

We returned to Biggin Hill triumphant. The rigger met me from my aircraft.

'Did you get anything sir?'

I shook my head.

'Oh well, better luck next time.'

I bumped into Claude who had also just landed and was also making his way to the dispersal hut.

'Fancy a pint later?' he enquired.

'Is the Pope a Catholic?' came my response, 'but there is something I need to do first.'

After I was stood down from readiness I made my way to the sergeant's mess where I spent a concentrated hour coming up with a pilots' rota that would allow us time away from the base without jeopardising operations. I presented it to the senior officers who eyed it with considerable suspicion and treated me like some kind of subversive because I dared to question the accepted way of doing things.

'You see, Sir, it doesn't make sense for those of us who live nearby to hang around the aerodrome when we are off-duty. We may as well take the opportunity to go home and see our families and, well, just have a break from it all. I've worked out a rota, so it's fair.'

I finished my homily for greater freedom and waited as the officers studied the rota.

'All right Sgt Corbin. We'll go along with your little plan, but one slip-up and that'll be the end of it.'

Amazingly, they saw sense and agreed to implement it. My grumbling may have earned me the nickname of Binder, but when the others realised that thanks to me they were going to get more leave, my popularity soared. The rota was great for those like me who lived close by and could return at short notice, but it was a bit tight for those boys who lived a long way away. They still had to remain on the base. Still, you can't have everything.

That confrontation, as far as I can recall, was the last time the Germans used Ju87s in such large numbers. It was a hugely successful day for the British and put the final nail in the coffin of Operation Sealion, Hitler's invasion plans. The RAF had arguably prevented a German invasion by not allowing them control of the skies, but it was too soon to wallow in victory. Days of triumph could so quickly turn to days of tragedy and defeat. Sorties didn't all go our way. No. 66. Squadron, in common with all the squadrons, still lost pilots, sometimes at a frightening rate.

On 28 November, during an interception patrol by B Flight, Sgt Peter Willcocks was killed in a mid-air collision with Sqn Ldr Dizzy Allen. Miraculously Dizzy survived after baling out. He was 20. Plt Offs Tucker and Heyton also crashed and were killed. I wasn't flying with them at the time and I didn't know them that well. Closer colleagues mourned their loss more than I did, but even so they didn't dare dwell on their deaths. To be honest, when I heard what had happened I felt sad for their families, but relieved for myself that it hadn't been me. My overriding desire in all of this was to survive. I did the job as well I could. I wasn't brave, but neither was I a coward. I fought, but I fought with the will to live, not to die in some spectacular feat of aerial courage that would be talked about for years to come. What good is glory if you're dead?

During December and January, the weather turned and the skies grew quieter. In two months I did a little over twelve hours flying. The only enemy activity during this time consisted of a few reconnaissance missions which were hard to detect in the bad weather, and on most occasions were intercepted by squadrons based on the coast.

With the Battle of Britain well and truly over we began to give the Germans a taste of their own medicine. On 10 January 1941 the RAF carried out its first daylight bombing raid over France with a fighter escort. Three squadrons, including 66, swept the Channel off Calais at about 15,000ft while three more squadrons went in with the Blenheim bombers and bombed Calais.

We took off from Biggin Hill. Anti-aircraft fire was intense over Calais and my little Spit rocked and shuddered as the shells exploded all around us. White puffs of smoke appeared and formed a wall of cloud. It was my first real experience of ack-ack fire and although we were five miles up in the sky, it felt uncomfortably close and I suspected it could do me and my machine considerable damage. The fact that shortly afterwards my suspicions proved entirely founded gives me no great pleasure.

At that time Adolph, or 'Sailor' Malan as he was famously known, commanded the Wing at Biggin Hill. A wing consisted of three Squadrons. There was 92, 74 and, ours, 66 Squadron, which all reported to him. No. 74 was Malan's own squadron and was known as the Tiger Squadron, a name acquired during the First World War due to the aggressiveness of its pilots.

Sailor Malan was a lovely man. He was very quiet, but very charming and very good in the air. At that time I only knew him by sight, but I got to know him reasonably well when I attended an advanced gunnery school at Sutton Bridge of which he was in charge. I was a warrant officer by then and also the only non-commissioned officer on the course, so I probably stood out. I also knew George Malan who was Sailor's younger brother and who I had the pleasure of serving alongside later in the war.

Sailor Malan – his nickname came from time he spent in the South African navy as a young man – already had something of a reputation as a great pilot and tactician in 1940. He first saw action over Dunkirk as well as the Battle of Britain and had already challenged accepted practices when he ordered that the machine guns on his Spitfire be re-aligned to converge at a distance of 250yd, instead of the recommended 400yd.

There was much debate around that time about the most effective flying formations from which to mount an attack. Arguments have also raged over who was first to come up with the formations of wings of three squadrons. As far as I am concerned Sailor Malan should take the credit. He quickly realised that standard formations of basic vics of three were adequate against unescorted bombers, but of little use against the German Messerschmitts. The German leaders had long realised this themselves and their tactics, due in part to practice in Spain and Europe in the 1930s, had evolved to a much looser formation of four aircraft. Sailor adopted the same tactics with 74 Tiger Squadron of three flights in a wide vic, each with four aircraft in line astern. It provided much greater manoeuvrability and reduced our chances of getting bounced from behind. As we moved from a defensive strategy to an offensive one and began to mount our own raids on the German airfields in France, as well as escorting our own bombers as they flew across the channel to attack pre-determined sites, we also began to adopt Malan's tactics.

In addition to his disregard for the accepted practice of formation flying, Malan also gave his pilots a list of ten dos and don'ts of flying which probably kept many a pilot alive, including myself. His ten rules for fighting were pinned up in the crew room at Biggin Hill. The first one was 'Wait until you see the whites of his eyes', which was a reference to the fact that you stood little chance of hitting an enemy aircraft if you were more than 200yd away. But it was the last rule that summed up aerial combat for me. Malan always advised us to 'go in quickly – punch hard – get out'. I held this edict close to me and hoped it would be enough to get me through the war. In time the RAF adopted Malan's rules as the official line. To me, Malan was one of the great heroes of the RAF in the Second World War.

February arrived, the weather cleared and the action resumed. Fighter sweeps were now becoming more frequent. It was 21 February 1941 and our last sweep before being posted out of Biggin Hill. Wg Cdr Malan ordered up three squadrons, including 66, in an offensive patrol over north-west France. In other words, we were looking for trouble and, sure enough, we found it.

We took off and were instructed to climb to 30,000ft which was bloody freezing. Our route had been determined as Dungeness, on the south coast of England, Cherbourg, Calais and then back to Biggin Hill. Our squadron was flying in pairs in one large loose vic formation, in line with Malan's thinking on this. I was flying alongside Pickles Pickering, which was always a good place to be as he had phenomenal eyesight. If there was something to be seen, Pickles invariably was the first to see it. That day, however, the sweep had been fairly uneventful and there wasn't much to see. We had set off in the direction of Dungeness. From there we had travelled on to Cherbourg. Now we were just rounding the French coast before heading back to base.

We had nearly completed our tour and were just off the coast of Calais when my aeroplane experienced a terrific jolt, the force of which lifted me from my seat. The whole craft wobbled precariously and a pungent smell pervaded the cockpit. I looked in my mirror, ominous black smoke belched out from my exhaust. I knew the smell was cordite, a combination of nitro glycerine and petroleum jelly used in ammunition, which meant a shell from the anti-aircraft guns down below had exploded too close for comfort. How the hell had they managed to hit me when I was 5 miles up in the air? It must have been sheer luck. I looked down below at the icy waters of the Channel swirling beneath me. I couldn't crash land on that and I was jiggered if I was going to bale out. There was nothing for it. I had to get her home.

My adrenalin was pumping furiously through my body. I tried to calm myself so I could think clearly. Panic would get me killed. Pilots got hit all the time and survived. Why shouldn't I? I quickly scanned all my instruments one by one: oil pressure, altimeter, rev counter. Thank God, they were all in working order. The plane stopped jerking and appeared to level out. I kept checking the dials and counters. Had I missed something? Was the Spit going to explode into flames without warning? No, everything seemed well, as far as I could tell.

The CO ordered us to change direction slightly to my relief and we increased our speed to dodge any further ack-ack fire and headed back to Biggin Hill. The airfield finally came into view and I felt that now familiar hit of elation as I landed and taxied the plane safely to a standstill. The ground crew raced over to me as I clambered out of the cockpit. One of them nodded at the fuselage where there was a large gaping hole where the shell had ripped it open. The rudder had also been hit.

'That one looked a bit close, Sir.'

'It certainly was.'

'Never mind, Sir, we'll have her right for you tomorrow.'

I made my way to the dispersal hut where Durex was already warming himself by the fire with a mug of tea.

'You all right Jimmy?'

'Just about. The Kite's a bit shot up. Anyone else run into bother?'

'Yes, apparently poor old Claude got hit the same time as you. He had to land at Manston. Be back tomorrow though. Can't keep a good man down, can you?'

Chapter Nine

FEBRUARY 1941 – DEVON AND CORNWALL

On 26 February 1941 my time at Biggin Hill came to a close. The German offensive had failed and the RAF deemed it unnecessary to maintain so many squadrons at the bump when they were needed elsewhere in the country. For us 'elsewhere' meant a posting to Exeter in south-west England.

I left Biggin Hill with a certain degree of regret. The airfield had undoubtedly been in the thick of the action and, at times, I admit that I yearned for some respite from the chaos that sometimes descended on the place. But Biggin Hill had been a lively posting for another reason. Its proximity to London meant that we often piled into the squadron jalopy and headed for the West End pubs and clubs. Even in the midst of the Blitz people were determined to enjoy themselves and we were no exception. It was all part of that feeling of not allowing the enemy to get the better of us. Somehow I doubted that Exeter would offer the same delights as Soho.

A second reason for not wanting to leave Biggin Hill was that we were forced to leave behind our beloved Spitfire Mk IIs. The Mk IIs were similar to the Mk Is, but had a Merlin XII engine that ran on 100 Octane fuel and used a Coffman cartridge starter instead of the old trolley accumulators. They also had armour plating fitted on the production line as well as bullet-proof windscreens, after Hugh Dowding, the head of Fighter Command, apparently said that if it was good enough for Chicago gangsters, it was good enough for his pilots. The Mk II had been a dream to fly and now we had to take on someone else's clapped out old Spit Is. All in all, our move to the English Riviera was a step backwards in every respect.

On our arrival the CO, Athol Forbes, briefed us on our new roles. I cast an eye around the room, we were a motley crew if there was one. Next to me sat Oxo, now DFC and fast developing into a formidable pilot. Next to him were Durex and Bogle, still playing the jokers on the ground, but totally professional in the air. Claude had safely returned from his crash-landing and was still on hand to deliver advice on the Spits. Pickles still looked undernourished, but remained a cracking pilot. Dizzy Allen, who had also had his fair share of scraps, was sat next to the CO. I trusted each and every one of them with my life.

Forbes began his briefing.

'Convoy patrols are now our stock-in-trade, boys.'

A groan went up.

'I know it's not the most thrilling of flying, especially after the bump, nevertheless it is essential work. These Merchant Navy boys have survived the U-boats lurking in the Atlantic to make sure you get fed, the least we can do is afford them a little protection as they continue on their journey through the English Channel to London.

'Our role is to escort them for a set distance along the south coast until another squadron further along picks them up and relieves us of that duty. All straightforward stuff, but Jerry are always looking to pick these ships off, so don't get complacent.'

He was right, of course. It was the least we could do. The Merchant Navy were the unsung heroes of the war. They endured horrendous attacks in their attempt to prevent Britain from starving.

Athol Forbes continued, 'In addition to convoy, we are going to be carrying out milk trains.'

Bobby Oxspring and I exchanged a frown. 'I've a suspicion, it's not going to be as pleasant as it sounds,' I whispered.

'When we get the call, we'll take off at dawn when it's semi-dark with orders to fly due west,' Forbes began.

'But that's the Atlantic,' someone said.

'Well done, it is and you will be flying over it to see if you can hunt down any German reconnaissance planes.'

'What are reconnaissance planes doing over the Atlantic?' Claude asked.

'Trying to spot the convoys so they can relay their positions to the U-boats and mount an attack before they reach the English coast.'

This time it was Pickles turn to ask the questions: 'So how far are we expected to fly to find them?'

'You could probably cover up to 150 miles offshore before having to turn back. Any more questions?' the commander replied.

Durex spoke up.

'Sir, there are rumours going around that we might do raids on France.'

'I've had nothing official yet, but we'll see. Right, good luck everyone.' CO Forbes ended his briefing.

Bogle turned to us.

'Don't like the sound of those milk trains,' he grimaced.

'Me neither,' I replied.

The thought of milk trains sent a shudder down my spine. I decided then and there if I was hit I would go down with the plane. Baling out of the aircraft was a far worse prospect as I would succumb to the freezing waters of the Atlantic and either die of hypothermia or drown. Either way my body would never be recovered.

True to CO Forbes's word, our time was filled with convoy patrols and milk trains which thankfully remained largely uneventful until early April.

On 15 April 1941 we were sitting in the dispersal hut waiting for the day's instructions. As usual, it was always the worst time of day. Even though the tide had turned on the political front and Britain had been saved from invasion, protecting the skies remained a dangerous job which none of us could take for granted. We had been on readiness since 4 a.m. Some of the pilots were catching up on kip, others played cards. A few sat and read the newspapers. Bogle sat staring ahead of himself lost in his own private world. Occasionally Durex got up and looked out of the window.

No one knew what the day had in store for them and that always put a damper on conversation. Outside our tatty old Spits, which had already been used and abused by other squadrons, had been prepared for take-off. Our flying kits had already been put in the cockpit by the aircrew and the planes had been revved to full power to check everything was in order. All we had to do now was wait.

The phone rang. The telephone operator called the flight commander over who listened to his instructions and nodded.

'There's a convoy off Dartmouth. We are to supply one section to fly over it until 09.00hrs. Scramble base.'

Sqn Ldr Forbes despatched Green Section to carry out the convoy. I was Green Two. The three of us quickly made our way to our aircraft. I nursed the cranky old Spit into the air and we headed out towards Dartmouth in south Devon. The flight commander was Oxo.

We reached 28,000ft and passed through the thick cumulus cloud. As we emerged a rush of sunshine filled the cockpit. It was a wonderful sight to see the bright light bouncing off the clouds. Up here the blue skies were flawless and the air so pure. I hated the thought of an enemy aircraft intruding on this perfect world, ready to smash the peace and tranquillity.

My mind returned to the job at hand and I craned my neck in all directions, as I suspected the other pilots were doing, trying to spot a Ju87 that might have thoughts of diving through the cloud to bomb the line of ships currently sailing up the Channel. There was nothing in sight. They have to be here somewhere. Tension began to creep into my body. Where were the bastards hiding? The CO called us up over the R/T: 'Nothing doing here, lads, let's fly down and let our boys know we are here. Fly round them, we don't want to scare them into thinking we are Jerry.'

We banked earthwards and dipped down through the clouds and spotted the convoy. It was an impressive sight of some twenty to thirty ships. Some of the vessels displayed battle scars acquired during their harrowing passage across the Atlantic that were either the result of a run-in with the German warships or their deadly cousins, the U-boats. But these were the lucky ones. They had made it. This time.

As I flew overhead, I felt nothing but huge respect for these people. They weren't soldiers, they were merchant seamen. The boats were defenceless except for the machine guns mounted on their decks which were largely ineffectual against the U-boats and the might of the German Navy. Even after the war, when thousands of servicemen were recognised for their role and decorated with medals and other military plaudits, no one seemed to spare a thought for the merchant sailors whose bravery saved the nation from starving.

I passed low over the last of the convoy as they zig-zagged through the water to avoid torpedoes. Suddenly from the deck house of one of the smaller ships a large man emerged wearing a vest and a pair of trousers. He put a bucket on the end of a broom and starting juggling with it. I smiled and continued on. The others often talked about some of the bizarre signals the sailors used to greet the RAF.

Then, suddenly, silvery streaks shot past the cockpit. Christ, there must be Hun in the area and they have caught me catnapping.

'Fool Jimmy, while you'd been admiring the ships, a 109 or Ju88 had come calling,' I told myself.

The firing continued. I swivelled around in my seat until my neck ached. I checked my mirror. There was nothing on my tail. I looked up and down, but I couldn't work out where the bullets were coming from. I broke into a sweat. This was serious. They could see me and I couldn't see them, which meant they had the upper hand which in turn meant, if I wasn't careful, it would be curtains for me. The best I could do was to try and take some evasive action. I pulled the Spitfire into a tight left-hand turn. Then a voice came over the R/T. It was the skipper.

'I don't believe it. The stupid bastards are shooting at us.'

I looked down. Sure enough, there were two men standing on a gun platform on one of the ships towards the front of the convoy. They were swivelling an enormous cannon that was pointed skywards and letting off rounds of bullets as we passed overhead. I couldn't blame them really. These people had been through hell. They hadn't crossed the Atlantic and avoided countless enemy ships and submarines, only to be sunk in the English Channel. They couldn't afford to take any chances and some of them had taken to shooting at anything that moved across the skies, regardless of who it was.

'Time for us to go, I think,' the Skipper said calmly and we climbed back up into the relatively safety of the clouds. From then on we never flew overhead, but always escorted the convoys from a safe distance or at least until we were absolutely certain they realised who we were.

By June 1941 we had been re-equipped with Spitfire IIs which were long-range Spits with a 30-gallon tank built into the starboard wing. It didn't affect the flying apart from when you were going downhill and then the excessive drag caused by the bulge meant it was difficult to keep the aircraft straight in a very fast dive. But, compared to the advantages it gave us, this was a minor complaint. The Spit IIs meant we could remain in the air for longer periods of time and so travel further into Europe. The new aircraft were certainly superior to their predecessors, but it was a double-edged sword as it also meant we could roam further afield in search of the enemy.

In the same way that convoy patrols and milk trains were a new experience for me, so too was the Rhubarb. I was first in the squadron to conduct a raid into Northern France, otherwise nicknamed a 'Rhubarb'. For some reason, Forbes chose me as his number two. I suppose he must have considered me a reliable sort and it was certainly a privilege to be selected. We were scheduled to take-off at dawn. As we prepared to leave, Forbes went over the mission again.

'We're going to shoot up Lannion aerodrome, it's only about 20 miles in from the French coast, but it will give them something to think about.'

'Yes, Sir, it will,' I replied.

'The success of the mission is down to the element of surprise. We can only achieve this by flying as low as possible above sea level to avoid being picked up by the German radar. If we make it to the French coast and the airfield, I will go in first, you follow as close as you can. Try and pick a target, but either way, just go in once and get out as fast as you can, stay in contact and good luck,' he added.

'Thank you, Sir, and you.'

We climbed into our respective aircraft and took off. Before long we were flying over open sea. Travelling a few feet above the sea was incredibly exhilarating and reminded me of those far distant days when I used to practise low-flying over the Peaks of Derbyshire. That was a lifetime ago, but that thrilling sensation of speed remained and for a moment I could forget the war and just enjoy the brief pleasure of flying my beautiful Spit II so low I could almost reach out and touch the waves.

Soon the channel gave way to land and we found ourselves in enemy territory. The green fields and small hamlets flashing past us appeared remarkably peaceful. I could only hope we had managed to evade the radars otherwise our reception committee would consist of anti-aircraft guns and the full might of the German Luftwaffe. But the land below us remained eerily quiet and our passage was ignored as we continued on our way towards our objective – Lannion aerodrome.

The airfield had been converted by the Germans into a fighter base. We knew there were a lot of aircraft on the field and that it would be infinitely easier to shoot them while they were firmly parked on the ground as opposed to circling each other in the air vying to get each other in our sights. Forbes's voice came over the airways.

'Lannion approaching, Blue Two. Take your pick.'

'Message received and understood,' I heard myself reply.

I checked my air-speed indicator which tipped 300mph. I knew the faster I could get the aircraft to go, the less chance I had of being hit myself by ack-ack fire.

Just short of Lannion, we pulled up to give ourselves some height from which to dive because, in order to shoot objects on the ground, the nose of the spitfire had to be pointing slightly downwards as we launched our attack. The CO went first. He dived down and opened fire on the airfield. A neat line of earth shot up as his bullets punctured the ground below him. An explosion told me that he had scored a direct hit. That was one less aeroplane for the RAF to worry about. Next it was my turn. My heart raced as I opened up the throttle and eased the stick forward. The nose of my Spitfire dropped down towards the airfield. Smoke was already drifting up from the airfield. Small figures now raced in all directions as chaos enveloped the aerodrome. There was no time to pick out a target. I set my course and went in hard and fast just as Sailor Malan had recommended. I opened fire and strafed the entire length of the airfield. The speeds were such that I have no idea what, if anything, I had hit. It was all over in seconds and we didn't dare risk a repeat performance as the Germans would undoubtedly be ready for us second time around.

I glanced in my mirror. Lannion airfield now receded into the distance and all thoughts turned to getting back to Perranporth in Cornwall, where the squadron was now based, as fast as I possibly could. I opened the throttle and the Spitfire raced homewards at 330mph. Any fear I had was now firmly replaced by my old friend, exhilaration. I had come through the madness again. Instinctively I touched my trouser pocket. Yes, the champagne cork was still there, of course, as I knew it would be.

In the distance I could see Forbes.

'Well done, Corbin. A good job.' His soothing words drifted through the R/T and we headed towards home.

We touched down at Perranporth and I rolled the Spitfire to a standstill. Sqn Ldr Forbes and I walked across the airfield to the dispersal hut where the rest of the squadron was idling away the time as best they could. The other pilots listened intently as we recounted the squadron's first raid into Northern France.

By now I had been operational for seven months and experienced just about every combat situation imaginable. I was no longer a sprog, as it were, but a highly experienced fighter pilot. In the May of 1941 I was promoted to flight sergeant and was often called upon to lead my own sections. But there was one aspect of my job that had eluded me. I had yet to bag my first 'kill'. I had never shot down an enemy aircraft.

In fact, I would have to wait just one more month before I could claim to have shot down an enemy aircraft. When it finally happened the experience didn't bring me any joy. Unlike those Polish pilots we had met, I didn't revel in any thoughts that their deaths might have been drawn out. For me, it was always a case of making sure I got them before they got me. Survival was my ultimate goal, always.

Up until that point I never dwelled on who I was shooting at or trying to kill. The Germans, like us, were encased in a flying machine and it was this contraption that we were trying to obliterate from the skies. The thought that they were flown by men and boys just like us never really entered the emotional equation. It made the fighting and the killing that less personal and, therefore, easier to cope with. But the fact that men got killed or wounded when their aeroplanes were sprayed with bullets really only came home to me one day in June 1941.

Sqn Ldr Forbes and I were scrambled on an interception patrol on 25 June. I was Red Two to Athol's Red One. An enemy aircraft had been reported at 1,500ft heading across Wales and towards the south west where no doubt they were aiming to escape back to north-east France.

Although it was summer, an early morning chill hung over Perranporth. Heavy dew had settled on the Spits and the erks were busy wiping down the damp cockpit hoods. As I climbed into my Spit, the night sky had begun to recede, but day promised a grey and gloomy start to our mission. The chances of us finding anything appeared slim.

'We've got a bomber just been bombing Liverpool. We think he's lost. He's headed down through Wales. We think he intends to turn left along the Cornish coast somewhere and head out to the Channel. Vector 140 degrees at 1,500ft.'

'Copy that.'

We took off and headed in a south-south-easterly direction as instructed. The light was particularly poor and made worse by a slight mist rising from the sea. Visibility was less than 500yd. Sqn Ldr Forbes called me up on the R/T.

'Red Two. We are not going to see much up here. Take her down to 700ft. You lead the way.'

I followed his orders. We cleared the cloud and I spotted the bomber almost immediately. He was just off Start Point and was on my port side.

'Red One, we have a bandit at 300 degrees.'

'Copy, Red Two. He's all yours. I'll follow.'

As I was nearest, I broke away from Forbes and came up behind the bomber.

'Red One. It's a Heinkel 111.'

'Copy, Red Two. Ready when you are.'

I remember thinking. 'It's a 111, there're a lot of men aboard inside those things.' The bomber was flying low, somewhere between 20 and 50ft, presumably to evade our radar system. In comparison to the Spitfire, the Heinkel was a heavy, slow aircraft. Without the protection of a bunch of 109s, he didn't stand much of a chance.

I got him in my sights and flicked the gun button and gave him a quick burst in a starboard forward quarter attack. Sqn Ldr Forbes was close behind me and came in for a port forward attack and his bullets raked the machine from end to end. From then on we took it in turns to fire on the 111. Evasive action for such an unwieldy beast of a machine was virtually impossible. All they could hope to do was shoot me out of the sky. I went for a further attack and the rear gunner who was on top of the plane returned my fire. I swung the plane from side to side to avoid the bullets and fired again. This time the gunner didn't return fire and I could only assume he'd been hit. The 111 then began to lose height and descend towards the sea.

It slipped into a steep dive from which I could tell there could be no recovery. Inevitably it disappeared into the sea fret, which was a thick mist that sat above the water. The event was recorded as a probable because we hadn't actually witnessed the aircraft's demise, but there was no doubt in my mind that the aeroplane would have crashed into the sea.

Several weeks later I took down my first Messerschmitt. It was 12 August. The day began with clear blue skies. The perfect weather conditions for what lay ahead. We had been ordered to fly to Southend on the east coast. There we were due to rendezvous with two other fighter squadrons, 152 and 234, at approximately 11.30 in the morning. The three fighter squadrons were to provide protection for a huge squadron of some fifty Blenheim bombers as they proceeded on to Holland to attack a pre-designated target. That number of bombers was certainly going to do some serious damage, but only if they could penetrate the German air defences.

We reached the Dutch coast and moved into line astern. We and 152 Squadron kept a height of between 200 and 1,000ft while 234 climbed to 2,000ft with the bombers sandwiched in between. We tracked the progress of the bombers, aiming to stay within about 400yd of them which, of course, made us targets ourselves.

A sprinkle of 109Es, 109Fs and Me110s made a half-hearted effort to stop us but the sight of three fighter squadrons must have been too much and they made little dent in our progress. Finally, we reached our destination of Waelsoorden. No. 152 Squadron went into a defensive circle around the Blenheims. No. 66 Squadron remained in open formation, weaving the whole time to prevent any enemy aircraft from approaching the bombers, and 234 Squadron circled overhead to prevent attacks from above. The operation went like clockwork. The bombers unleashed their awesome fire power. Thousands of bombs tumbled from their innards and in seconds the ground was a mass of grey explosions. The Germans returned with their deadly flak, but there was little they could do to repel an attack on this scale.

After ten minutes the wing commander ordered our return to base. No. 234 Squadron attached itself to the first wave of Blenheims and escorted them home. We attached ourselves to a further 19 Blenheims and headed for the coast of England.

We had just passed Neuzen and were approaching Holst when a Messerschmitt 109 appeared from nowhere and shot past my starboard wing. His presence threw me for a moment as I hadn't seen him coming, but I was also struck by the sheer foolishness of his decision to overtake me in this manner. Maybe the pilot assumed he could out-fly me, but it was a suicidal move as it placed him perfectly in my sights. I had had more testing targets than this in my training days at Hawarden. It was all too easy. All I had to do was fire my guns which I did. I gave him a good two-second burst from dead astern and watched my ammunition strike his fuselage. Suddenly the plane fell from the steady course on which it had been travelling and into a steep, uncontrolled dive. There was no smoke pouring from the aircraft and I assumed that I, in fact, had shot the pilot. The Me109 flew from view. As we were following the bombers, I didn't have time to check that I had definitely downed it, so on my return to base it was recorded as a 'probable'.

Overall it was a successful mission with thirty-seven out of the fifty-four bombers returning safely to their base. We flew back to Perranporth and only then did we realise that we had also suffered casualties. One of our pilots, Sgt Stevens, had gone missing off the coast of Holland. He never returned.

By the end of August, although I didn't know it, I was coming to the end of my posting with 66 Squadron. I had been with them for a year. I had seen boys become men and I had seen boys who had lost their lives and would remain forever young. I was now the old, experienced hand because, quite simply, I was still alive. The powers that be had decided, without my knowledge, that for the time being I had done my bit and I was due some time out from the madness that was war. But before I left 66 Squadron, fate dealt one last blow.

It was 20 August and I had been detailed to fly another escort for a group of Blenheims on a bombing raid to Holland. I arrived at the dispersal hut as usual and the CO called us together to go through the operation. It was a straightforward mission, similar to the previous ones I had flown in. Our role was to provide cover while the bombers did their job.

I was all set to go, when the Skipper called me over and told me that he was going to stand me down for that particular mission. I can't remember why, but it wasn't unusual for last-minute changes to be made to the line-up. 'I've decided to send Claude Parsons up in your place,' Forbes informed me.

'OK, Sir.' I thought little of it. The squadron took off. I loafed around the base until they returned. The pilots filtered back to the aerodrome on a high. As the noisy rabble filled the dispersal hut it became clear that operationally it had been another hugely successful mission.

'The bombers did a superb job, scored a direct hit on the steelworks at Ijmuiden in Holland. The factory was completely destroyed,' said Bobby Oxspring.

'Yeah, I saw it, it looked completely wrecked,' added Durex.

'Where's Claude?' I asked.

The pilots looked around them as if they expected him to be present.

'He's probably landed somewhere else. I saw someone bale out as we crossed the Channel. Maybe that was Claude, I don't know,' offered Pickles.

'Don't worry, Jimmy, if anyone knows how to get their kite back, it's Claude,' said Dizzy Allen.

It turned out that the pilot who baled out was a chap called Durrant who had joined the squadron earlier that year. Miraculously he was picked up 80 miles off the coast, alive and relatively unhurt.

Flt Sgt Claude Parsons, the squadron's leading expert on Spitfires and all-round good sort, never made it back. He had been with the squadron since the Battle of Britain days. Poor old Parsons – that wonderful source of Spitfire knowledge – was gone. He had already survived being hit by anti-aircraft fire. Dear Claude, who had taken my place in the line-up that day at the very last minute without a second thought, had been shot down and killed.

Chapter Ten

SEPTEMBER 1941 – LLANDOW, SOUTH WALES

At the end of September 1941 I became what was known rather brutally as 'tour expired' and was posted off operations. I had been in the frontline for a year now and the Air Ministry decided it was time for me to have a much needed rest. This came in the form of a spell instructing other young pilots to fly. Just as I had been taught at Hawarden to fly Spitfires by those pilots taking time out from the war, now it was my turn to get young men operational as soon as possible.

My posting came through and I found that I was to be sent to Llandow, which is near Swansea in South Wales. Naturally, the squadron gave me a big boozy send off. Then Forbes, myself and the other lads piled into his Humber Brake and took me to the railway station. The train was already in the station waiting to leave. The boys all clambered on board with me, insisting that they find me an appropriate travelling companion. And sure enough they did. Sitting alone in one of the carriages was a pretty young WAAF.

'Right, Corbin, in you go,' said Sqn Ldr Forbes. I squeezed past the grinning members of 66 Squadron, who were by now blocking the doorway to the carriage, and I took my seat opposite the lady.

The boys looked at the young lady and winked at me. The whistle blew, indicating that the train was about to leave. My fellow pilots bade me a noisy farewell. Forbes turned to the WAAF and said, 'Now then, young lady, look after him, he's very important.' And with that they left. As they waved the train out of the station, still winking and nudging each other, it occurred to me that I probably wouldn't see any of them ever again.

On my arrival at Llandow, I was shown my sleeping quarters. As I made my way to the mess, I spotted a tall thin chap talking to some pilots on the airfield. I shouted at the familiar figure of Flg Off Pickering.

'Pickles!'

He turned in response to hearing his nickname called and waved back. He excused himself from the group he was talking to and made his way over to me. We shook hands.

'Jimmy, it's good to see you! Welcome to 53 OTU. I had no idea you were coming here.'

'That's the RAF for you, always full of surprises. It's good to see you too.'

Pickles had arrived several weeks before me. He was younger than me and of slight build. In his school days, he had been a superb athlete and had been the 100yd sprint champion for the public schools. Most of all, he was a thoroughly good chap who would be good company in what promised to be a dull posting.

'So, what's it like?' I asked.

'OK, it's nice to have a break from it all, to be honest, and as you are a teacher you won't have any problems with this lot,' he nodded towards the groups of young men standing around on the airfield.

'What are they like?'

'Keen and green,' replied Pickles. 'It's quite a tough place for young pilots to train. We're near Swansea and just south of the Welsh hills and mountains which can be hazardous if you don't know what you're doing.

1. Flt Lt Jimmy Corbin DFC.

2. Walter Corbin, the author's father.

3. Daisy Lizzie, the author's mother.

4. The author aged about 4, in a cart made by his father.

5. The author, aged about 15, and a friend at the Scout Jamboree in Mote Park, Maidstone.

6. Shoreditch College: the staff and class of 1934–8.

7. The propeller tip of the Miles Master pranged by the author at 14 AFTS. It was presented to him when he completed the course at Cranfield.

8. No. 1 War Course, Burnaston, Derby, 1939–40.
9. (Opposite) The author outside 'The Dorchester' at Burnaston in the winter of 1939–40.

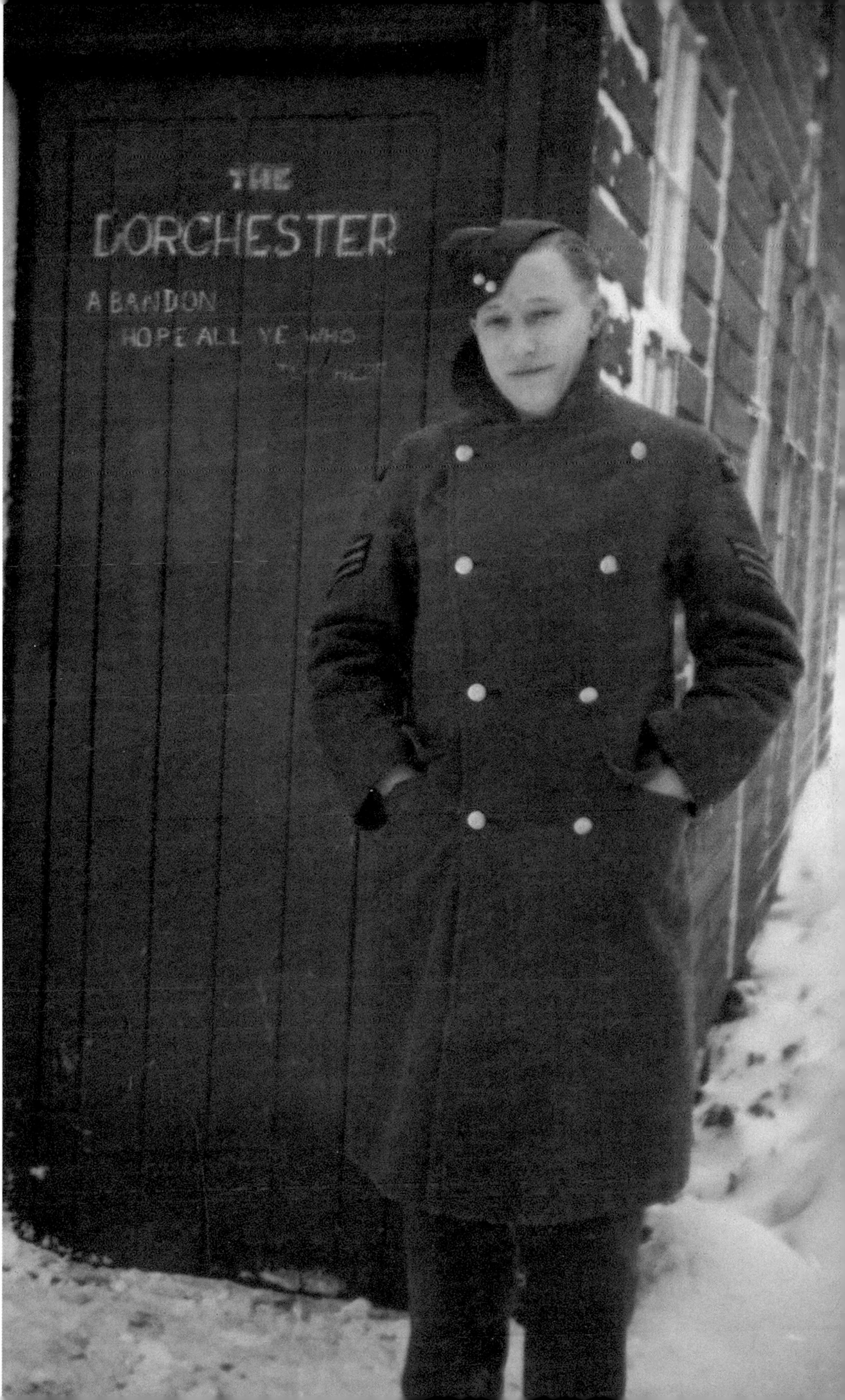
THE
DORCHESTER
ABANDON
HOPE ALL YE WHO

10. Flt Lt Hubert 'Dizzy' Allen DFC, 66 Squadron.

11. Left to right: Plt Off John 'Durex' Kendal, Rastus, Plt Off Hubert 'Dizzy' Allen and Pookie.

12. No. 66 Squadron, Gravesend, October 1940. Left to right: Plt Off H.W. Reilley, Plt Off C.A.W. 'Bogle' Bodie, Flt Lt G.P. Christie, Sqn Ldr R.H.A. 'Lucky' Leigh, Plt Off A.B. 'Watty' Watkinson, Flg Off Bobby Oxspring, Plt Off H.R. 'Dizzy' Allen.

13. Flg Off Peter King, 66 Squadron.

14. 'Dizzy' Allen and John 'Pickle' Pickering, 66 Squadron, 1941.

15. Sqn Ldr Athol Forbes DFC, 66 Squadron.

16. The author as a sergeant pilot, sitting in the cockpit of a Spitfire, 66 Squadron, 1941.

17. No 610 Squadron, Acklington, September 1940.

18. Long-range Spitfire Mk II, Portreath, 1941.

19. Central Gunnery School, Sutton Bridge, with its CO 'Sailor' Malan, April 1942.

Flying log book — **YEAR 1940** / **AIRCRAFT** / **PILOT, OR 1ST PILOT** / **2ND PILOT, PUPIL OR PASSENGER** / **DUTY (INCLUDING RESULTS AND REMARKS)** / **SINGLE-ENGINE AIRCRAFT** / **MULTI-ENGINE AIRCRAFT** / **PASS-ENGER** / **INSTRUMENT FLYING**

Month	Date	Type	No.	1st Pilot	2nd Pilot / Passenger	Duty	SE Day Dual	SE Day Pilot	SE Night Dual	SE Night Pilot
						TOTALS BROUGHT FORWARD	87.45	166.00	2.05	2.40
NOV	10	SPITFIRE II	P7433	SELF	BIGGIN HILL					
NOV	13	SPITFIRE	P7740	SELF	SOLO	MAIDSTONE PATROL		1.30		
NOV	14	SPITFIRE	P7540	SELF	SOLO	INTERCEPTION PATROL		1.25		
NOV	14	MAGISTER	R1504	SELF	SOLO	MAIDSTONE PATROL		1.20		
NOV	15	SPITFIRE	P7538	SELF	FLAT GREEN	WEST MALLING + RETURN		.30		
NOV	16	MAGISTER	P2705	SELF	FIRST PARKER	INTERCEPTION PATROL		.66		
NOV	16	MAGISTER	P2703	SELF	SOLO	TO CRANFIELD		1.00		
NOV	21	MAGISTER	P7538	SELF	SOLO	FROM CRANFIELD		.55		
NOV	21	MAGISTER		SELF	SOLO	INTERCEPTION PATROL		.20		
NOV	23	SPITFIRE	P7538	SELF	SOLO	READINESS PATROL		1.40		
NOV	23	SPITFIRE	P7538	SELF	SOLO	INTERCEPTION PATROL		1.25		
NOV	24	SPITFIRE	P7538	SELF	SOLO	MAIDSTONE PATROL		1.20		
NOV	24	SPITFIRE	P7538	SELF	SOLO	PATROL MAIDSTONE		1.25		
NOV	24	SPITFIRE	P7538	SELF	SOLO	INTERCEPTION PATROL		1.00		P/O ALLEN 407
NOV	26	SPITFIRE	P7538	SELF	SOLO	INTERCEPTION PATROL		1.50		109 W/R CRAWFORD
NOV	26	SPITFIRE	P7538	SELF	SOLO	INTERCEPTION PATROL		.75		
NOV	27	SPITFIRE	P7638	SELF	SOLO	INTERCEPTION PATROL		1.40		SGT WILLOCKS KILLED
NOV	28	SPITFIRE	P7440	SELF	SOLO	INTERCEPTION PATROL		1.00		ALLEN BALED OUT
NOV	29	SPITFIRE II	P7518	SELF	SOLO	MAIDSTONE PATROL		1.50		
						TOTALS CARRIED FORWARD	87.45	188.25	2.05	2.40

Summary box:

TOTAL ALL TYPES	DUAL	SOLO
	89.50	191.35

HOURS

TYPE OF AIRCRAFT	FLYING DURING MONTH DUAL	SOLO	TOTAL FLYING AT UNIT DUAL	SOLO
1. SPITFIRE	-	21.00	-	30.45
2. MAGISTER	1.55	-	1.55	-

O.C. 'B' FLIGHT

O.C. 66 SQUADRON

Remarks: P/O TURNER AND P/O HATTON CRASHED

GRAND TOTAL [Cols. (1) to (10)] 281 Hrs. 25 Mins.

20. The author's flying log book entries for November 1940 with 66 Squadron at Biggin Hill.

21. No. 72 Squadron at Souk El Chemis, North Africa, 1943.

22. No. 72 Squadron pilots with a visiting VIP.

23. Left to right: the author, Jupp and Le Cheminant, North Africa, 1943.

24. The author's flying log book for 1943 and some of the silk escape maps he carried.

25. A British fighter shot down over North Africa, 1943.

26. Miles Martinet of No. 11 Armament Practice Camp (APC), Fairwood Common, 1945.

27. Crews at No. 11 Armament Practice Camp, 1945.

YEAR 1942		AIRCRAFT		PILOT, OR 1ST PILOT	2ND PILOT, PUPIL OR PASSENGER	DUTY (INCLUDING RESULTS AND REMARKS)
MONTH	DATE	Type	No.			
—	—	—	—	—	—	TOTALS BROUGHT FORWARD
DEC	1	SPIT V/B	812	SELF	—	TO SOUK EL ARBA
	1	"	812	"	—	SHOT UP TANKS AROUND DJEDEIDA
	2	"	812	"	—	AERODROME PATROL
	2	"	812	"	—	SWEEP DJEDEIDA & TUNIS
	3	"	812	"	—	SWEEP - RETURNED A/C U/S
	3	"	812	"	—	AERODROME PATROL
	4	"	812	"	—	AERODROME PATROL
	5	"	812	"	—	SWEEP TABOUBA MATEUR AREA
	6	"	812	"	—	SWEEP TUNIS AREA
	7	"	812	"	—	SWEEP SCRAMBLED COCK-UP.
	8	"	812	"	—	AERODROME PATROL
	9	"	812	"	—	SWEEP BIZERTA 20,000'
	11	"	812	"	—	DAWN PATROL
	13	"	812	"	—	SWEEP MEDJEZ EN BAB - TUNIS ROAD.
	18	"	812	"	—	ESCORT BOSTONS & FORTRESSES
		"	812	"	—	TO MATEUR SIDINGS & AERODROME
	18	"	812	"	—	R/T CHECK O/K.
	20	"	812	"	—	AERODROME PATROL
	21	"	811	"	—	ESCORT HURRICANES ON TAC. R.
	22	"	812	"	—	ESCORT HURRICANES ON TAC. R.
	24	"	811	"	—	AERODROME PATROL
	24	"	812	"	—	AERODROME PATROL
						TOTALS CARRIED FORWARD

GRAND TOTAL (Cols. (1) to (10)) 850 Hrs. 35 Mins.

28. The author's flying log book entries for December 1942 with 72 Squadron at Souk El Arba.

29. The author at home in Kent, 2006.

30. The author after the war in his demob raincoat.

31. The staff of Maidstone Technical School in 1957. The author is in the back row, third from the left.

To be honest, we have had a few flying accidents. It's worse in bad weather when the mist and fog descend from nowhere. Some of them just get hopelessly disorientated and fly straight into the sides of hills and mountains. It's a terrible waste.'

'I see I'm going to have my work cut out here, then.'

I quickly got into my new role, but the novelty of instructing others soon wore off and as the months slipped by I felt I was beginning to stagnate and it became hard to stave off the boredom of teaching others to fly. It's difficult to explain, because I didn't want to be in the frontline risking my life on a daily basis, but I didn't want just to fester at Llandow either.

Once at the training unit, I was quickly transferred to X Squadron, which is the gunnery squadron. I enjoyed the gunnery school more than the formation flying. Although it was less than a year since I was the pupil trying to get to grips with keeping the plane in position, I really didn't like taking young and inexperienced pilots up in formation flying. They flew too close and were too unpredictable for my liking. But I suppose my instructors thought that about me.

Life in the gunnery squadron was less hazardous, but only just. My job was to take a pupil up in that old faithful, the Miles Master II, and show them how to attack a drogue which was like a big wind sock. This was pulled along by another aircraft at about 100mph. The idea was that you would approach the aeroplane towing the drogue from the opposite direction with the intention of getting slightly above it and to one side. Then at the right moment you had to turn your aircraft through a 120-degree angle and open fire at the drogue. The tips of the bullets were dipped in paint so you could check your score afterwards to see if you had hit the drogue. This was all fine except that occasionally I would have to pull the drogue, which was never a pleasant experience as these trigger-happy pilots often seemed to fire at random and the bullets went all over the place. I am not sure how they managed to avoid hitting me.

After one particularly hairy experience, I returned to the instructor's mess. A big bear of a man with a shock red hair and moustache was sitting by the window. He grinned at me as I entered.

'Bloody hell, that looked a bit close for comfort,' he said.

'You're telling me. Bloody lunatics, some of them, don't know their arse from their elbow,' I replied.

The man held his hand out.

'Gerald Le Cheminant. Call me Chem, it takes less time.'

'Jimmy, pleased to meet you. French?'

'Certainly not,' he replied indignantly. 'I'm from Guernsey.'

'You seem familiar. Were you at Biggin Hill?'

'92 Squadron.'

'I thought so, I was in 66. Bit rough for a while.'

'Certainly was. Fancy a drink?'

'After that lot, I think I deserve one,' I replied.

We requisitioned a couple of bikes and headed off into the village nearby for a few pints.

'So, you got a girl, Chem?'

'She's called Eileen, lives in Twyford, near my family,' he replied as he fished out her photograph and showed it to me.

'Serious?'

'Thinking of asking her to marry me.'

'Now, that's serious.'

'What about you?'

'No, it's the bachelor life for me. I dabble from to time to time, but that's about it.'

That was the beginning of a great friendship between Chem and me. On leave I often travelled with him to his parents' home in Berkshire. His family were delightful and treated me like a second son. In fact, I seemed to get on better with them than I did with my own family. I also met Eileen who was a very attractive girl and very much in love with Chem. They made a perfect couple.

One weekend I remained at the base and Chem went home for the weekend. He returned on the Sunday night, bursting with news. He announced that he and Eileen were getting married which, of course, was much cause for celebration, so we all set out for the local pub to toast the prospective groom.

We were in the pub enjoying a beer when Chem sidled up to me. I shook his hand.

'Well Chem, congratulations to you and Eileen. It couldn't have happened to a nicer bloke.'

'Thanks, Jimmy. Look a mate of mine in the Navy was down to be my best man, but he can't make it. I wondered if you would do the honours.'

'Chem, I'd be honoured.'

So, second choice or not, I became Chem's best man. The wedding was a very grand affair and we all had a great time. I executed my duties as best man without any serious mishap and I spent the day with Chem's sister who I had a bit of a soft spot for. Afterwards I returned to Llandow and Chem and Eileen went away for a few days' honeymoon. It had been refreshing to escape Llandow for a short time and enjoy something as normal as a mate's wedding.

The day after my return life as an instructor resumed its boring self. I went up in an old Lysander with a flight lieutenant by the name of Greenaway. We carried out a routine defence exercise. He was a keen student and was progressing well. It wouldn't be long before he joined the fight. We came into land and, after debriefing the pilot on his performance, I returned to the instructor's hut. I sensed an atmosphere I hadn't known since my days on the squadron. An air of gloom had settled on the place. One of the other instructors looked up as I strolled in.

'Have you heard?'

'Heard what?' I asked.

'Pickles is dead.'

'What?'

I was incredulous. I couldn't believe what I was hearing. On the squadron, you expected to hear the news that one of your companions had gone down, so you were always prepared to for the worst. But here in the safe environment of a training school it came like a bolt from the blue.

'How?'

'A mid-air collision with a chap called Polton. They were doing some low-level aerobatics and, well, clearly he didn't see the other chap coming.'

It was a wretched and tragic end to such a talented and likeable individual. Pickles was just 21 years old. He had survived so much. He had fought so bravely for his country in the Battle of Britain and this was how it was to end for him.

Several days later Pickles was buried in a cemetery near Llantwit Major. It was an honour to act as a pall bearer at his funeral. To think he had survived the very worst the Luftwaffe could throw at him, only to end up like this. As they played the Last Post at his funeral, I helped lower his coffin into the grave and I'm not ashamed to admit that I shed a tear for Pickles.

PART TWO

THE
Battle for North Africa

Chapter Eleven

AUGUST 1942 – GIBRALTAR

Spring became summer and I began to feel I had spent a lifetime at Llandow as an instructor. My job of teaching others to fly had become increasingly tedious and dull. And, although I didn't crave to be 28,000ft in the air with a Messerschmitt Me109 on my tail, I did wish for some excitement in my life. To make matters worse, Chem, my closest friend and fellow instructor at Llandow, had received news that he was to join 72 Squadron which was stationed in Ayr at Scotland. Rumours abounded that 72 was going overseas and I envied him the opportunity to have a break from the monotony of instructing.

We gave Chem a noisy send-off, but I was deeply disappointed to see him go.

'Well Chem, I'm going to miss you mate,' I said to him at his leaving party.

'Might not be over yet. I'll see if I can put in a good word for you with the CO,' he replied.

'Thanks, mate, I would appreciate that. Anything has got to be better than Llandow.'

We toasted to each other's success and the thought of not seeing him again was a depressing one. I didn't hold out much hope of being able to join him in Ayr. The RAF work in mysterious ways, but rarely gave you what you wanted. No, for the time being, I was stuck at Llandow.

Two weeks later I was called to the CO's office and informed that I had been posted to 72 Squadron. I sensed Chem had had a hand in this and I was grateful to my old chum for remembering me. I packed my bags and left Llandow for good, ready to rejoin the war. When I reached Ayr, Chem was there waiting for me with a big grin on his face.

'I assume I've you to thank for this,' I said.

'I've no idea what you are talking about,' he smiled, 'but there's someone here who'd like to meet you. Someone you know well,' he added mysteriously.

Chem showed me to the CO's office where another surprise greeted me. A young man looked up from his desk.

'Hello Jimmy, it's been a while, hasn't it?'

'Bobby Oxspring!' I exclaimed.

We shook hands warmly. Bobby had been a flight commander at 66 and was now the CO of 72, which was a well-deserved promotion. He was a terrific pilot and the only man I knew who could detect and shoot down enemy aircraft at night. I suspected that Chem had told him I was also at Llandow and Bobby had got on to the Air Ministry to get me transferred into his squadron, which I took as a huge compliment, although neither of them ever admitted to anything.

Over the next few days the rest of the team assembled. There was Flg Off David Cox, or Coxy, who was a bit of a short arse and probably didn't weigh much more than 10st. But he was a very good pilot and rightly went on to command his own flight. He had a DFC and Bar, and an AFC. He wasn't a man you could warm to, but you respected him as a pilot and leader.

Flg Off Owen Hardy was from New Zealand, but had moved to England in the 1930s where he married an English girl and opted to stay in Britain and joined the RAF. He was a good pilot, honest and straightforward. He was a good-looking chap, and a good friend and drinking partner.

Daniels was a pilot officer and a big, red-headed Scotsman who I grew to like immensely. He was always up to mischief. Plt Off Johnnie Lowe had been posted to 72 Squadron straight from OTU and was on his first tour of operational duty. Poor kid, he reminded me of when I was a sprog.

Chas Charnock, who was a warrant officer, was at 37 the oldest of the group and always referred to me as Uncle Jimmy, because at 23 I was the second oldest member of the squadron. Chas was one of those chaps who was seemingly fearless and got himself into all sorts of scraps. But he was a lovable rogue and a hugely popular member of the group. Chas was a good sort to have around and his crazy antics always boosted morale.

Robby Robertson was also a pilot officer and became another great friend of mine. Roy Hussey was a sergeant pilot. He was a nice boy and an excellent pilot who shot down quite a few enemy aircraft. We flew in pairs then and he was number two to Robby. When Robby got shot down he blamed Hussey for it. Robby lost an eye in the process and after that he never flew operationally again.

Pete, Frampton, Mottram, Pierson, Piggott and Browne, Chem and myself made up the remainder of the squadron. Flt Lt Ford Krohn was our flight commander who had a penchant for writing poetry.

By now we knew we were definitely going overseas, although we still didn't know where. The next seven days were spent knocking us into shape as we trained hard for our mission. We went on cross-country runs and route marches as part of the toughening-up process. The operations record book states that spirits in the team were high and we threw ourselves enthusiastically into the training. I think this was true. We knew it was going to be tough, maybe as tough as the Battle of Britain had been. But there was one difference. We were experienced pilots. We knew what we were going into. This time we would be prepared.

From Ayr we were moved to Ouston in Durham where we waited for our much hoped for embarkation leave. This didn't happen and one flight was told to return to Ayr for readiness while the other was sent to Hartlepool, as part of some mind-boggling bureaucratic nightmare that the RAF excelled itself at.

After ten days, we were all recalled once again to Ouston. By now it was 11 October. A few of us managed to scrounge five days' leave, but after four days the telegram came through and we were recalled on 18 October. The CO filled us in on as much detail as he could.

'Sorry for the delay, lads, but we've heard that there's a ship ready to take us. I can't tell you where for obvious reasons, but you should pack only the barest essentials such as flying kit, some toiletries, and just one change of clothing.'

'Christ, forget getting killed by the Hun, we're all going to die of BO,' Chas Charnock said.

The CO ignored him and continued.

'The flight is to be divided into groups and you'll travel in separate convoys to the initial destination where you'll reform as one squadron before moving on to our final destination.'

Johnnie Lowe leaned over to me.

'Why is that then?'

'If we get torpedoed on the way, the whole squadron gets wiped out. By splitting up, at least one half has a chance of getting through and carrying on with the fight,' I responded.

Lowe looked a little shocked.

'I wish I hadn't asked now.'

'Right, first things first, we need you all to have some jabs. After that, pack as quickly as you can and be ready to leave at dawn.'

A series of hasty inoculations followed, including one for yellow fever which sparked a lengthy debate among us over our possible destination. I packed my essentials as ordered, but included an extra travelling companion – my champagne cork. I didn't ask the others, but I suspect they too slipped in the odd lucky mascot. I also took my prized Rolls razor that Ken Baker, my old school chum, had given me for my 21st birthday. God only knew where he was and whether he was still alive.

When the time came we said our goodbyes to the others and Krohn, Cox, Hardy, Daniels, Robertson, Lowe and myself went ahead alone. We caught a bus that took us, along with 93 Squadron, to the Manchester

Ship Canal where we spent a grim day in the pouring rain waiting for our ship to come in.

At around 5 p.m. in the afternoon our transport appeared. It was an ageing 4,500-ton unladen merchant cargo vessel, called the SS *Staffordshire*. Our aircraft had already been dismantled and stored in numerous crates which were now being lifted onto the ship by huge cranes and lashed to the decks by the ship's crew.

We boarded the *Staffordshire* and carried out the first essential task – locating and inspecting our sleeping quarters. These turned out to be in the top hold which was crammed from floor to ceiling with narrow bunk beds. I bagged myself a top bunk and found that if I got out of bed too quickly, my head collided with the ceiling.

The *Staffordshire* set sail along the canal towards Liverpool. There we joined a coastal convoy and steamed up the Clyde. By the Friday morning we had collected scores of other ships and the convoy was ready to move out. Fifty or more ships sailing in a line must have provided an impressive sight. From the deck of the *Staffordshire* we identified an aircraft carrier and several frigates and destroyers which all counted among our line up. This led to inevitable comparisons and debates about the merits of travelling in the various different vessels which led to grumbles of discontent, mainly from me.

In true RAF style, the officers were allowed to travel on one of the flashy new destroyers while the rest of us had to make do with a cramped and decrepit old merchant ship. I had long grown used to the blatant favouritism shown to those of an officer rank and it rarely bothered me anymore, but this time I felt rather piqued as I had always fancied a trip on one of the warships, especially a destroyer.

During the next few days, the convoy ploughed through the dark seas in a westerly direction. If our destination was Gibraltar, as we had now begun to suspect, then ordinarily we could have completed the journey in two to three days. But during the war sailing a direct course via the Bay of Biscay was nothing short of suicide, because German U-boats lurked beneath the surface waiting for information from their reconnaissance planes which would betray our position and lay us open to attack. The convoy could only travel as fast as the slowest ship, making it an easy target for the U-boats. But by steering an erratic course, the commanding officer of the convoy hoped to confound the enemy and prevent them from predicting our course, so they could not lie in wait for us. As a result it took us twenty-one days to sail to Gibraltar.

The ship's officers and crew gave us a free rein and we passed our time exploring the ship with almost childish enthusiasm. By the end of two days we had familiarised ourselves with every nook and cranny of the vessel several times over and the novelty of being seaborne was starting to wear off. It wasn't half as exciting as flying.

Then one night we climbed into our bunks, exchanged the usual banter and drifted off to sleep. Sometime later we were shaken awake by a terrific noise. Someone shouted in the darkness, 'We've been hit.' Chaos ensued. We all dived out of our beds and headed for the bridge as fast as we could, as being below deck in a sinking ship didn't strike us as the smartest place to be.

Once on deck it became clear that we had not been torpedoed as first thought. In fact, a gangway had broken loose in the heavy swell and was flapping all over the deck, crashing against the side of the ship. A storm was in full force and waves the size of a house broke against the side of the ship. I smiled at the thought of the officers in their shiny new warship being buffeted by 30ft waves. I realised then that by opting to travel on a destroyer which was a lot smaller than the *Staffordshire*, they had consigned themselves to weeks of being tossed and turned by the sea. They probably spent more of their time below sea level than above it. Perhaps the *Staffordshire* wasn't such a bad place to be after all.

Relieved that we hadn't been attacked by anything other than high winds and water we returned to our beds. But the experience had unnerved us and this false alarm prompted us to organise our own two-hour watch which also helped to break up the monotony of sea life. It was a surprisingly popular job and the ship's bridge was often awash with keen-eyed pilots with nothing better to do than spend their days scouring the horizon for tell-tale periscopes sticking up above the water.

When not on watch we struggled to find ways to amuse ourselves. We grew bored and restless and even a sweep on who would be the first to be struck down by sea sickness, which turned out rather satisfyingly to be the wing commander, did little to relieve the tedium.

Five days into the journey and the inevitable happened when a group of pilots are thrown together: a poker school was set up. Night after night, we huddled below deck swigging beer around a makeshift table bathed in the blue haze of cigarette smoke. I enjoyed poker. Hours of sitting around airbases perfecting my technique had made me a proficient player and I fared well enough to keep myself in cigarettes and alcohol. As the dealer shuffled and dealt the cards we chatted about all sorts.

One night the conversation turned to matters of love, which was quite a popular conversation topic among pilots. Johnny Lowe, who was on his first operational tour of duty with 72 Squadron, had married shortly before we had set sail. I decided to give him the benefit of my experience with women, only to be interrupted by the others.

'What do you know about love, you're not even married, Jimmy?'

'I don't see what that's got to do with it,' I replied.

'Well, old boy, it's a case of you can sit in the car and watch the driver, but that doesn't mean you know how to drive the car yourself, if you get my drift.'

'But at least I can put the brakes on the car and leave it, unlike you married types,' I retorted.

At this point the captain of the ship interjected.

'Look, none of you know anything about love. You're all wet behind the ears. When you've visited as many places as I have and met as many women as me, then you might know something.'

It was difficult to argue with him and the conversation drifted off at a tangent leaving poor old Lowe none the wiser in the ways of love.

The night ended with two of the COs and the ship's captain becoming increasingly inebriated. This in turn led to them to bet ludicrously wild amounts of money. The captain of the ship finally triumphed. Defeated, the two COs excused themselves and staggered off in the general direction of their quarters.

Daniels and I helped the swaying captain scoop up his winnings and guided him back to his bed.

After a week at sea, it became clear that we were indeed heading south. The weather improved enough for us to build sunbathing into our daily itinerary. Coxy, Robby, Johnny Lowe and I contented ourselves reading and playing poker while Fordy volunteered repeatedly to keep watch from the bridge. As he wisely pointed out: 'I tell you it's the safest place to be. I'd rather be on deck if the jolly tin fish appears than down below with you lot.'

He had a point, the U-boats had begun to take an unhealthy interest in us and we now wore our Mae Wests every day as a precaution. One day towards the end of October I came across Fordy in his usual position on the bridge.

'See that,' he said pointing ahead.

I squinted at the horizon.

'Nope.'

'The convoy is splitting up. They're heading south, I reckon they're going to Sierra Leone.'

'What direction are we heading in?'

'West, I think.'

'West? But there's nothing between here and North America.'

'Must be a decoy to shake off the U-boats. I reckon we're headed for the Rock.'

'Gibraltar?'

'Yep.'

'Well, there are worst places, I suppose.'

Fordy, pilot-turned-amateur-sailor, was right. Some hours later our ship turned east again confirming suspicions that we were headed for Gibraltar.

On Friday 6 November, we sighted the coastline of Spain and Morocco. Shortly afterwards we entered the Straits of Gibraltar and steamed into the bay. The remaining twenty-three ships continued on their journey through the Mediterranean, but the *Staffordshire* anchored just off the Rock along with one of the other ships.

We stood on the deck and looked across the bay. The Rock of Gibraltar rose out of the sea and stood so tantalisingly close to our ship that I could almost have swum to it. When we were transferred to a Spanish tug we thought that at last we were going to sample its undoubted pleasures. But, no, life is never that simple, especially in the RAF and we ended up on another bloody troop ship this time alongside some Americans and other air force types. We stood on another deck of another ship and stared longingly at the lights of Gibraltar which winked at us in the distance. Our only consolation was that the ship's bar was noisy and boisterous and the hooch was cheap and palatable.

Two days later we were finally released from the ship and stepped onto solid ground. It felt good. We were taken to a secret camp for security reasons, which was on the eastern side of the Rock facing the Spanish border. It was a bizarre decision, as a stone's throw away on the other side of the border with Spain sinister-looking German agents would sit in a hut and monitor our every move, such that it was. Interestingly, if they could have seen around the whole of this little rock they would also have noted that once landed we hit Gibraltar with gusto.

We boozed extensively at either the Cottage Victory Inn or the Bristol Hotel, where I bumped into David Niven, the film star, who was in the Army at that time and enjoyed a drink as much as we did. In the afternoons we took a break from our lunchtime sessions and went to see a decent film at the local flicks, such as the wonderful *Casablanca* with Humphrey Bogart and Ingrid Bergman which was out that year. Finally, we headed back to our camp for a game of cards and more booze and cigarettes.

A few days after we arrived, the second batch of pilots from 72 sailed into port and the squadron was together again. Chem, Chas, Pete, Hussey, Frampton, Mottram, Pierson, Piggott and Browne were all there and in fine spirits. It was a rowdy reunion. Confidence was running high in our ranks. We were ready for anything.

Now we were all together, the pace picked up and talk of our impending operation began. The following day we attended a lecture from Wg Cdr Simpson on the campaign. There was an air of excited anticipation.

'Right men, you're part of Operation Torch which is a combined land, sea and air campaign to kick the Germans out of North Africa. Its primary objective is to make landings in Morocco and Algeria which is 500 miles east of Gibraltar. Those who land at Algiers will then drive eastwards towards Tunisia and try and occupy the German stronghold of Tunis, its capital, as soon as possible. There they'll be met by Monty's Eighth Army which is currently to the south of Tunisia, fighting its way up from Egypt.

'As the British First Army pushes through North Africa, they will secure airfields on their way for use by the Royal Air Force. We will in turn operate in support of the land forces until victory in North Africa is secured. In short, gentlemen, it's going to be a rough ride. The Germans aren't going to give up North Africa without a fierce fight.'

Chem turned to me.

'I heard the RAF boys are already having a tough time of it in Algiers. I was told pilots have to sleep in their cockpits. They're flying around the clock.'

Wg Cdr Simpson saved the best news until last.

'You'll all be given the requisite rations and escape packets, including your "blood" ticket.'

Chem and I exchanged a frown at the mention of blood. The wing commander put us out of our misery.

'This is a small purse containing five gold coins that will come in handy if you need to buy your way out of trouble in enemy territory. One thing you'll quickly learn about Arabs is that everything is negotiable.'

Our CO, Bobby Oxspring, attended a further briefing for senior officers by the Air Officer Commanding Gibraltar, who explained in detail the operation plans. He reminded the squadron commanders that the timing of the air support forces was crucial as the commandos had just six hours to capture the important airfield of Maison Blanche, near Algiers. The area was controlled by Vichy French forces and there would be no guarantee that the first fighter squadron, timed to arrive six hours after the initial land assault from Gibraltar, would receive a friendly welcome. Also, by the time they got there they would not have sufficient fuel to divert elsewhere, so they would have to land and face the consequences.

According to Bobby, Mickey Rook, the CO of 43 Squadron, made a crack along the lines that it all seemed rather dicey. To which the AOC agreed, adding, 'The first squadron in will be 43.' Apparently Rook took the information to heart and secreted a murderous array of knives and pistols about his person before his departure for Maison Blanche.

Where 43 went, 72 Squadron was destined to follow and our next task was to make sure our aircraft were combat ready. We went to the aerodrome at Gibraltar which was a huge area covered in some 600 aircraft of all different species. The Royal Engineers had even extended the North Front runway by some 500yd out to sea to allow aeroplanes to land and take off. It was an impressive feat.

Our disassembled aircraft had arrived from the ship still in crates. Each Spit was in various stages of reconstruction. Their body parts were spewed out across the airfield. A small team of Army engineers buzzed around the shells of the aircraft, puzzling over the various pieces that lay around them. It didn't fill us with confidence.

The relationship between the Army and the RAF has always been an uneasy one and we would have preferred to have seen our own trusty RAF engineers putting the Spits together, but they had yet to catch up with us and so the task fell to the Royal Engineers. As we watched the brown jobs, as we called them, pondering over the engines and the fuselage an uneasy feeling came over us. These chaps were more used to fixing tanks. What did they know about aeroplanes? As it turned out, quite a lot. A test flight around the Rock told us that we had done the army engineers a great disservice by doubting their abilities. They had, in fact, made an excellent job of putting the aeroplanes together. I take back everything I ever said about the Army.

As our time in Gibraltar drew to a close, a few of us made the most of the dying embers of our last days on the Rock. Chas and Fordy had a final fling at the Cottage Victory Inn and got so drunk that Fordy lost his way back to the camp and rang up to ask if the squadron had moved on without him.

We assembled at the airfield in our full flying gear, hangovers and all, on 16 November ready for the next stage of the war. I had not seen combat for well over a year. The milk trains, the rhubarbs, the convoy patrols and the dogfights were little more than distant memories. A large part of me wanted to get back up there and do my bit. But, similarly, I didn't know what lay in wait for me. I had survived the Battle of Britain when many hadn't. My next test was to be the Battle for Tunis. Would I come through this unscathed? Or would this be my finest, but final hour?

I stepped into my Spit. It was good to get back into the cockpit. I hadn't flown properly since I had left Llandow. I strapped myself in, carried out the usual checks and moved along with the rest of the squadron towards the runway. The weather did not bode well for us. The rain lashed the runway and streamed down the outside of the cockpit making visibility particularly poor. I taxied along the runway which jutted out to sea with the Mediterranean lapping either side. The Spit gathered speed, then I throttled back and she rose up into the air.

It was a shaky take-off. We were now flying the Spit Vb, which had two cannons and four machine guns and a more powerful engine. The Spits had been tropicalised for use in the sandy conditions of North Africa and had been fitted with a Vokes engine air intake dust filter which knocked off a bit of speed, but, as most of the upcoming action was to take place below 20,000ft, this made very little difference to their overall performance. They also carried 90-gallon fuel tanks which were jettisoned when empty, but they made taking off a bit tricky because of the heavy fuel load.

I reached 15,000ft and levelled out. The plane stabilised and settled down to a comfortable cruising speed of 300mph. The weather finally began to clear and I took the opportunity to take in the sights below me. I had never seen so much sea, but littered all along the entire route were shipwrecks from both sides of the war and evidence of the fierce marine battles that had taken place. The mangled carcasses of naval vessels were an uncomfortable reminder that the war had proceeded happily in my absence and looked as if they had been positioned there intentionally to guide me back into the fray once more.

Several hours later an aerodrome, if you could call it that, came into view. It was Maison Blanche and it was not half as attractive as its French name seemed to suggest. A flat featureless airfield, it bulged with aircraft of all types. There were Spits, Blenheims and Beaufighters, USAAF Lightnings and DC-3s, and some Italian planes. I assumed the latter had been captured at some point. The airfield was basic in the extreme and I described my first impressions of the place in my diary as 'nature in the raw'. At least the rain had stopped, for the time being.

We saw to our Spits, as the ground crew still had not arrived, and spent the rest of the day learning how to cook in preparation for the hardships that lay ahead. Usually the airmen cooked for us and we received regular food parcels from the Ministry, although by the time they reached us all the decent stuff had been pilfered and we were left with biscuits and sardines, the charms of which wore pretty thin after a few months.

At around 11 p.m. that night we were told once again to pack what few belongings we had been allowed to bring with us. The next morning we would be moving to our forward base wherever that was. We were briefed on the next stage of the campaign and issued with yet more maps. We gave three cheers for the success of the campaign and went to bed, if you could call it that.

The only bedding I could muster was a couple of small blankets which provided meagre cover and no warmth. We bedded down on the hard, cold concrete floor of a French Air Force hangar. It was a miserable beginning to my time in North Africa and I had the strongest suspicion that it was unlikely to get much better. But I was too hungry and too tired to moan and finally I drifted into a fitful sleep.

During the night I was woken by the distant thud of bombs exploding. The Luftwaffe had come to pay someone a visit. I worked out that their target was probably the harbour at Algiers, which was only about 3 miles away from Maison Blanche. Our naval ships replied with their cannons and the fierce exchange continued for some minutes more. As I lay in the dark, the noise reminded me of that day when I watched Tilbury Docks being bombed out of existence. Now here I was, once again, back in the thick of it all. It felt like I had never been away. Just like last time, there would be no telling what the result would be. I hoped it would all go in my favour. A loud crash nearby shook the hangar and dust sifted down from the roof onto my face. Welcome to North Africa.

Chapter Twelve

NOVEMBER 1942 – SOUK AL ARBA, NORTH AFRICA

The next day began early with the usual checks on the Spits to make sure they had survived the previous night's bombing. This was followed by my usual breakfast of a couple of cigarettes and a hot drink to shake off the miserable effects of too little sleep. As I nursed a mug of steaming tea, my commanding officer, Bobby Oxspring, approached me.

'Jimmy, I want you as my number two, today. We're going to go up to Bone to do a bit of reconnaissance. It's an airfield further up the coast toward Tunis and it's under Allied control, but it's a port as well, so it's attracting a lot of attention from the Jerrys. We have had reports that there were 109s patrolling in the area. So keep a look out.'

'Yes Sir. What time are we leaving?'

'Be ready to leave in ten.'

We took off shortly afterwards. Sqn Ldr Oxspring took the lead and I followed closely behind. My take-off was again a little shaky due to the loose rubble on the strip of ground masquerading as the runway. It was still an unfamiliar and unnerving experience and one I hoped I would grow accustomed to it as there was little prospect of the quality of the runways improving. This was new territory for me and my Spitfire. I knew how they performed on English soil, but here in desert conditions, I was less certain. A layer of dust permanently settled on every surface and seemed to seep into every crevice. Grit constantly swirled in your mouth. God only knows what damage it was doing to the aeroplane.

I steadied the aeroplane and climbed to about 10,000ft before levelling out. Thankfully, by now, the ridiculously tight formations we had flown in during the Battle of Britain had been scrapped. Sense had finally prevailed and we now flew in pairs, or sometimes in a line of four spread out across the sky to give us the best possible chance of spotting the enemy.

As Bobby and I flew on towards Bone, my perspex hood became oiled up and I made a mental note to get it fixed on my return. It was the last thing I needed as it reduced my visibility to dangerously poor levels, especially as Bobby had warned me that the enemy was highly active in the skies all around the area. There was little I could do other than hope I didn't run into a gaggle of Me109s, because the chances of spotting them first through the smears on my windscreen were slim. Incredibly something so seemingly insignificant as a dirty hood could cost me my life, I thought ruefully. But fortune smiled on me as we flew into a light storm which seemed to clear it, allowing me to relax a little.

Our two Spits hugged the coastline of North Africa. Every now and then we passed one of the many small fishing villages that dotted the shoreline until a large collection of buildings on the horizon signalled we were approaching the port of Bone.

We drew nearer and I could see the harbour was a frenzy of activity and crammed tight with the familiar blue-grey vessels of the Royal Navy. The ships were spewing out scores of men and machinery belonging to the British First Army as quickly as they could, but a quick scan of the skies revealed no trace of enemy aircraft.

Bobby's voice came over the intercom. He suggested we circled the aerodrome, which was on the outskirts of the town, before coming into land. I followed him in and we taxied to a standstill and climbed out of our Spits. Pete Hugo, the commander of 322 Wing, was there to greet us. He and Bobby saluted each other.

'Morning Sir, I'm Sqn Ldr Oxspring and this is my No. 2, Plt Off Jimmy Corbin. The rest of our party are still at Maison Blanche.'

'Glad to have you both here, Sqn Ldr Oxspring.'

The pleasantries were quickly dispensed with as the conversation was interrupted by the distant and unfamiliar drone of aeroplanes which were not ours. Instinctively we turned to look in the direction from which the noise was coming. Above the buildings that made up Bone we could just make out a number of German bombers, Ju88s, approaching the harbour. Seconds later, the familiar sound of explosions followed as the enemy aircraft released in turn their lethal bombs and weaponry on the un-suspecting town.

The wing commander reacted immediately and barked his orders.

'Right, get the kites refuelled. We'll take them up and do a sweep over Tabarka and see if we catch up with them there.'

We were already running for our aircraft. Wg Cdr Hugo took off first, closely followed by Sqn Ldr Oxspring and myself. Within minutes we were airborne and searching the skies for our quarry. A year of instructing others melted away in an instant. It had started again. I was a fighter pilot once more.

By the time our aircraft reached the harbour, the bombing had ceased and the Ju88s had made themselves scarce, but this didn't deter an old war veteran like Hugo. He decided we could still hunt the bombers down and make sure they could not bomb our men again, if we knew where to look for them. Hugo ordered us to turn towards a place called Tabarka which is just east of Bone and just inside the Tunisian border.

'With any luck, we will find the blighters lurking somewhere in that area.'

We had been airborne for just eight minutes and were travelling at a height of around 8,000ft when, in the distance ahead of us, a lone Ju88 crossed our paths in an act of total folly. He didn't stand a chance. His position was relayed over the R/T and we went in for the kill.

Sqn Ldr Oxspring went first and squirted the aircraft with a short burst of machine gun fire. I followed suit. But it was the wing commander who rightly claimed the kill. As he approached the bomber, he let rip with his machine guns and sprayed the aeroplane end to end with bullets. There was a slight hiatus before the aircraft exploded in a ball of flames and showered debris across the sky.

'I don't think he'll be giving us anymore trouble,' a voice came over the R/T and we headed back to the base.

We returned victorious to Bone, but as always our triumph was short-lived. Throughout the day the Luftwaffe continued to mount wave after wave of attacks on the little harbour in a relentless effort to disrupt the Allies' crucial supply lines.

The aerodrome was the scene of frantic activity as we hastily dug slit trenches for our own protection in between sorties and the ground crew hurriedly serviced our Spits so the pilots could take off and try and intercept the bombers as they flew towards their target at Bone. It was all too reminiscent of the Battle of Britain.

Later that day the rest of our squadron finally arrived to join in the fray and on the second day, during a dawn patrol, Owen Hardy, the New Zealand lad, achieved the accolade of being the first member of 72 Squadron to shoot down an enemy aircraft in North Africa.

Hardy had been scrambled and was patrolling over Bone when he spotted a Me109 and launched an attack on it. As his bullets sliced into the German aeroplane's fuselage, its propeller just seemed to disintegrate and it crashed spectacularly into a hillside just outside the town.

By nightfall the bombing had eased and we were called to a briefing by the wing commander.

'Tomorrow you'll be leaving Bone and going to another airfield further south from here.'

'Further south? That takes us nearer the frontline, doesn't it?' Chas Charnock enquired. The senior officer ignored his question.

'Just be ready to leave at 09.00 hours.'

As we filed out Chas spoke first.

'You know what? I think we should treat ourselves to a night out in Bone. I have a suspicion it's going to be the last opportunity for some fun.'

We all agreed and headed for Bone. The narrow streets of the town thronged with soldiers of the British First Army all filling time before they were moved on.

Despite the crowds, I managed to book myself into a hotel and enjoyed my first decent meal and slept in my first decent bed for a month. What I didn't know then was that it was also destined to be my last for many, many months.

The following day we left Bone for a place called Souk Al Arba in Northern Tunisia, south-east of Bone. The move took us nearer to our ultimate destination of Tunis, which was still firmly under German control. Souk Al Arba was the most forward of all the airfields and, as such, was less than 30 miles from the frontline.

Our approach to the airfield revealed that our instincts that Bone might be our last brush with civilisation for some time appeared correct. The airfield seemed to me to be worryingly deserted.

We touched down one after the other, brought our Spits to a halt, climbed out of our aircraft and looked for signs of life.

'Where is everybody?' asked Hardy. 'I thought the Army boys were meant to meet us.'

'Looks like we might be the advance party,' Chem said grimly.

'Chem's right. I think we might've beaten our boys here,' Bobby added.

'That makes us the frontline,' I chipped in. I looked up at the sky and nodded towards a number of 109s circling over ahead like vultures. 'Do you think anyone has told them?'

And so, for a few short hours, 72 Squadron unwittingly became the Allied frontline in Northern Africa, which wasn't a particularly comforting thought.

The airfield at Souk Al Arba was even more depressing than the ones at Bone and Maison Blanche. I never realised that the desert could be so bleak. In fact, 'aerodrome' was a wild exaggeration of what lay at our feet. It was just a bare expanse of rough stony ground that stretched as far as the eye could see. The only interest was the occasional bush that broke the monotony of the dirty yellow landscape.

Nearby was a local village which was little more than a huddle of low buildings, the inhabitants of which took no interest in the aircraft and pilots now disconsolately mooching around a piece of unused rough ground nearby. I didn't think we would find much to entertain us there.

As we were the first to arrive, nothing had yet been built at Souk al Arba. There were no accommodation blocks or mess halls or even tents. It was a far cry from Biggin Hill with its comfortable dispersal huts and conveniently placed local hostelries. But there was something that reminded me much more of home than of the desert.

Dark clouds sat low over the airfield. It was cold and it had been raining. The airfield was a sea of sludge, the like of which I had never witnessed before or since. The earth was basically sandy, but must have had a lot of loam mixed in with it, because when it rained it produced a substance that had amazing adhesive-like qualities. As I walked around the site, great clods of earth stuck to me like glue and wouldn't come off. The thick dirt was so cloying that I could hardly lift my foot up.

'What is this stuff?' I grumbled.

'What's the matter, don't you get dirt in Maidstone?' Chem grinned.

'Not like this we don't.'

I tried to knock the mud from my boots and a thought occurred to me.

'This stuff is going to be a nightmare for the Spits,' I grumbled.

'Why?'

'Well, if we aren't careful, the whip of the airscrew will just churn up the mud and throw it back and clog the radiators and oil coolant, which means we won't be going anywhere.'

Soon after our arrival, other squadrons began to make an appearance until 111, 93, 152 and 225 (a reconnaissance squadron equipped with Hurricanes), were all assembled on the field with us. An enterprising commanding officer from one of the other squadrons managed to persuade the French Foreign Legion to donate some of their tents and cooking equipment so we could at least set up camp while waiting for the paratroopers to turn up.

Later that day, the British 1st Parachute Battalion arrived to a warm reception from us. They quickly secured the airfield for us, which was ironic as we had now been standing around on it for some time. The commandos dug the trenches and sorted out the cookhouse with lightening speed, making us pilots feel rather redundant. The Pioneer Corps, who were mainly a non-fighting unit that undertook all the building jobs, also busied themselves putting together a makeshift runway of about 30 to 40ft wide and 400yd long. This they did by laying Sommerfeld tracking, which were large square wire meshes of approximately 6in square and ¼in thick. They were slotted together and laid on the ground in an effort to hold the mud together so an aeroplane could take off without its wheels getting bogged down in the sand. That was the theory, anyway.

While the commandos undertook the lion's share of the work we refuelled our aircraft. As we only had 4-gallon petrol tins and the Spitfires carried a full load of 90 gallons of fuel this was a long and onerous task which took up most of the rest of the day.

Finally, after a meal of watery stew containing largely unidentifiable ingredients, we all settled down for night in a large bell tent. Our parachutes became makeshift pillows and the one thin blanket we each had was little more than a nod towards comfort. It was going to be a long night. The desert temperature plummeted and I thought I would die of hypothermia as I lay shivering under an over-sized tea cloth. It was a miserable night and tomorrow I would be expected to get into an aeroplane and fight.

Those early days at Souk Al Arba were as hectic as any I'd known during the Battle of Britain. The Germans poured fighters and bombers into the area in their determination to hold onto North Africa. It was our job to intercept them and take down as many as possible while we waited for the Eighth Army, under the command of the British General Bernard Montgomery, to sweep up from the south and meet the First Army, which we were covering as they came down from the north.

Geographically, the distance between us and the Germans was similar to what it had been during the Battle of Britain when we were fighting to prevent an invasion. But there at least we had the English Channel which acted as natural barrier between us and the Germans. This time we were separated by just a few short miles of sand, which made it feel like the enemy was a lot closer to us than they had been before.

It was now November 1942 and there was no let-up on either side in this North African theatre of war. Strafing had become the favoured method of attack for both us and the Germans. Our Wg Cdr 'Sheep' Gilroy was particularly keen on it. Often we would be dispatched to search out German supply lines and airfields. Wg Cdr Gilroy would then order us to fly in low and shoot them up. It wasn't without its risks. German anti-aircraft fire was frighteningly accurate and always ferocious. To make matters worse, we were now flying at much lower heights than we had flown in Britain. If they could hit me at 28,000ft in the air as they had done once before, what damage could they wreak on me at 8,000ft? It didn't bear thinking about.

German Me109s or Italian Macchi M202s would also visit the airfield at Souk Al Arba as many as five or six times in a day. We almost became used to being bombed, as far as you could be used to someone trying their hardest to kill you. That said, the first time we were strafed still ranks among the most terrifying episodes of the whole war for me. Quite simply I thought I was done for.

One Sunday in November, I took off to carry out a patrol with the rest of the squadron. We had been in North Africa for two weeks and had scored a few kills, but more importantly we had not sustained any casualties ourselves. That was all about to change.

Twelve of us took off at 8 a.m., led by Sqn Ldr Oxspring. We swept up from Souk Al Arba east to Lake Biserta, which was less than 30 miles from Tunis and well into enemy territory. There we searched the skies, but unusually there were no enemy fighters in sight.

The CO then ordered us to turn south towards Mateur to try our luck. There we came across six unprotected German military trucks which were travelling on the road heading north out of Mateur. It was too good to be true. We flew down in turn and strafed the entire line. The vehicles exploded one after the other. A huge ball of flames shot high up into the air, which seemed to suggest that the trucks had probably been carrying fuel. This only added to our victory.

The formation reformed some distance from the attack. The CO's voice came over the airways.

'That's enough for one day. Head for base.'

'Pryth' Prytherich, who had only recently joined 72, called the CO up on the R/T.

'Skipper, I don't want to worry you, but I've oil on my windscreen and I reckon it's coming from you.'

'Thanks Pryth. I am not going to make it back to the drome. Fordy, you take over from here.'

'Yes, Sir.'

'Try and get a handle on my position, so the Army boys can pick me up. I will see you lot later.'

I watched as Bobby Oxspring guided his aircraft down. He crash landed the Spit on its belly. A huge cloud of dust billowed out from underneath the craft. We circled overhead for as long as we dared, but there was no sign of life. Fordy called over the R/T to head back.

I landed and got out of my Spit. Chem was ahead of me and I caught up with him as we walked back to the tents.

'The CO's landing looked clean enough to me. I reckon he should have got out alive,' I said to Chem.

'Yes, I think so too. Only problem is, we were still close to Beja and that's in enemy hands.'

As the afternoon wore on I spent the time relaxing in my tent, writing home. Letters home were a surreal affair as we could say nothing of note and really they were just a way of telling our families we were still alive. Chas put his head round the opening to my tent.

'Jimmy, 153 Squadron are due to arrive. Do you want to join the reception committee to greet the new boys?' I dragged myself from my bed and accompanied Chas out onto the airfield. We stood and studied the skies. A number of other pilots had also gathered on the field to wait for the new squadron to arrive.

'There they are,' Chas shouted and pointed to the sprinkle of black dots heading in our direction.

I shielded my eyes from the glare of the sun and squinted into the distance. Sure enough, 153 Squadron were heading our way and would be with us in a matter of minutes. I decided I would wait on the field and welcome them in.

'Wait!' Chas shouted suddenly.

We both froze and studied the incoming aircraft intently. The dots became aeroplanes and the clear outline of their silhouette told us we were staring a dozen 109s in the face.

'They're not ours, get down, get down,' Chas shouted more urgently. But it was too late, we were under attack.

More screams and shouts of 'get down, get down' were drowned out by a deafening high-pitched drone as the twelve 109s prepared to dive down to bomb and shoot us into the next life.

Chas, I and one of the younger pilots hit the deck, not that it would do much good. We were in the open and completely exposed. We didn't stand a chance and we knew it. Was this it? Was this how it was going to be? Shot dead as I lay in the stinking sludge of Souk Al Arba aerodrome, a place I had never heard of until four weeks ago.

I looked across the aerodrome. Chaos had broken out. I couldn't see Chem anywhere and I hoped that he had found himself a safe bolthole. Many people were still searching for cover as the first wave of enemy aeroplanes swooped down. The screaming aircraft was enough to burst your ear drums, even if the bullets didn't get you. I covered my ears and squeezed my eyes shut trying to block out the noise and the fear.

The Messerschmitts were now less than 500ft overhead. It would be any moment now. Even with my hands clamped over my head, I heard the sickening thud of bullets as the 109s opened fire and streaked the field. I heard explosions all around me and knew the Spits were going up in flames as plane after plane dived down and raked the ground with machine gun fire. The bullets were so close that pellets of earth spat at my face and showered my body. The next bullet would hit me for sure. I pressed my hands even harder against my head to try and block out the chaos around me. I'm not a religious man, but I was truly terrified and I prayed as hard as I could. Please God, let me survive.

For some reason I dared to open my eyes momentarily. I looked up and saw a figure get up just ahead of where I was lying, as bombs fell and bullets punctured the ground all around him. It was one of the younger pilots whose name I don't recall. I was stunned by the stupidity of his actions. What the hell did he think he was doing? Was he mad? All right, we weren't that safe where we were, but standing up was far more dangerous. He knew that, of course, but he had panicked and lost the battle to control his most basic instinct which was to run and hide from the danger and not lie still in the open, waiting to get killed.

The young man sprinted towards the tents on the edge of the field. That wouldn't save him. He had unwittingly made himself an easy and attractive target for the next Luftwaffe pilot who was probably lining him up in his sights right now. He was as good as dead and would be cut down at any moment. There was nothing any of us could do for this poor boy. If I chased him it would cost me my life too. I prayed the German pilot was a poor marksman.

Unbeknown to me, Chas had also noticed this kid making a dash for it. What occurred next was typical of Chas, who was quite a remarkable man. Without a moment's hesitation he stood up, took out his revolver from his belt and bellowed at the boy

'Get down, you little bastard, or I'll shoot you myself.'

Knowing Chas, he would have carried out his threat. The boy thought so too as he responded instantly by dropping to the ground and there he stayed until all twelve 109s had finished with us. He almost certainly owed his life to Chas Charnock.

It was all over in a few minutes. The Messerschmitts disappeared into the clouds, leaving us to count the cost of the damage. It was bad news. Three local people from the village had been passing at the time of the attack. They had jumped into a drainage ditch that ran alongside the road without realising it was full of fuel cans. The ditch was bombed, igniting the fuel, and they had been burned alive.

Our casualties were surprisingly light. Coxy was hurt, but not seriously. Everyone else emerged from their various hide-outs unscathed. And, unbelievably, Krohn had even managed to get airborne and bring one of the 109s down.

The news on the Spits was less encouraging. Eight Spitfires had been completely destroyed in the attack and our campaign in North Africa hadn't even started. We surveyed the burnt out carcasses that sat smouldering on the field. It was a total disaster that left us completely vulnerable to attack, an observation that was not lost on the Germans. Forty-five minutes later they returned and we were strafed again. This time it was a group of Fw190s that bombed and machine-gunned us over and over again. We could do nothing other than lie in the dirt and pray to be spared.

An hour after the second attack, 93 Squadron, who had arrived at Souk Al Arba the day before, were hit by a number of Ju87 bombers being given cover by an Italian M200, some German 109s and 190s. At least the squadron managed to get into the air where they shot down two 109s and claimed several 'probables'. No. 72 Squadron could do nothing but watch. We were completely impotent. We just didn't have enough planes to get off the ground and repel the attack, although this didn't deter Daniels who found a Spitfire and managed to coax it into the air, only to crash-land in an area close to the airfield. Thankfully Daniels survived his admirable display of courage.

That night we moved our tents further from the airfield in the hope they would be safer. It had been a terrible day. Spirits were low as we knew it would be sometime before our replacement Spitfires arrived. In the meantime we would be easy pickings for the Germans.

The mood lifted when Bobby Oxspring, who had crash-landed that morning, rolled up in a Humber flanked by a couple of infantrymen. The CO regaled us with his tale of survival, which had been as eventful as ours.

'I landed the plane quite easily and got out unhurt, but as I got out of the cockpit, a bullet whizzed passed my ear and ricocheted off the Spit. It took me a moment to realise I was being shot at. So I leapt over the nearest low wall to take cover and sat there wondering what the hell I was going to do next. All of a sudden I heard this loud whisper call out "Over here, mate".'

'I looked over and saw the tin helmet of a British soldier appear above a hole in the ground nearby. He beckoned to me to join him, so I crawled along the ground on my stomach and jumped into the trench alongside the soldier. I asked him where I was and he said it was an observation post. "Sir," he said, "This is the forward outpost of the frontline. You landed slap bang in the middle of no man's land. If you had run the other way you'd be on your way to a POW camp".'

The soldier led Bobby back to his camp where an Army lieutenant-colonel lent him his Humber staff car to transport him back to the airfield. En route they had to stop and dive into a ditch as a bunch of 109s, in fact the same ones destined to shoot us up at the airfield at Souk Al Arba, tried to take them out by strafing the road they were travelling on.

It was good to have Bobby back, but he was by no means the last of our number to go missing. Not all were as lucky as Bobby. Some never returned.

Chapter Thirteen

DECEMBER 1942 – SOUK AL ARBA

The attacks on the aerodrome cost us dearly and it wasn't until early December that the call came through to say our replacement Spits were ready. A few of us were taken in a DC-3 to Maison Blanche to collect our new aircraft and fly them back to Souk Al Arba.

It felt good to get our hands on the new aeroplanes. A pilot without an aircraft to fly isn't much use to anybody. Tempers were also becoming rather frayed as we sat around the camp all day long with nothing to do but moan about our situation and wait for our aeroplanes to be delivered.

When we returned with the Spits there was no time to familiarise ourselves with our new toys as we were quickly propelled to the centre of action once more. Several days after our return from Maison Blanche with the aircraft we were sent on a patrol over Mateur. It was a normal day, well as normal as it can be in combat. The squadron was flying at around 7,000ft. The skies were clear. Then the CO's familiar voice suddenly pierced the airways causing me to start.

'Bandits at 12 o'clock!'

I squinted into the sun for as long as I could bear, but couldn't detect any aircraft. The blinding sunlight stung my eyes, forcing me to look away until I heard Chem on the R/T.

'I see them, there's at least ten.'

I looked once more into the sun and this time it was a different story. Straight ahead of me, emerging directly from the sun's rays, were at least twenty 109s. And they were heading straight for us.

The Germans always aimed to attack whenever they could from the direction of the sun, as we did. The blinding white light made it very difficult for anyone to detect their presence until they were practically on top of us. This was a textbook attack.

'Break,' came the CO's command and we peeled away from each other in preparation for the attack.

A familiar knot tightened deep in the pit of my stomach in antici-pation of what was to come. No time to think. The squadron quickly broke from the loose formation we had been travelling in as ordered by the skipper and vied for some height advantage over the enemy as we took up our positions.

A burst of machine gun fire shot past my cockpit as the enemy flew towards us in the first wave of attack. Then both sides adopted the usual merry-go-round of trying to take out their opponent until they realised they were being attacked themselves which meant switching to evasive action. Aeroplanes dived and climbed, screaming and squealing as they were pushed to the upper limits of their capability. Bullets pelted from our wings and whizzed across the skies.

It was a far cry from my first taste of combat over Dover when I didn't even fire a bullet. Then I had blacked out before I had time to pick my quarry, or shake off my attacker. When I woke up, it was all over and had seemed more like a terrifying dream. Now I was in the thick of it. There would be no blacking out. I would be in this until the end. I checked my mirror. Damn it. A Me109 had latched onto my tail. My reaction was automatic. I turned the Spit into steep roll as I had done many times before and the Hun disappeared from my rear view. Free from my would-be assassin, I searched the skies for a possible target. I had not yet had a kill since I joined 72 Squadron. As I swivelled around in the cockpit for a likely candidate, I saw Chem pass just below me. To my utter horror, he was closely followed by another Me109 that had locked on to him. He was still flying in a straight line which meant he hadn't seen the aircraft now stalking him.

I got on to the R/T straight away.

'Chem, you've got one right up your arse, mate.'

But I was too late. Chem reacted to my call and had started to turn his machine, but not before a line of tracer bullets raked his fuselage. Time seemed to stand still for a moment until his wounded aircraft began to turn to one side and plummet earthwards through the low-lying clouds until it disappeared out of sight.

'No. Chem!' I shouted.

I tried to raise him on his R/T, but there was no response. This couldn't be happening. Not to Chem. Not to my closest friend. Not to one of the best pilots around. He was just 23, a year younger than me, and he had been married less than a year.

I wanted to fly down and check to see if my old friend had landed safely somewhere, but such an act would have been suicidal. Feeling slightly numb, we chased off the remaining Me109s and the boss ordered us to reform and return to base. A terrible realisation came to me. I had to leave Chem behind.

Back at base, as I climbed out of the cockpit, I saw the two ground crew who serviced Chem's machine. Their necks were craned as they searched the skies for him. I thought it only right that I should speak to them.

'Chem ran into a spot of trouble. I think he might have crash-landed his kite somewhere.'

The two of them nodded and exchanged a knowing look. I made my way to my tent where I lay on my bed and thought about Chem. I desperately hoped that he was out there somewhere – alive. I knew that the longer time went on the less chance there was of a safe return. Pilots who crash-landed didn't hang around, especially in the desert. They quickly made their way back to their squadron, rather like homing pigeons.

I discussed with the others what might have happened to Chem.

'He looked like he was still in control as it went down, Jimmy,' said Chas.

'I'm not sure. He didn't respond when I called him up.' I replied.

'It's still early days. Plenty of time for him to turn up yet,' said Pryth.

I returned to my tent. Now the only thing I could do was hope. I could only hope. I couldn't get thoughts of Chem out of my mind. How the hell was I going to tell Eileen? She was expecting their first child in the New Year. She would be devastated. Another child raised without a father. I had promised her I would look after him. I had been his best man at his wedding. Why hadn't I spotted that 109 sooner?

I had known so many men who had gone missing and never returned and it was always a sad moment, but I never allowed myself to mull over their loss too much, otherwise I simply couldn't have done my job. The more superstitious pilots thought that dwelling on death would hasten their own demise and so death, although ever present, was rarely discussed. When someone was killed, most of us were just thankful it hadn't been us. That feeling now deserted me. This time it was personal. Chem was my closest friend. I didn't want him to die. Bobby put his head through the opening to the tent.

'Jimmy, are you ready to go?'

'Yes, of course.'

There was no time to grieve. The squadron needed pilots in the skies not moping around on the ground. I knew that despite how I felt I had to concentrate on the job in hand. Worrying about Chem could prove to be a fatal distraction and the RAF could end up losing two pilots in one day.

We carried out some further strafing, I can't remember where, and then returned to base. Night fell and it wasn't looking too good. I sat in my tent, picking disconsolately at some sardines in a tin. It was 7 p.m. There had been no news. Daniels came in.

'I heard about Chem. He'll turn up, Jimmy.'

I hoped he was right. Hope was all I had.

Just after 8 p.m I was disturbed by a loud commotion just outside my tent. I went out to see what all the noise was about just in time to see a French Foreign Legion truck pull up in front of the tents. A few of us gathered around to see what was going on.

The flaps at the back of the truck were suddenly pulled back and the huge, dishevelled figure, covered in dust but otherwise unhurt, appeared. It was Chem.

He grinned broadly and jumped down from the truck.

'Hello everyone.'

'Chem, you old bastard, you had us worried there for a moment.'

I hugged him. I don't think I've ever been quite so relieved to see anyone before. I was elated to have him back as was everyone else. We scrounged some beer and drank to Chem's return. It had been a long and terrible day with the best of endings.

Chem had returned safely from his adventure, but some pilots seemed to make a habit of going missing. For some it was almost an occupational hazard. The week after Chem's return, it was Chas' turn to disappear. We had taken off despite the heavy mist. Our orders were to provide protection or top cover, as we called it, for fifty-odd American A-20 Bostons and B-17 Fortresses that were being escorted by P-38 Lightnings at 17,000ft. It was a successful mission. Some railway sidings at Mateur were bombed, as was an aerodrome which had a fair number of 109s parked on it.

During the trip my radio transmitter had gone down, leaving me with no means of communication, which meant I couldn't warn the others of the presence of enemy aircraft and they couldn't warn me. My number two had also gone back to the airfield which left five of us to patrol the route. By now we had ditched the tight formations of the Battle of Britain and flew in a line, several hundred yards apart from each other. I was on the wing, the last in the line and quite vulnerable, especially with no means of communication. Sure enough it was as if the enemy had sensed my vulnerability because as we cleared the low cloud I was jumped by two 109s. Both of them clung to my tail. I kicked the rudder, putting the Spit into a tight turn to try and shake them off. This succeeded in getting rid of them, but the sharp manoeuvre meant I couldn't get myself into a position where I could fire on them.

I looked across and saw an Me109 had latched onto Coxy, but he carried out a similar turn and managed to evade him. Then suddenly an explosion ripped across the sky. It wasn't one of ours and I guessed that one of the other pilots, Robby as it turned out, had destroyed one. Fragments of the aircraft floated down from the sky. The remaining German aircraft seemed to lose their appetite for a fight and drifted off, but Chas was not content to let them go and, in typical style, was last seen climbing skywards heading towards a large number of 109s. His kite was badly shot up and his engine suddenly seemed to seize and he fell from view.

This was the second time in a week Chas had gone missing. Several days earlier, we had been on a patrol with Daniels, Cox and Chem, who each got a 109, but their success was blighted as Chas failed to return to the airfield. He was our most experienced pilot and it was a huge blow to the squadron. We waited that night, but there was no sign of him. I went to bed thinking what a loss he was to the squadron, not only as a pilot, but as a great friend. In the early hours there was a loud racket outside the tent and some of the lads piled in to my tent with Chasy boy in tow. A crowd of noisy pilots fell onto my bed and in their enthusiasm they broke one of its legs. Much as I was pleased at Chas's safe return, I spent the rest of my time at Souk Al Arba sleeping on a lopsided bed, but perhaps it was a small price to pay to have Chas back with us.

Now it was the second time that Chas had gone missing. I hoped that his luck would hold out and that he would return once more. How much luck could one man have? But, that said, Chas was different. He was a remarkable man, a real one-off.

I remember looking in his log book once just after he had baled out of his plane. In it, he had done a drawing of a pencil-man on a parachute falling through the air with little bullets being fired at him from German-marked planes. The figure was Chas. He didn't like that. A week or so latter, I looked at his log again and this time there was a similar drawing. But instead of the stick figure labelled as Chas, it was the other way round. Chas was in the aircraft firing at the parachutist who was presumably German. That was the sort of man he was. He would fight fair, but only if others did.

When I got back from the patrol, a gloom had already settled over 72 Squadron. Chas was a big character and his absence sorely felt. I spent the rest of the day quietly testing my RT. Just as I had finished an excited Chem called me over to the dispersal tent.

'Jimmy, come and check this out.'

I found Chem and Coxy in the tent admiring a small box in front of them. It was a gramophone, the first glint of civilisation we had had in weeks. Chas was missing, but life went on so we put on a few records and enjoyed a lively jazz session until the early hours. For a short while the music lifted the despondency hanging over the camp.

The following day we received news that Chas was badly wounded, but alive. He had turned up at a hospital in Bone having walked miles across the desert. Not only that, the old dog had destroyed two 109s before he went down. To say that the man had guts was an understatement.

But of course not everyone came back and just a month after our arrival in North Africa, our squadron's death toll began to rise. Death was as unpredictable as it had ever been. We would go weeks without anyone receiving so much as a graze then several pilots would be wiped out in quick succession.

It was late November and I had briefly joined the list of casualties when I received my only injury in the entire war. My mishap was somewhat less glorious than Chasy boy's. It happened while I was opening a tin of sardines. My hand slipped and sliced my palm open. It meant I couldn't fly for few days because I couldn't grasp the controls and so the doctor grounded me. My one attempt to fly before it had healed led to the wound re-opening and the medic signed me off for a further two days.

As I moped around the camp, the others continued the job of trying to keep the skies clear of enemy aircraft. We were also still short of aeroplanes, but in one day the rest of the squadron managed to undertake five sweeps of areas near the airfield which was an incredible achievement.

During one of these sorties, before he went missing, Chas shot down a 109F and scored a probable. Chem and Hussey also got a 'probable' each and Robby took out a Ju88. The squadron was jumped twice, but managed to escape unharmed. Jubilant at their success, they returned to Souk Al Arba. But by the time they reached the aerodrome the boys began to realise that no one had neither sight nor sound of Johnny Lowe.

Johnny, the promising young pilot who had got married just a week before we sailed for Gibraltar, had gone missing. He was on his first operational tour of duty and had shot down his first plane several days before. It was a Ju88. Now nobody could work out what had happened to him. We waited, just as we had done for Chas, Chem and Bobby, for Johnny to re-appear, but hopes faded into an unspoken understanding that he wasn't coming back. Some days later Johnny was found still strapped into his Spitfire. It had crashed into some hills not far from Souk Al Arba. He never would find out what married life was like after all.

About a week after we lost Johnny, the doctor passed me fit to fly and I was up again with the others. We were carrying out a dawn sweep over Tunis where we had encountered flak and a number of 109s, which we were certain were Gs – the latest variant of this German fighter.

The skipper, Pryth and Sexton, who was another new boy, squirted one of them and it exploded in flames. By that time another 109 had fastened itself on to the tail of one of our boys. Between us we tried to drive it away and finally it got the hint and disappeared, but not before it sprayed the Spitfire with bullets. The aircraft caught fire and I watched anxiously as it hurtled towards the earth. This time it was Sgt Mottram. In truth, it didn't look too good, but maybe he would be able to crash-land the aircraft somewhere and make his way back to the squadron. There was always hope. You couldn't assume anything until a pilot's death was confirmed or it became obvious they were not coming back.

Too often I had seen pilots step from the wreckage of an aircraft which should have by rights become their tomb and marvelled at how anyone could survive such an impact.

The remaining 109s faded away into the skies and the CO ordered us back to the airfield. In turn, we all responded as normal to the skipper's request over the R/T. No one referred to Mottram. It was as if the mere mention of him might adversely affect the outcome. For now we had to believe he was still alive.

As we flew on back to the drome, I realised that Browne had committed the cardinal sin of leaving his transmitter switched on. This meant that none of us could communicate with him. Nor could we talk to each other, which put the squadron in a perilous position if we were bounced again by a group of 109s. Browne, who was completely unaware that he had an audience, broke into song. It was bawdy number which began with the line 'Rip my knickers away' and rapidly deteriorated. I was annoyed that his performance was blocking the airways, but I couldn't help but smile over his choice of lyrics. I am sure the others were enjoying his performance as much as me. Then as he reached half-way through the chorus, his voice stopped altogether. At first I thought he had just forgotten the words and would burst into song once more when he had recalled the correct lyrics. But the pause became a long ominous silence at the end of the R/T. Browne had gone. Browne was a sergeant pilot, like I had been. Now he was no more.

On landing we discussed what had happened to poor old Browne and we concluded that he must have fallen victim to unseen flak coming from the German's ground defences. We never did find out the truth. That was the way it was. One day they were there and the next they weren't. Sometimes you knew their fate, but more often you didn't.

As the day wore on Mottram also failed to materialise and it became obvious that 72 Squadron had lost two fine men in one day. I recorded the events in my diary and added that it had been 'a damn bad' morning. It reminded me of my days at Kenley and Biggin Hill when it wasn't unusual to lose a couple of pilots in one trip, although I noticed a trend had begun to emerge in North Africa.

During the Battle of Britain and the early days of aerial fight, death was not a fussy customer when it came calling. There seemed no logic to those who were shot down and those weren't. Experience didn't necessarily win you a reprieve from the Luftwaffe. Personally, I always believed that it was purely luck that saved some and not others. If you found yourself in the wrong place at the wrong time, you joined the ever increasing roll call of death. It was as uncomplicated as that. But this cruel randomness that marked the early days of combat began to change as the war progressed. In North Africa, a pattern, such as it was, had begun to develop and it became clear that experience did count for something. Survival was greatest among those of us on our second operational tour of duty. Johnny, Browne and Mottram had one thing in common: it was their first time out against the enemy. Whatever the rationale behind their deaths, their loss hit us hard. On our return to the airfield, Chas, Pryth and I procured some cheap red wine from some local Arabs and got very drunk, which dulled the dreadful events of the day and marginally increased our prospects of getting a full night's sleep.

Despite these losses, the frequent strafing, the absence of sleep and the dearth of Spits, November had been a successful month for the squadron. Many of the pilots, some of whom later lost their lives, seemed to find their stride and most of them shot down an enemy aircraft in those early weeks.

In the space of just one day, Robby and Dan both scored a kill. Krohn and Frampton got one and Krohn claimed a damaged. By the end of the day, 72 had undertaken four patrols and had scored five confirmed kills, two probables and one damaged. It was a phenomenal achievement. In fact, it seemed everyone had bagged an enemy aircraft except me. In my diary that day, I wrote: 'I will get results later. My luck is not so good, but plenty of time.'

As it was, I only had to wait another day for my turn. On the last patrol of the day, Pete, Robbie, Johnnie and I jumped two 109Fs. There may have been a time when a new enemy fighter plane straight off the production line would be cause for concern, but we always felt a Spit could out-do anything the enemy could throw at us. The 109Fs were no match for the Spitfire anymore than their predecessors had been.

We were 8,000ft up when we spotted the two enemy aeroplanes below us. Frampton was nearest to them and went in first. He managed to get a shot at one of them but the aeroplane accelerated away from him unscathed. Pete then peeled his Spitfire away to prepare for an attack, but he couldn't get into a position from which he could get a shot. Next it was my turn.

I came in close behind Pete, determined to pick up where he had left off. The German fighter plane tried to out-fly me, which was a foolhardy thing to do as I just opened the throttle and stuck with him. At the same time I nudged him into my sights. I lined him up, flicked the gun button up on my joystick and pressed the tit. A quick two-second burst of machine gun fire spat out from my wings. The bullets struck the 109's engine and its fuselage in a perfect deflection shot. Glycol bled profusely from its nose and black smoke streamed from its wounds. The aircraft dived at an angle of about 40 degrees and slid vertically towards the ground, protesting all the way. I watched as my first 'kill' fell from the sky and I felt nothing but a sense of achievement and success. My job had been done. I had broken my duck. We returned to the airfield. The other pilots slapped me on the back and congratulated me. We adjourned to my tent where we perched on my still broken bed and drank to the squadron's success.

As the month wore on into December, there was little festive spirit to be found in the camp. The rain came down in sheets and the airfield became a sea of sludge and deep muddy pools. It was a depressing time as the bad weather confined us to long periods of sitting around doing nothing other than trying to beat the boredom and wishing we were anywhere but Souk Al bloody Arba. Christmas was approaching fast, but it failed to deter either side from chasing the ultimate prize of victory in North Africa. If anything, both the British and the Germans stepped up attacks when the weather permitted and became more aggressive in their determination to obliterate the opposing side. Christmas Eve 1942, in particular, saw an immense amount of aerial activity.

On 24 December, two squadrons, including 72, either carried out repeated tactical reconnaissance flights or protected the aerodrome in the face of the latest intelligence that the Germans planned to blitz the airfields and take out our runways. I carried out a dawn patrol, but was quickly recalled as the weather rapidly began to deteriorate. The rain had become torrential and the place was a quagmire. On my return, I jumped down from the Spitfire into a morass of mud which clung to my boots forcing me almost to wade across the airfield to my tent. Happy Christmas, I thought. The only saving grace was that somehow we managed to procure forty-eight halves of beer, six bottles of whisky and two bottles of gin. With flying suspended until the weather eased our only option was to hole ourselves up in my tent and spend the rest of the day working our way through our liquid rations, which at least would make the day bearable. Rain battered the canvas for most of the day and we toasted Christmas.

The atrocious weather continued on throughout Christmas Day. I decided to skip breakfast which proved a good move as the cookhouse had been flooded during the night. This meant Christmas dinner consisted of the same stew we had been served with since our arrival two months previously, only now it was even more watery.

Later on in the day we succeeded in procuring more booze from the NAAFI which had been set up in the village. From there we decanted to a house where we had a sing-song which went some way to lifting our spirits. Drunk on cheap booze, we finally staggered back to the camp, laughing and cheering at Pryth's unsuccessful attempts to remain upright on the mud.

On Boxing Day the skies cleared and we were airborne once again, which was preferable to sitting around the camp wallowing in the tedium. The skyways were mercifully quiet and we patrolled the whole area unchallenged.

By 30 December it had become a different story. The brief hiatus from the action was over. The war was back on. Eight Huns in 109s pitched up overhead in the morning and dive-bombed the camp, damaging three planes in the process. We all ran for cover except one poor pilot who had the shock of his life. He had been spending some quiet time in the toilet, or latrine as we called it, which was a tin hut situated on the edge of the field. The attack had taken us completely by surprise, leaving him no time to finish his ablutions. As the bombing began, he decided the latrine was no longer a safe refuge, so with his trousers still wrapped around his ankles he shot out of the hut and stumbled awkwardly into one of the slit trenches. He survived. So did the latrine.

New Year's Eve approached. Frustrations began to mount because we seemed to be undertaking endless patrols and little else. We wanted to take the offensive, but decisions had been taken elsewhere that we should remain at the base in order to protect it. So we stayed put while the Germans attacked us as and when they could.

By now we were getting very tired. Exhaustion threatened to engulf us. We were a long way from home, we had been fighting non-stop since the beginning of November and some of us didn't even have a proper bed to sleep on. In short, we had had enough. To cap it all, our food for New Year's Eve was a tin of sardines and some dried biscuits. Life was a bind and we sat around the camp bemoaning our lot, until Daniels decided to take the initiative.

The big Scotsman headed off in the direction of Souk Al Arba village wearing a rather stoic 'I may be sometime' look on his face. A few hours later he returned carrying a large roasted turkey.

'Well boys, we can't go through Christmas and New Year without a turkey now, can we?'

'Where on earth did you get that from?' I asked.

'Ah, now that would be telling. Red or white meat anyone?'

We never did find out where he got it from, but six of us quietly disappeared into one of the tents and gratefully sat down to tuck into the bird. We washed it down with ample quantities of the cheap red plonk that Chas had bought us before he went AWOL and siphoned into the 4-gallon petrol cans that littered the airfield. Chas hadn't bothered to clean them out, but that didn't stop us. Grog was grog, with or without a hint of petrol, and we drank it without complaint. We forgot about the weather. We forgot about the war.

Chapter Fourteen

JANUARY 1943 – SOUK EL CHEMIS, NORTH AFRICA

O n 6 January 1943, word came through that 72 Squadron had been awarded the mantle of highest scoring squadron in North Africa with 31 confirmed 'kills'. The news lifted our somewhat dampened spirits and seemed to bode well for the long months ahead. We knew we were good, now everyone else knew it too.

Hussey and I heard about our success as we recovered from a dose of dysentery which we had both caught simultaneously a couple of days previously. We both knew the culprit was Chas's cheap booze and the fact that he hadn't bothered to wash the petrol cans before decanting the *vin rouge* into them. Blissfully unaware of this oversight, we had knocked back a lethal combination of petrol and alcohol with total abandon. Chas was no longer around to blame as he was still recovering in a Bone hospital after having been shot down. Besides, even if we had known we probably still would have drunk it. Nevertheless, despite feeling vaguely guilty that we had more than amply contributed to our current predicament, Hussey and I didn't think it was our place to contradict medical science and so accepted the doctor's diagnosis of dysentery and his subsequent recommendations for treatment.

Our illness, albeit self-inflicted, meant a prolonged stay in Ghardimour rest camp which was near the airbase. The camp was situated in an olive grove at the foot of some hills and was very peaceful. It felt like a million miles away from the fighting. Hardy was already there when Hussey and I arrived and was taking a well-earned rest away from combat.

Removed from the frontline, I filled my days with a little idle rifle practice and when the weather was kind enough I went for long walks in the near by hills.

It was the first time I had stepped out of the theatre of war since I had come to North Africa and it was during those few restful days that I came to realise just how much I was in need of a break. In fact, if the doctor hadn't ordered us to Ghardimour to recuperate from dysentery, I suspect the CO would have recommended that I take a few days off from the fight.

In my diary I admitted to feeling a little 'shaky' at times and 'unnecessarily jumpy'. These were classic signs of fatigue resulting from constantly living on my nerves day in, day out. It caught up with everyone sooner or later. I remember one highly experienced pilot who one day taxied to the end of the runway before to take-off just as he had done hundreds of times before, but the aeroplane failed to take off. A number of us rushed over to see what had happened only to find him staring down at the controls. He had simply frozen. He just couldn't face taking off. He just couldn't face going into unknown that day. Maybe he felt he had had more than his fair share of luck and that it had to run out sooner to later. Who knows? We never talked about it. But after a short time away to recuperate, the pilot returned to action as if it had never happened. I never froze like he did, but if I hadn't been given a long overdue opportunity to enjoy the relative peace and serenity of Ghardimour, maybe I would have been next.

Despite our fragile states, after a few days in Ghardimour Hussey and I crawled from our sick beds and returned to the squadron.

Our motives were to join in the squadron's upcoming celebrations over the announcement that we were officially the highest scoring squadron in North Africa. The party began life in Chem's tent and turned into a double celebration when Chas appeared unannounced at the airfield, still sporting a bandage around his head.

We greeted him warmly, although we were not expecting him for some time, given the extent of his injuries.

'Good to see you, mate. What the hell are you doing here?' Chem ventured.

'That's nice. I got fed up lying around in a hospital bed and discharged myself,' Chas grinned.

'What, with all those nurses to look after you? You must be mad,' Daniels added.

I pulled up a crate we were using as a makeshift chair.

'Well now you are here, sit yourself down, mate, have a drink and tell us what happened.'

Chas's tale was straight out of a *Boy's Own* story. After he was hit, his plane came down near a place called Djebel Abiod which Chas knew was enemy territory. Despite his injuries, he managed to crawl from the wreckage of his aircraft when a local Arab man found him. Chas gave him one of his gold sovereigns, from his blood ticket, on the condition that he took him back to the British lines. The man agreed and they set off.

'We had only gone a short distance when I thought this bastard is shooting me a line. This isn't the way back. So I pulled out my pistol and shot the ground in front of the bastard. I can tell you he quickly changed direction after that and led me back to a British Army patrol,' Chas said.

Chas's injuries had been severe enough to keep him in hospital for two months before he decided to discharge himself. Unsurprisingly, he was awarded the DFC for his bravery. He was truly a one-off.

'Well done Chas, mate. I reckon we should celebrate in style and head into Constantine,' announced Pryth.

'Great idea, Pryth, only we haven't got any money,' I added the voice of reason.

'I know. Let's tell the CO that one of the tents went up in flames in the strafing and suggest we use our blood money to go into town and buy some new tents.'

'Brilliant, Chem. Off you go.'

It worked. The CO fell for it and gave us permission to go into Constantine in search of canvas. In fact, our search began and ended at a bar where we converted our blood money into beer money.

After some not very hard negotiation, the barmaid agreed to take the five gold pieces we all possessed as part of our blood ticket in return for a not inconsiderable sum in Algerian francs which, to show our gratitude, we then duly spent in her establishment.

As we handed over the sovereigns, Hardy observed ruefully.

'I guess this means none of us can afford to land in enemy territory.'

A couple of people nodded in agreement, but the thought wasn't enough to stop us parting with our gold sovereigns. At that moment the enemy felt a thousand miles away. Chas had returned to the fold. The squadron was all together once again. We had shot down more planes than anyone else in North Africa and, with a little additional input from the booze, we thought we were invincible.

The night was ours. The drink flowed and we could have been a bunch of friends enjoying each other's company in any bar in any part of the world. We weren't the only people who were pleased with ourselves that night. For a time afterwards there was a very attractive French barmaid from Constantine sporting rather large earrings made out of gold sovereigns, courtesy of the RAF.

We returned to Souk Al Arba several days later minus our blood tickets and the 'replacement' tents, which thankfully didn't seem to register with the CO. A permanent gloom now hung over the base which matched our own as we recovered from the effects of too much alcohol. Heavy rains continued to lash the airfield and the aerodrome became badly bogged down. All flying was suspended and finally the decision was taken to move to another site in the hope of finding better soil to build our runways on.

The search ended at Souk El Chemis, about 10–15 miles away. Here the land was sandier with a fast-draining surface which increased our chances of getting the Spits off the ground and not getting stuck in the mud. It also had the added advantage, from the RAF's perspective, of being 15 miles nearer the frontline.

Four new airfields were quickly constructed at the site using the same Sommerfeld wire track runways that had been used at Souk Al Arba. Once built, they were christened, rather incongruously, with the names of London railway stations; Euston, Paddington, Marylebone and King's Cross. No. 72 Squadron operated from Euston.

By the time we arrived at our new base, 111 and 93 Squadron were already well ensconced. A quick look-see revealed that Souk El Chemis appeared to offer not only better flying facilities, but better mess facilities too. No. 93 Squadron had already commandeered a farmhouse for their billet. It was a luxurious affair compared to our flimsy tents at Souk Al Arba. The excellent meal I enjoyed there was such a high point among months of dreadful dried biscuits and pickled fish that I even recorded it in my diary. I wolfed down a wonderful steak and kidney pudding, followed by pineapple and apricot. For a man who has always enjoyed his cooking, it was bliss.

We quickly settled into our new surroundings and set up permanent camp in a disused railway station which became the officer's mess. It was a great deal more comfortable than sleeping under canvas and I even managed to get myself a bed that wasn't broken. Suddenly life was looking up. There was only one downside: Daniels and I were lying on our beds when I heard a snuffling noise, followed by a deep, almost scornful grunt. I thought Daniels had fallen asleep, but when I looked across he was absorbed in reading a letter.

'Did you hear that?' I asked.

'What?' Daniels looked up from his letter.

The snorting noises came again. We looked over the side of our beds and found a sizeable pig, caked in dirt, sniffing the floor.

We both jumped up. The pig squealed with alarm and darted out of the room and back to his home which was the farm next door. The discovery of stray pigs searching for food became an irritatingly frequent occurrence at Souk El Chemis. The pigs seemed to think they had a right to roam through the mess unchallenged and we found ourselves constantly having to shoo them out. I was just getting used to eating decent food for the first time in months and I certainly wasn't going to share it with a bunch of pigs.

Apart from our presumptuous neighbours, our accommodation was a marked improvement on Souk Al Arba. Unfortunately, the weather wasn't. The torrential rain and storms continued to beat the newly laid airfield and hamper operations. It rained for days on end and, at times, the rain became a more formidable enemy than the Germans were and claimed almost as many lives.

Finally, in late February, news arrived that briefly dispelled the air of despondency. Our Spitfire Mk IXs were ready and awaiting our collection from Gibraltar. An aircraft was organised to take us back to the Rock via Algiers and Constantine. Like eager schoolboys who had been holed up in boarding school for too long we set off in excited anticipation to pick up our new toys.

When we reached Algiers we were told the Spits weren't ready and we would have to wait there until further notice. This didn't faze us. We had escaped camp life and we were in no hurry to return so we took the unplanned stopover in our stride.

Algiers was a pretty town with much to offer the entertainment-starved pilots of 72 Squadron and it wasn't long before we filled our social timetable. The boys and I quickly made ourselves comfortable in a school that had been requisitioned for our use and in true RAF style we went off in search of a decent pub.

An American bar provided a comfortable backdrop for much of our stay, and Chem, Pryth, myself and the rest of the crew enjoyed several sessions on egg flips there. We finished off our evening rather satisfyingly with a trip to the casino. Suddenly we were in no hurry for the new Spits to be ready. Waiting around for something to happen was an event that all servicemen learned to adapt to, often with gusto.

Our days spent loafing about Algiers began to trip into each other and became an unending round of late mornings, liquid lunches at bars like Alletti, rounded off by a spell at the poker tables or a film at the local flicks. The highlight for me was that one night at Alletti I got talking to an English nurse. It is a mark of how starved of female company I was that I even remember her name. She was called Daphne Stevens and she was the first Englishwoman I had seen in months. In fact, she was the first woman I had spoken to in ages. The experience was a revelation. Several hours talking about nothing in particular with Daphne was the just the tonic I needed after months of rain, dirt, broken beds and dried biscuits, not to mention the odd engagement with a German 109E. One brief conversation with a member of the opposite sex made me feel more human than I had been in months. I thought back to when I took the presence of girlfriends, such as Audrey from Derby, for granted, never realising what a rarity the sight of a woman would become.

Tens days of sampling the delights of Algiers to excess and we were beginning to run out of money and our normally limitless enthusiasm for boozing and chasing women was on the wane. In short, we were fed up, bored and itching to get at the new Spits.

Finally, the call came through on 10 February and we were told to proceed to Gibraltar where our new steeds were now ready. I couldn't wait. The Spit IX was a class above the Spit Vb, which had served us well. It was more powerful than its predecessor and the presence of two 'blowers' meant we had the same power at 20,000ft as we had at ground level.

On arrival in Gibraltar, the squadron quickly familiarised itself with the new Spits, a marvel of modern engineering. They combined a Spitfire Mk V airframe with a Merlin 61 engine. These fighters could reach speeds over 400mph and heights of 43,000ft. Their arsenal included two 20mm cannons. They handled beautifully and would be a formidable addition to our campaign. Surely there was nothing to match their capabilities?

I climbed into the cockpit, pulled the cover shut, ran through my checks and waited for the off. Several minutes later we were all airborne and I sat back and enjoyed the ride.

The skies had turned dark and threatening by the time we left Gibraltar and, although we didn't know it, were a portent of what was to come. We landed safely at Algiers, where we spent the night in the Hussein Bay stables on a hard concrete floor with damp blankets and woke to a revolting breakfast the following day.

Confusion seemed to set in, which wasn't unusual for the RAF, but was nevertheless frustrating as we all wanted to get back to Souk El Chemis as quickly as possible. By mid-morning we still hadn't received our orders to proceed. As a result, we hung around for most of the day. Hussey and I enjoyed a cigarette in the doorway of the stables.

'What a bloody shambles,' I commented to Hussey.

'Typical RAF, you'd think we'd be used to it by now.'

Passmore, a sergeant in the squadron, appeared in the doorway.

'Good news, lads, we've been given the all-clear to head back to Souk El Chemis.'

'About bloody time too,' I stamped out my cigarette and headed for my plane.

We took off and headed for base. Our designated route took us over the old airfield at Souk Al Arba. It was there that we ran into an enormous electrical storm, the like of which I had never seen before. Hailstones the size of golf balls pelted the hood of my cockpit, threatening to smash the perspex. Lightning flashed and forked across the black clouds and crashed around the aircraft as the torrential rain teemed down the sides of the aircraft.

My Spitfire rocked and bumped and protested its way through the maelstrom as it battled against the extreme conditions. I gripped the control column hard in an attempt to hold the aircraft steady, but it seemed to have little effect.

The airwaves were silent as all of us fought to keep control of the aeroplane. Suddenly, what felt like such a solid, dependable aircraft now appeared vulnerable and fragile up against the thunder and lightening that crashed all around us. This didn't look good at all.

After an age I spotted Euston runway. A sense of relief swept over me, although I was experienced enough not to let the whiff of safety affect my concentration. Visibility was diabolical and I considered what limited options I had. In the end, I had no choice but to attempt a landing. I couldn't stay aloft any longer as it was far too dangerous. One lightning strike and I would be dead.

I eased back on the throttle and began my descent. The aircraft swung wildly as the high winds continued to buffet it. Rain streamed down the hood distorting my vision.

Finally the wheels made contact with the ground with a hard jolt. I knew instantly something was wrong and my problems were only just beginning. The Spitfire's undercarriage seemed to drag in the mud and the machine began to career along the runway. I wrestled with the column to keep her straight and on course so she didn't veer off into the quagmire that surrounded us. But I needn't have bothered, the runway was completely waterlogged. The wheels continued to drag in the deep mud and slush and I realised that unless I did something quickly I would nose over. I tugged the Spit slightly from side to side to free it from the boggy runway, but it made no difference. The aeroplane was still travelling forwards at a speed of 60mph when the inevitable happened. Its wheels had trapped themselves firmly in the mud and the whole aircraft tipped over onto its brand new nose and came to a halt.

The wretched rain beating down on the cockpit told me I was still alive and in one piece. It was the straps that had saved me from falling forward and smashing my head on the instrument panel. It was a close shave. I instinctively called up my number two and told him not to land. One smashed up Spit is quite enough.

Carefully, I undid the buckle, slid the hood back, eased myself out of the aeroplane and jumped down onto the ground which was now a mire. I surveyed my machine which was wedged at a pitiful angle, nose down in the mud. An erk who had braved the weather ran over to me.

'Are you all right, Sir?'

'I'm fine, but that isn't.'

I nodded at the mangled mess in front of us. The brief euphoria I experienced on discovering I was still alive was replaced by a rising anger. We had waited months for these new models and I'd damaged mine, possibly even written it off on its maiden voyage. I was furious with myself, the weather and the whole damn war.

'It's totally fucked up, isn't it?' I sighed.

'It's not the worst, sir,' replied the erk. 'Two made it successfully at Waterloo. Five came down at Paddington and four are still missing. We have heard nothing from Sgt Passmore and Sgt Hussey.'

It was then that I realised just what a total disaster it had been. I returned to the mess. A pig seeking shelter in the doorway received my boot. It flinched and darted off into the darkness. Bloody pigs, I thought. I lay on my bed and waited for news of the others. Word quickly came through that Hussey had crash-landed his Spitfire at Ghardimour and was unhurt. Two more landed safely at nearby Tingley. But Sgt Passmore spun in as he landed and crashed. He was killed instantly. What a waste of a life and all because of the bloody weather which was rapidly becoming our worst enemy.

An inspection of my aircraft revealed a burst tail wheel tyre that had added to the drag I experienced while travelling along the runway. My spectacular flipover into the mud didn't cause a lot of damage and all the aircraft needed to get it airworthy was a new airscrew. The news didn't console me much. It was a terrible start to our stay at Souk El Chemis.

The delivery of the new Spit continued to be more of a curse than a godsend when the engineers found they hadn't been tropicalised. In other words, they weren't equipped to fly in the hot dusty atmosphere of the desert which shouldn't have been a problem given that we had been beset by rain for months on end. But as sod's law dictates, the weather began to improve and hailed a return of dust and grit which seemed to swirl constantly across the base.

Our salvation came in the form of the engineer officer who was a remarkable man called Farish. Within twenty-four hours he had designed and made a mesh which fitted over the air intake for all ground operations. But it could not be carried in flight because it would restrict the air to the engines at altitude. So Farish invented a system that meant we could fly low over the end of the runway, pull on a cable and jettison the air filters. These were then collected by the ground crew and reused. He was a genius and his idea kept the Spitfires aloft and even managed to lift our spirits.

As we moved into the spring of 1943, our battle tactics began to change. The Germans continued to strafe us, although their attacks were becomingly increasingly ineffectual. One afternoon, a group of 109s appeared in the sky and dive-bombed us as they had done many times before. However, this time a number of us managed to get airborne and in return shot down four 109s and damaged another. It was a far cry from that terrible day in Souk Al Arba when the Germans bombed the base and I could do nothing other than pray for my life to be spared. This latest attack seemed indicative of what was happening across North Africa. The Germans were becoming increasingly ineffectual and we seemed to be nearing our objective which was to push them out altogether.

No. 72 Squadron continued its successful run, but undertook fewer strafing attacks. This was mainly because Wg Cdr Gilroy's initial enthusiasm for this method of attack had now waned somewhat. On a patrol over Beja, the CO went in to shoot up a line of enemy trucks. As he passed over the trucks, a shell about 1in in diameter shot up through the floor of his cockpit and out through the roof, missing him by inches. He lost interest in strafing soon after.

As a result, tactical reconnaissance flights, or escorting the bombers as they bombed Tunis and Bizerta, became the mainstay of our daily routine. 'Tac R's' as we called them were straightforward missions and often we didn't see any enemy aircraft. By then it is fair to say the Germans were becoming markedly less aggressive in their attacks on us.

The bombing missions we escorted during this period were nearly always American aircraft which was a nerve-racking experience that usually left us wondering just whose side they were on.

On one occasion we were ordered up to look after a group of American bombers who were going to bomb Bizerta. When we reached the rendezvous point they were nowhere to be seen.

'Can anyone see them?' Bobby Oxspring's voice came over the radio.

'Nothing, sir,' someone replied.

'Keep looking, they're travelling at 10,000ft so they have to be here somewhere.'

I could sense the frustration in his voice. We were told to rendezvous with the bombers, but there was no sign of any of them which was strange as they were usually difficult beasts to miss. We stooged around for a while trying to locate them, but with no joy. Then, by chance, I looked up through the hood of the cockpit. It was a bright clear day. There were no aeroplanes, but I did notice a thin line of silver fishes in the distance. I watched them as they came down towards me. What the hell was it? Then, in an instant, I knew exactly what they were. They were bombs. I screamed over the R/T to the others: 'Christ, let's get out of here, they are bombing us.' In a fraction of a second, six Spitfires roared away to escape the American-made bombs that were tumbling indiscriminately from the sky.

The reason I hadn't known what the silvery specks were was because fighter aircraft protect bombers by flying above them, for obvious reasons. The Bostons should have been below us, but for some reason they had climbed an extra 2,000ft above their designated position and failed to see the need to inform us. And now, to add insult to injury, they were bombing us. Thankfully, no one was hit, but from then on nobody enjoyed the company of the American bombers.

But it didn't necessarily take an enemy aircraft or even the Americans to damage us or our Spitfires. We were quite capable of doing that ourselves. During this time, we all had our fair share of mishaps, including me which, thankfully, I survived.

The whole squadron had been patrolling the skies above Cape Bon. Below us we could see the fierce fighting taking place on the ground between the British First Army and the German Afrika Korps. Despite the ferocity of ground battle, there was very little activity happening in the skies around us so we turned for home.

Pryth came into land first followed by me. I was several hundred yards behind him and as I touched down I expected him to taxi to the end of the runway and then turn into the dispersal area, as we always did. But for some reason, Pryth slowed his aircraft right down, but remained on the runway. I thought to myself, 'Pryth, look in your mirror mate, I am right up your backside', but it was too late. He was obviously unaware of my presence. I was too close to him to avoid hitting him and although I pulled up as hard as I could, my Spit ploughed straight into the back of his.

Pryth was fine, if a little shaken up. My own kite was damaged, but the only thing that was really hurt was my pride. Both Pryth and I were ordered to appear in front of Air Commodore Cross who was the senior officer in charge and who I fully expected would tear a strip off me.

The following day Pryth and I found ourselves outside the Air Commodore's office like a couple of naughty school boys. I can't remember which of us went in first, but when I went in and presented myself to the officer, he looked up and me and growled: 'So, you're another one of these ex-sergeant pilots who think they know it all,' and he proceeded to give me a rollicking for my carelessness.

I was, in fact, a pilot officer by then, but the RAF never let you forget where you had come from. Still, the Air Commodore had a point. We were experienced pilots and I shouldn't have had an accident. It was bloody careless and I didn't do it again. The prang I had with Pryth could have been a lot more serious and there were others who were not as fortunate as me.

On 1 May, shortly before Tunis was captured by the Allies, we were ordered to fly south to Kairouan then head west before returning home. It was a long way, but a good trip with a lot of cloud cover. Daniels managed to hit two German lorries, otherwise it was an uneventful operation. In the afternoon of that same day, we escorted a group of Hurricane bombers while they bombed Jefara station, but they bombed the wrong place behind the lines making us very unpopular with the Army.

As we headed back from this escort, Stone and Smith, who hadn't been with us long, flew too close to each other. Their wings clashed and they collided and spun into each other. The two aeroplanes went down separately and we hoped the pilots would return, but it was not to be.

Two days later another collision occurred between Wg Cdr Gilroy and a new flight lieutenant from 111 Squadron. The wing commander baled out at 800ft, but the other officer was killed. Even though the tide had turned and the Germans were in retreat, pilots were still getting killed.

The spring months were long drawn-out affairs for us. There was a pervading sense of monotony. Adverse weather conditions meant missions were still cancelled on a regular basis which left us with very little to do other than carry out tests on the aircraft. The evenings revolved around drinking cheap wine and beer when we could get it and playing cards. On one occasion, I was invited to 154 Squadron's mess where I bumped into a number of former pupils from my days at Llandow which provided a pleasant release from the mounting frustrations and irritations of squadron life.

The weather improved and we became active once again. By the end of spring we were now so close to the frontlines we could hear the bombing and the gunfire as the Germans slugged it out with the allies. The frontline couldn't have been more than 4 miles away from Beja. The air was just as busy. Hurricanes flew over, as did Mitchells and Spits in their dozens, giving cover as they headed to strafe the Germans at Mateur. The Hurricanes dropped 66,000lbs of bombs in just two days, causing immense damage to Tunis and the surrounding areas. Our patrols moved onto Cape Rosa, which was near the city where the lion's share of fighting was happening.

Pete Fowler and I were sent up to patrol the area. By now the rain had subsided to be replaced by scorching heat. It was a case of going from the sublime to the ridiculous. We undertook frequent patrols of the aerodrome which meant that two aircraft had to be on a constant state of readiness so they could be airborne at a moment's notice. I would taxi with another pilot to the end of Euston runway and sit in the cockpit waiting for someone to give me the signal to take off. The sun beat down on the perspex cockpit with an intensity I had never known. The temperatures would soar in excess of 100 degrees while we sat in the cockpits for anything up to half an hour at a time. Finally, the local ops centre would ring through with our orders. In the distance, by the dispersal tent, someone would emerge and fire a Very pistol into the air, similar to the ones used on ships and aircraft. That would be our signal to take off and carry out the patrol. But by then the atmosphere inside the Spits was sweltering and sweat streamed down our faces as wet palms tried to grasp the joystick. Our shirts would be soaked through and it was a relief to take off just so we could cool down.

I sat in the stifling atmosphere of the cockpit and waited until finally a red flash appeared in the sky and I could take off. Pete and I climbed to around 8,000ft and headed towards Tunis. We scoured the area but without success. There were no enemy aircraft in the vicinity as far as we could tell.

'Nothing doing here Pete, let's get back.'

'Copy that Jimmy.'

The two Spits turned towards Souk El Chemis. It was a perfect day for flying and visibility was excellent which is probably what enabled me to spot the Me109G so easily. He was about 200yd to my right and just below me. He must have had his finger in because he clearly wasn't aware of our presence as he made no attempt either to escape or challenge us. I was nearest to him so I radioed Pete.

'This one is mine, Pete.'

'Go ahead, Jimmy. I'll watch your back.'

In truth, I didn't have to do much other than just catch him up a bit. When I had him in my sights, I pressed the gun button and the orange-white tracer bullets streamed from my wings. It was probably the first indication the German had of my presence. Fool, why wasn't he checking his mirror? The bullets hit his fuselage and his nose dipped downwards. The aircraft fell into a steep dive. The pilot was out of control. In seconds he would crash into the ground. I felt a surge of success. It was my job to shoot down Germans. When I did, it meant I had done my job well.

'Well done, Jimmy, it doesn't look like you need any help from me,' Pete's voice came over the radio.

'Thanks, Pete, let's head back.'

I resisted the urge to go down and double check the fate of the Me109G. It was tempting to confirm this as a kill as opposed to a probable, but it was a dangerous distraction. Often pilots were so caught up making sure they could claim to have shot down an enemy aircraft that they were shot down themselves. You could never take your eye off the ball.

We returned to Souk El Chemis. I wandered back to the mess and found Daniels sitting on his bed filling out his log book. He looked up when he saw me come in.

'Good day, Jimmy?'

'Certainly was. I'm sure I got one this time, a 109G.'

'Excellent. The Germites must be running out of planes by now.'

I pulled up a chair and sat down next to Danny. We talked about my kill, but were interrupted, as we often were, by the sound of grunting and shuffling. We both looked down to see a pig come lumbering through the door heading in our direction.

'For Christ's sake, those bloody animals,' sighed Danny.

Then all of a sudden he pulled out his revolver, aimed it at the pig and fired. A shot rang out. The pig gave a short indignant squeal and keeled over. Its body twitched for some moments and then it went still. Blood oozed from a neat wound in its side. Dan and I looked, open-mouthed, at the dead pig.

'Bloody hell, Dan, you've shot it. What did you go and do that for?'

'I don't know. I didn't think I'd hit it. I was just messing about.'

'What the hell are we going to do with it now? And who is going to tell its owner?'

Word quickly spread throughout the base of the pig's assassination. A number of us gathered in the mess and debated what to do with the pig's carcass which was still lying on the floor and attracting attention from flies.

'Daniels, you'll have to do the decent thing and tell them you shot it by accident,' I suggested.

'Tell them you thought it was a spy.'

'Shut up, Chem.'

There was a knock at the mess door and we fully expected to see an angry farmer brandishing a rifle on our doorstep.

'OK, just tell him it attacked you and you killed it in self-defence.'

The door opened to reveal a young airman who I'd never seen before.

'What do you want? We're a bit busy at the moment,' Daniels said.

'I thought I might be able to help you boys out. I used to be a butcher.'

The airman was ushered into the room and the door quickly closed behind him. He took one look at the dead pig and grinned.

'No problem, just as long as I get a piece.'

'Of course.'

In no time at all, the man had skinned the animal and cut it up into a range of joints.

That night we sat down to a huge meal of the most succulent pork. We tucked into the juicy chops, although Daniels, the man responsible for our feast had failed to show.

'Perhaps he feels guilty,' said someone.

'Oh well, all the more for us.'

Just then the door to the mess opened and Daniels walked in, closely followed by the farmer and his wife who ran the pig farm next door. The couple nodded to the gathering and a couple of us offered a few 'Good evenings' in return, possibly to head off what clearly was going to be trouble.

Daniels showed the couple to two empty seats at the table and invited them to sit down. He piled two clean plates with the cooked pork and placed them in front of the farmer and his wife. If they knew they were eating their own livestock, they didn't show it. Without so much as a pause, they smiled and thanked Daniels before tucking into their feast.

Dan came and sat near me and Hussey who was staring open-mouthed at what had just taken place. But Daniels just shrugged and grinned at us.

'Well, it just seemed the decent thing to do. It's their pig after all.'

Unbeknown to us the tide of war was turning. The Germans were now surrounded on all sides. It was only a matter of time before Tunis fell, which meant it was now only a matter of time before I could go home.

Chapter Fifteen

MAY 1943 – TUNIS, NORTH AFRICA

On Thursday 6 May we were put on readiness. The skies were filled with the menacing drone of Allied bombers as they headed towards Tunis and Bizerta. I estimated that by 8 o'clock in the morning, somewhere in the region of 150 bombers had passed overhead. As I wrote in my diary, that many bombers were going to leave 'a hell of a mess' when they hit Tunis and the surrounding areas.

It turned out to be a busy day for 72 Squadron, too. We began by escorting a group of bombers on their operation to attack Tunis, the final stronghold of the Germans. It had been a beautiful city surrounded by orange groves. The air was thick with the smell of their blossom. It was here that our intelligence led us to believe that the Germans hid their tanks and aircraft and so it was here that we dived down onto the orchards and strafed the long lines of trees, hoping to hit the machinery concealed beneath their foliage. The resulting explosions revealed our information had been spot on and we had been successful in wiping out numerous enemy aircraft. Resistance from the Germans was waning.

We returned to base to refuel and take off again. Our second sortie yielded nothing more than some minor flak. On our third sortie we ran into twenty odd 109s, 7,000ft over Tunis. The enemy was always a formidable one, but by now it was becoming clear to us that there were not many German aces operating in North Africa. These pilots were inexperienced and not as well trained as those who we had fought at the beginning of the campaign. It made our job much easier and our tally rose rapidly as a result. Between us the squadron destroyed five aircraft and damaged three. None of us was hurt. On our fourth mission of that day, we bumped into a few 109s and recorded one damaged.

We returned to base having flown four separate missions in support of the land forces. I was exhausted by the day's exertions, but I found the energy to write in my diary that the Army 'can't moan' about Air Force protection now. And it had been incredible. The onslaught against the Germans was huge and relentless. It had been months in coming. We had spent long days doing very little, which had led to mind-numbing boredom and frustration with the whole campaign. We had bemoaned our tactics and were critical of our apparent lack of progress. But now the reasons became clear. Monty was biding his time, delaying his offensive until he could be assured that victory in North Africa would be his. When it came, the sheer scale of the attack was overwhelming and I felt like the smallest cog in a massive military machine that was unstoppable. Rommel, the German commander in North Africa, and his soldiers would not be able to repel us this time.

On Friday 8 May it came as no surprise to learn that the Allies had captured Tunis. Our job now was to shoot up the road between Tunis and Bizerta to prevent the Germans from evacuating the area. Tebourba was also captured. I took off at 18.18hrs to strafe the enemy soldiers who were in retreat and by doing so I noted in my diary that I would be 'reversing Dunkirk'. I was, of course, referring to the event three years previously where thousands of British soldiers were stranded on the beaches of Dunkirk sandwiched between the English Channel and the advancing German Army. Now it was the turn of the thousands of German soldiers who were caught between the British First Army charging forward from the west and Monty's Eighth Army, including my old school chum Ken Baker, who were attacking from the east.

The following day I took off at 07.00hrs to patrol the area. I came across a line of enemy lorries at Zaghouen. I lined them up in my sights and dived down towards them. There was surprisingly little flak around. I opened fire and sprayed the column of vehicles and men with bullets. A couple of trucks went up in flames.

It was a far cry from my first strafing expedition in Lannion in northern France two years previously with Athol Forbes. Then I had been tense with fear and anticipation and my only aim had been to go out as quickly as I could and get home intact. I didn't have time to line up my target and I had no idea if I had hit anything at all. Now the adrenalin still pumped through my veins and my overriding desire was to get out alive, but I was in control. I knew what I had to do and I did it. During the Battle of Britain I had been a novice, feeling my way, hoping I would survive. In North Africa it was a different matter. I was an experienced pilot. I knew the limitations of my aircraft. In combat situations, I had the upper hand. North Africa was my war.

From Zaghouen, we flew onto the port of Carthage, where enemy ships were waiting to collect the German soldiers, just as the British Army had evacuated our men from the beaches of Dunkirk in June 1940. Here at least the flak was intense with 109s and 190s weaving around the sky. I had to hand it to them, defeat may have been breathing down their necks, but some of the German pilots were determined not to give up without a fight.

I picked out a motor torpedo boat in the harbour and flew towards it. As it grew nearer I put the Spit into a slight dive. When I was nearly upon it, I opened fire and accelerated away from the port. The boat exploded and an enormous ball of flames shot up into the air. The noise was deafening and made me start. I could almost feel the heat from the explosion.

When we landed at the base at dusk, we counted the cost of the day to our own squadron. It was minimal. One of the squadron, a relatively new chap, had crash-landed at Medjez, but he was safe. Griffiths, another recent addition to the squadron, picked up a hole from all the flak, but had successfully nursed his Spit back to Souk El Chemis. The rest of us were fine. The damage to the enemy, on the other hand, had been immense. I was credited with destroying two trucks and killing ten soldiers. The squadron's tally was five kills and three damaged.

By now the RAF dominated the skies. What enemy aircraft were left became reluctant to engage in combat with us. Lying off the coast, the Navy continued to do its bit by shelling Tunis. Below us, the two sides fought it out in the streets of Tunis as the Germans tried to break their way through to their own ships moored off the Cape Bon peninsula, north of the city, so they could get out. By the time the fighting ended towards the second week in May, tens of thousands of Germans had been taken prisoner. Even we could tell it had been a triumph of military coordination that had routed the Germans from North Africa.

A sweep on 17 May over Tunis and El Aoinna aerodrome showed large numbers of damaged aeroplanes. Enemy activity in the skies above Tunis was scant and there was now a strong sense that it was all over bar sporadic gunfights in the city as some Germans decided to take a brave last stand. These petered out, as did the last remnants of resistance in the area north of Tunis. The Allies had won. We had done what we had come to do. And I had survived once again.

That afternoon I treated myself and travelled with a few others to Tebourba on the coast where we swam and lazed around on the dunes. The warm waters felt glorious against our unwashed bodies and our spirits were sky high. The fighting was over, for the time being.

Over the next few days, life in 72 Squadron became increasingly routine. We carried out a number of uneventful convoy patrols at La Sebala. We were still put on readiness at dawn or just after, but our forays into the skies yielded no evidence of enemy aircraft. When we did come across a stray 109 or 190, we were able to chase it away. It seemed the enemy's spirit, in the skies over North Africa at least, had been broken.

The squadron moved on from Souk El Chemis and took up residence at an aerodrome at La Sebala which was in good shape. It had previously been occupied by the Germans and its tarmac runways had been our primary targets just days before. Curiosity got the better of us and we toured the entire aerodrome. Pryth went into one of the hangars and shouted for us to join him.

Inside we found a brand spanking new 109 sitting in a dispersal bay. I ran my hand down across its sleek body and over the iron cross emblazoned on its side. It was the closest I had ever been to an enemy aircraft. It was a beautiful machine, but in the end it was no match for the Spitfire.

With fighting now confined to Zaghouan, some 60 miles south of Tunis, we pilots had time on our hands. Scrase, who had joined the squadron some weeks earlier, Chem, a few others and I decided to investigate the city that we had patrolled for so many months. We managed to 'borrow' a Jeep (I have no idea where from) and began our own victory tour of Tunis. Scrase had scrounged a bottle of whisky which we took in turns to swig from. It didn't quench our thirst, but it made us merry enough until it was hard to distinguish if we were intoxicated by victory or the alcohol.

As we drove through the streets of Tunis, the sun beat down on us and the temperature hit 100 deg F. The damage to the city was immense. It was incredible to see what the bombers had done. There was really very little left. Entire streets had disappeared completely leaving behind piles of dusty rubble and the occasional wall on which pictures of family life in happier times still rested. Elsewhere buildings were pockmarked with bullets as the two sides had battled for dominance.

Despite the devastation, and undoubtedly the deaths that had occurred over the last few months, the Tunisian people turned out in their droves to wave and cheer us on. Their spirit was indomitable.

As we rounded the corner of a street on the outskirts of the city, we were confronted by an incredible sight that silenced our carousing in an instant. Scrase stopped the Jeep and we all got out. In front of us was a prisoner-of-war camp. It was a huge compound hemmed in by thick curls of barbed wire that stretched as far as the eye could see. Inside, row upon row of defeated German soldiers sat cross-legged in the heat and dust in eerie silence. Some of them looked up at us as we approached. Others stared at the ground. Their faces were expressionless. Their uniforms were ripped and dirty. They looked unkempt and crushed. In among them I knew there would be Luftwaffe pilots.

We stared at them. So, this was the enemy. This is what it had all been about. These were the people I had fought against in the skies over Kent. These were the people who had killed my friends and my compatriots. These were the people who wanted to invade my homeland. Suddenly they didn't seem quite so formidable anymore. I took a swig from the bottle and said out loud to no one in particular: 'I don't know whether I should hate them or feel pity for them.'

My comment broke the silence and sparked a debate in which everyone aired their personal feelings about the enemy. On balance I think I felt sorry for them. They were sons, fathers and brothers, just like us.

We drove away from the camp and continued our exploration of Tunis. Scrase, who joined the Air Force after the Battle of Britain, was a young pilot officer. He spoke fluent French which he now put to the test as he pulled up next to a couple of schoolgirls and fell into an easy conversation with them.

The two girls invited us to their house to have a meal with them and their parents by way of thanks for what we had done. It was a remarkable act of generosity. The Tunisians had suffered a great deal themselves, but still wanted to prove they were excellent hosts and insisted on sharing what little food they had with us. We accepted their invitation and enjoyed a superb meal with their families.

On 20 May Tunis played host to an official victory parade. While one of the other squadrons provided the spectacle of a low flypast, I remained on readiness and carried out a couple of patrols over Tunis to make sure no Germans crashed the party.

By now it was clear that our job had been done. A sense of boredom began to seep into the camp while we waited to move onto the next stage of the war, whatever that was going to be. We spent days hanging around and rumours of us returning to England began to circulate. Several members of the squadron had already been told they were going, including Chem.

In early June, I headed to Constantine to find out my fate. There I learnt that I would be recommended as a flight commander in the coastal defence squadron which I was more than pleased with. Ironically I had wanted to join the Coastal Command way back in 1940 when I was at Cranfield. It seemed now I was finally going to get the chance.

At the end of the month my turn had come and I was called into Air Commodore Cross's office. I didn't know where I was going, but I knew it meant that I would be posted and would not be staying with the squadron as they pushed up into Sicily and Italy.

The Air Commodore's tone was somewhat different from the one he had used when I crashed into Pryth's Spitfire earlier in the year.

'Flg Off Corbin, you have notched up 450 operational flying hours which is an impressive record for any man and one you should be proud of. You're more than ready to be given command of your own squadron here in North Africa, if you wish. The other alternative is that you could return to England and take over a squadron there. Do you have any preference as to where you'd like to go?'

If I stayed in North Africa then the next stop would have been Sicily as the Allies pushed up through Italy and on into Europe. I had already given this some thought and I had decided that I didn't want to be bringing up the rear. When the time came to launch an invasion of France and reclaim the territory from the Nazis, I wanted to be leading from the front.

'Sir, I would like to return to Britain and take up a squadron there, if you wouldn't mind.'

'So be it, Flg Off Corbin.' Perhaps he sensed that if I returned to England I wouldn't be going back on operations, but he said no more and I left.

My final days in North Africa wound down. I barely wrote anything in my diary because there was nothing to report. My time was taken up swimming in the beautiful Mediterranean and playing poker in the evenings which was pleasantly uneventful.

Other squadron members began to leave. Chem went to Gibraltar and then on home. Then after several orders to standby and be ready to leave followed by several cancellations, I boarded the SS *Samaria* and finally departed the shores of North Africa on 28 June 1943, eight months after I had arrived.

The journey to Gibraltar was excellent. I hit my poker form on that trip and I won the incredible sum of £1,200, mainly from the Americans. After a brief two-day stop at Gibraltar we sailed on to England, when not only were we attacked several times en route, but worse still, my form deserted me and I lost the entire £1,200 I had won on the first leg of the sea journey.

We docked in England early in the morning of 24 July 1943. I was given a travel permit which took me back to Maidstone where I enjoyed a spell of leave. It was great to be home, but in truth I found the little terraced house on Bower Street quite claustrophobic after the RAF. As a result I spent most of my time amusing myself in Maidstone.

I had been on leave for several weeks when I received the telegram telling me to report to RAF Eshott in Northumberland. When I arrived my spirits sank as I discovered that I was destined to become an instructor once again at an operational training unit. This time I was in the gunnery flight. The only upside was that Bob Doe was in charge of gunnery and I was second in command. It was a privilege to have him as my commanding officer. He was one of the highest scoring aces of the Battle of Britain and a superb pilot.

In some ways it was disappointing not to be given my own squadron to lead, but it didn't happen and I have long since learnt not to regret things in life, but just to get on with it.

I exchanged my beautiful Spit IX for a jaded war-weary Mk V which had been handed down to the OTU by one of the fighter squadrons. I was instructing in a Miles Master II and spent my days showing the young pilots how to shoot at a drogue, as it was being dragged along by another aircraft which was generally flown by a very nervous instructor.

One day I received some surprising news. The day began as so many others had at Eshott. I strolled out of the instructors' hut and approached the gaggle of young men kitted out in their flying gear. I introduced myself to my class. By this time the RAF was awash with pilots who now came from as far afield as Canada to train to become fighter pilots. Their training proceeded at a far more leisurely pace than mine had and they were rarely posted on to a squadron until they completed at least three months at the OTU. It was a far cry from my days at Hawarden when I just managed to scrape together twenty-nine hours flying time on Spitfires in just twelve days at OTU, before being dispatched to fight in the Battle of Britain.

I began my usual spiel. 'Right, this is what we're going to do. The drogue will be towed by the Martinet which is over there. Make sure you always attack the drogue as you approach from the opposite direction. Remember your speed will be much greater than a towing aircraft. When you get yourself into the right position, turn into the drogue. Make sure you get slightly above it so you can fire from an angle of about 40 degrees to about 20 degrees. And for God's sake don't hit the aircraft. Any questions?'

This manoeuvre was known as a quarter attack. Of course, it never worked in combat unless you found yourself in a similar position above the aircraft you wanted to shoot down. But that was the advice I was told to give and this I did, day in and day out.

The exercise proceeded thankfully without mishap and we finished the day and went our separate ways. I walked into the instructor's hut and one of the others handed me *The Daily Telegraph*.

'Here, Jimmy, you kept that a bit quiet, didn't you?'

I frowned at him and looked at the paper which was full of columns of names and I ran my finger down one line until I came across the name: W.J. Corbin. It was under the section headed 'Distinguished Flying Cross'. I had been awarded the DFC for my services in North Africa. Before I left Tunis, Bobby Oxspring had mentioned to me that he was going to recommend me for a DFC, but after I returned home I thought nothing more of it until I saw it in the newspaper that day.

Shortly afterwards I was invited to Buckingham Palace to receive my medal. I travelled down to London from Eshott and I was allowed to take one member of the family with me so I asked my youngest sister, Lily, if she would like to join me.

My family were proud of my achievement although I never discussed my experiences with them. It was a bit like Sir Alan Cobham's Flying Circus. They really wouldn't have understood. Only those who lived through it knew what it was to experience extreme fear at being attacked and extreme joy at being spared. How do you begin to explain that?

We went to Buckingham Palace where King George VI presented me with my medal. It was a very moving moment and I felt extremely proud to be in the presence of the King. The DFC set me apart from other pilots. It was recognition that my contribution made a difference. It gave me a feeling that I had done something extra, something that was a little bit special. Without it I was just another pilot. I can't deny, to be awarded the DFC gave me a lot of personal satisfaction.

Afterwards I returned to Eshott where life continued. It was a world away from North Africa and the fighting, but I tried to look on the bright side and, as always, it had its advantages. For a start there were women on the base. One day I was taxiing along the runway when one of the WAAF girls pulled out in front of me. She was driving a yellow peril. A lot of the transport was driven by WAAFs and it was their job to avoid the aircraft. This time she got in the way when I was taxiing and we crashed. I gave her a bollocking which developed into a conversation and I ended up asking her out. She was the daughter of a farmer and I went to her house for evening meals and a bit of snogging.

In June 1944, a year after I had returned from North Africa, the D-Day landings took place. The Allies made an all-out assault on northern France and the fight to liberate Europe once and for all was on. But I was still well away from the action. With this latest offensive, I was half expecting to be given command of a squadron, but it was not to be. Instead 11 Armament Practice Camp (APC) at Fairwood Common near Swansea was beckoning me and that is where I finished the war.

On balance, I suppose I was relieved not to be operational any more. Of course, being in the thick of the action does have its thrills, but these were tempered by moments of utter terror. My time at Eshott and Fairwood may have had its dull moments, but at least I now had a good chance of living. For me, the war had finished, so to speak.

My job at Fairwood was to instruct the pilots who were taking a break from squadrons that had been involved in the invasion of France. For them it was a refresher course which involved flying in the morning, with ground firing practice and instruction. The afternoons would be free and their favourite hobby was to take a group of WAAFs down to the beach.

As a chief instructor, Fairwood was rather pleasant for me too. I had my very own beautiful Spitfire Mk IX with the letters 'JC' inscribed on its body. I had the authority to fly to France to visit a squadron and could tell the ground crew to 'Get the aircraft ready' and I would be away.

When I wasn't teaching some of the instructors, Gooch, Farmer, Hulbert and I used to go into Swansea for a night out or to have a quiet drink in a pub near to Fairwood. It was here that I met Joan. She was a flying officer at Fairwood. She was good looking, slim and for a while, she became the love of my life. We had a great time together and, for a time, I thought she would become my wife. She certainly eased the dullness of instructing others to fly, day in and day out.

Then one day the war ended. Europe had already fallen to the Allies, but the Japanese held on for several months more until the Americans dropped the A-bombs and they surrendered. There was a huge global sigh of relief that the war was finally over. I was sitting in the instructor's hut on the airfield at Fairwood when the news came through. A chap, I can't recall who it was, turned to me and said: 'Here, Jimmy, let's have a final beat up of the airfield. Just for a laugh.'

He was referring to the practice of taking an aircraft up and swooping down low over the airfield. But I had decided long ago that I wasn't going to take any chances because that's when you got killed, when you were being silly and had your finger in.

I turned to him and said, 'Not bloody likely, I'm going up the mess for a drink.'

The end of the war in 1945 signalled the end of my service as a volunteer reservist in the RAF. So much had happened to me since I joined in 1938: the snow fights at RAF Burnaston, the parties at Biggin Hill, seeing Chem shot down, the rain and mud in North Africa. It had been a crazy roller-coaster of a ride. Now I had to decide if I wanted to get off. Bizarrely it was a difficult decision to make. The way had been horrific, but fun. It had been terrifying, but hilarious. It had been my life. In the end I knew what I wanted to do. I applied for a permanent commission. I was a rare breed among pilots in that I was not only a general duties pilot, but I had also completed an armament course which made me valuable property to the RAF.

Several months later I received a letter from the Air Ministry telling me that I had been accepted. This meant that I would finally shed my reserve status, which I had held throughout the war, and become a regular member of the Royal Air Force. The RAF was moving towards an exciting new stage of rocket technology. A great career was waiting for me.

The offer of a commission came through while I was at Fairwood and I went to visit Joan, my gorgeous girlfriend, to tell her the good news. I was stunned that she did not share my enthusiasm.

'Darling, I don't want you to join up. I don't want to be a pilot's widow.'

It was the same argument I had used with Audrey all those years before when I was training to be a pilot in Derby.

'But the war is over, Joan. I'm not going to die.'

'You know as well as I do that you don't have to be in a dogfight to get killed in one of those things.'

I deliberated over whether or not to stay. I couldn't ignore Joan's pleas. Like a fool I listened to her and I turned down the commission and left the RAF for good.

In January 1946, my demob papers came through and Flt Lt W.J. Corbin, as I now was, became plain Jimmy Corbin once more. My demob number was 18. We were demobbed in sequence so I was one of the first to go, because I had been one of the first to be called up. It was a case of early in and early out. My time as a fighter pilot was over. Shortly afterwards, my love affair with Joan also ended. In March 1946, more than a year after I had listened to her pleas and decided to leave the RAF, she told me she had fallen for someone else and she left me.

As I prepared to leave Fairwood for good, I had a very strange experience. I had many close shaves during the war, but there is only one occasion when I was flying that a real anxiety pervaded my whole being and a sense of foreboding swept over me. Ironically it happened far away from any combat situation.

I was flying my own Spitfire, 'JC', and was taking her up for a height test. We had just reached 41,000ft which was the highest I had ever flown. At that height the clouds, let alone the earth, are a long way down. Bright, almost ethereal sun streamed into the cockpit and warmed my face. Above me was just a wide expanse of blue skies. It was beautiful and I felt lulled by the sensation of being miles from the ground. Suddenly a wave of not quite panic, but certainly discomfort and apprehension, washed over me. I couldn't understand what had bothered me so much, particularly as I wasn't in any danger. The plane was flying like a dream. There was no chance of bumping into enemy aircraft up here. But something told me that I was too high up. I was too close to heaven, too close for my liking, anyway.

Without a moment's hesitation, I rolled the Spit over and we went into a gentle dive until the altimeter touched 30,000ft and I knew I was in more familiar territory. I levelled out again and flew back to Fairwood. To this day I cannot explain what came over me. I just looked up at the great blue wastes of sky that had swallowed me up and said to myself,

'That was just a bit too close, Jimmy, old boy. It's time to go down.'

Chapter Sixteen

FULL CIRCLE

I left the RAF and returned to my home town of Maidstone to consider my future on civvy street. I was sure of one thing: I didn't want to return to teaching. The reason for this was mainly pecuniary. I left the forces with ambitions of earning £1,000 a year, but with a teachers' salary at £350 a year there was no way I was going to achieve this in the classroom. I was considering a number of job offers, one of which was working for Halladlo which supplied equipment to hauliers, when I received a telephone call towards the end of 1945 which changed the course of my life irrevocably.

My mother answered the telephone. She nodded solemnly into the receiver and then handed it to me.

It was Mr Probert, the head-teacher of Collier Road School.

'Hello Mr Corbin. Mr Probert here. I am sorry to bother you. I heard that you were back in Maidstone and I was wondering if you would like your old job back.'

I was flattered that he wanted me back at the helm, but my mind was set on a career outside education.

'Thank you for the offer, Mr Probert, but I am considering other options at the moment.'

There was a pause at the other end of the telephone.

'The thing is Jimmy, things have got a bit lax around here lately and we could really do with someone who's good on discipline and can keep the boys in line. We also need people qualified to teach in the classroom as well as the workshops.'

I detected a certain desperation in his voice, but I decided to stand firm. The thought of being stuck in a classroom held no attraction for me. Although I was qualified to do so, I found the experience boring and restrictive and not on a par with the enjoyment of working in the school's workshops.

'I understand what you're saying, Mr Probert, but I've made up my mind.'

'I understand, have you started your new job yet?'

'Well no, not yet.'

'How about you just come in for a term to help us out a bit? It would make all the difference to us.'

The slight tone of desperation in his voice weakened my resolve. Also, I knew that Mr Probert's son, Gurney Oliver Probert, who had been a major in the army, had been killed in action in 1944 and I couldn't help but feel sorry for him.

'OK, I'll come back, just for one term, just to help sort the school out.'

And so I returned to Collier Road School as a teacher. The old place had taken quite a hammering in the war. Two of the workshops had been destroyed in the bombing. As the term wore on, other teachers who had been called up to fight began to drift back, including Sam Smart who I had bumped into in quite a surreal moment in North Africa.

Soon after my return, it became clear that Mr Probert was right. Discipline was lax. A problem I soon sorted out. When you have faced the Hun at 30,000ft, a bunch of hormonal teenage boys holds few fears. One morning the boys were practising countermarching in the hall. They were mucking about and even foolishly began to take the mickey out of me. I identified the ringleader, a boy by the name of English, and clouted him hard and then turned to the rest of the group who fell instantly silent and looked away. I glared at them for a few moments.

'Any one else want to play?'

Needless to say, no one took me up on my offer. Some years later, the boy I had batted approached me, just before he was due to leave the school. He took my hand and shook it hard.

'I just wanted to say thank you, Sir.'

'What for?'

'For straightening me out. That time in the gym hall.'

It was the one and only time I struck a pupil. It was the one and only time I had to.

Somehow my one term at Collier Road stretched to ten years. Plans to earn £1,000 a year after the war faded as my temporary position took on an air of permanence. Although I returned to my pre-war occupation as a schoolteacher, I still felt a faint pang of wanting to soar above the clouds. I began to yearn for that wonderful sensation of flying an aeroplane and I ached to get back up into the air, to feel the power of a Spitfire at my command and the pleasure of having the whole sky as my playground. I had spent so long training to become a pilot it seemed a shame to waste the skills that I had had to endure so much to acquire.

I also had some unfinished business that I had to attend to. Aerobatics remained uncharted territory for me. I had never been taught. From time to time I found myself having to perform the odd slow roll, but when I emerged from the manoeuvre I was invariably all over the bloody place and ended up cursing the fact I couldn't do it properly. For me there was little consolation in the irony that I had flown through the Battle of Britain and the Battle of Tunis. I had instructed others in the art of combat flying, but to my embarrassment I couldn't do anything fancier with an aircraft than a shaky roll. I had long admired pilots like Chas Charnock who could roll a Spit with breathtaking ease. I have no doubt that I would have been a better fighter pilot if I had been instructed in aerobatics. Now I just wanted to learn to do it properly.

In the end there was nothing for it, but to rejoin the RAF Reserve. My plan was to qualify as an instructor and for that I had to master aerobatics. The letter of acceptance came through telling me to report to Rochester aerodrome which had been the scene of my first tentative steps as a young pilot back in 1938, almost ten years previously. This time I was part of No. 24 Reserve Flying School. I had finished the war in the hard-earned rank of flight lieutenant, but the war was over and so too was my official standing in the RAF. Ranks held by those of us in the Reserves were known as war substantive and were removed from us once the war was over.

On the day I was due to return to flying, I decided to treat myself with a slap-up lunch at my local, the Star Hotel in Maidstone. Harry, the landlord, served me up a beautiful lobster salad for the princely sum of 5s. It was a far cry from that morning in 1938 when I reported to airfield with a mixture of fear and excitement at the prospect of my first ever flight. Then I was racked with anxiety that my fear of heights would overwhelm me and put paid to my dream of becoming a pilot.

After lunch I caught the Maidstone and District bus for 1s 1d to Rochester aerodrome. It still had the same grass airstrips from when I was training back in 1938. Rochester aerodrome had been spared by the war, mainly because it was not a combat base. Instead it was used by Short Brothers, makers of the flying boats and Stirling bombers, to test aircraft.

The bus dropped me off outside the airfield. I had already been told I would be going up in a Tiger Moth so I quickly identified the small craft and headed over to where it was parked to wait for my instructor. The Tiger Moth was built by de Havilland. It stood about 8ft 10in tall and had a wingspan of around 29ft. Its maximum speed was about 109mph and it was not a patch on the Spitfire. During the war it had been used mainly to train pilots.

Before long a figure emerged from the instructor's hut and began walking towards me. I realised with delight that it was dear old Vic Arnold, my very first instructor. I couldn't quite believe it. It felt like a lifetime has passed since our last meeting. I hadn't seen Vic since I was mobilised and left Rochester aerodrome in 1939. He hadn't changed a bit. He still had his dark moustache and he still looked the dapper man that he was. We shook hands warmly.

'It's good to see you, Jimmy. You came through it then.'

'Just about, Vic,' I replied.

'Well, you'll have to tell me all about it.'

'Not much to tell, really.'

Vic, it transpired, had remained a flying instructor throughout the war teaching young pilots like me. His superb flying skills were too precious to waste in combat especially as the RAF was short of instructors at the start of war and, as far as I was concerned, they didn't come much better than Vic Arnold.

Vic quizzed me on my war exploits and listened to my tales of the Battle of Britain and North Africa with interest. He seemed particularly impressed to hear that I had been awarded the DFC for my efforts. When I finished he frowned slightly and said to me, 'Well, Jimmy, you're obviously a very experienced fighter pilot, I don't think there's really much I can teach you.'

But there was. There remained an outstanding issue for me: aerobatics. I wanted to learn to do it properly and as I was going to become an instructor I had to get to grips with it. But there was more to it than that. I had always found a joy in doing things properly and flying was no exception.

'Well, Vic, that's where you're wrong. The truth is I'm not that experienced. I can't do aerobatics. I can just about manage a couple of ham-fisted rolls, but I'm all over the bloody place. You see, I was never taught properly and so I never learnt.'

Vic threw his head back and laughed.

'How the hell did you survive?'

I shrugged my shoulders.

'Just muddled through, I suppose. The point is Vic, I want you to teach me aerobatics.'

He paused and then said, 'Right, no time like the present. Let's get in. Oh, and make sure you do your straps up tightly.'

I climbed into the aeroplane. The champagne cork that I had kept throughout the war and which now resided permanently in my flying jacket pressed against my chest as I fastened my straps.

Vic and I took off and soared high above the aerodrome. With no hood, the wind whistled passed me, drowning out the sound of the aeroplane's engines. Our height barely got above 2,000ft. Our speed was little more than 70mph, closer to the Magisters I had flown than to the Spitfires which regularly topped 400mph, but it was still great to be back in the air once more.

We flew towards Gravesend which was only about 10 miles away. When we reached the town, the plane banked slightly and we began the return journey. By now I was beginning to think it was all very pleasant, but not very challenging. In truth, this was a bit basic for me as I was more than capable of handling a Moth.

Then suddenly the plane flipped over and we were travelling upside down. The straps seemed to strain at keeping me in my seat. Blood rushed to my head. I looked down and realised that nothing stood between me and the county of Kent. This was the first time I had experienced negative G. In all my flying experience, I had only to deal with positive G forces. Now it felt like my whole body was being dragged back down to earth. We stayed in this position all the way back to Rochester, gradually losing height. As the aerodrome came into view Vic righted the aircraft in one smooth roll and we were upright once again. My body composed itself as Vic brought the Tiger Moth into land. We taxied along the runway, just as we had done all those years before.

The Moth came to a standstill. Vic unfastened his straps and hauled himself out of the aircraft in one easy move. My movements were less nimble as I was still slightly disorientated. Finally, I jumped down from the aircraft to where Vic stood waiting patiently for me to join him.

He grinned at me. The years of combat experience melted away in an instant and, once again, Vic Arnold was my flying instructor and I was his pupil.

'Right, Jimmy,' he said, 'that was your first lesson.'

EPILOGUE

In 1955 I received a letter from the Queen thanking me for my contribution in the service of my country, but adding that the RAFVR would no longer be requiring my services.

The last aircraft I flew was a de Havilland Chipmunk on 19 March 1952. The Chipmunk was a light aircraft, a monoplane, unlike the Tiger Moth. It handled beautifully and was great for aerobatics which I had become quite proficient at. I knew my days as a pilot were over and so I made the most of my last flight. I could have stayed up there for ever, but I knew all good things must come to an end.

For the final time I collected my flying log which I had kept religiously from my first flight to my last. Vic Arnold, my instructor, had noted in it that my flying was now 'above average' which made me smile. My final appraisal was a considerable improvement on 'average, with a tendency to be careless' which I had received back in 1939. So, some things had improved, I thought ruefully.

For some time afterwards I missed flying dreadfully. I missed that feeling of absolute freedom and exhilaration. I missed the technical challenge of raising a machine off the ground and keeping aloft through my own abilities. Not everyone can do that and do it well. Although my career as a pilot ended in 1952, those farfetched dreams I had dared have as a working-class boy from Maidstone had become a reality and for that I will be forever grateful. I had realised my ambition and there are not many in this life who are given the opportunity to do just that. Sometimes I muse over the kind of career I might have had if I had remained in the RAF. But life is far too short to dwell on what might have been. Time moves on and it has been a long, long while since I yearned to be up among the clouds again.

At the end of the war, I resumed my second joy which was teaching and continued my career in education. After ten wonderful years at Collier Road School in Northfleet, I got a job at Maidstone Technical School where I had once been a pupil myself, as well as a laboratory assistant when I was training to become a teacher. I retired as a senior master at the school in 1980 and have spent the last twenty or so years improving my golf handicap.

After Joan left me in 1945, I resigned myself to life as a bachelor and remained footloose for nearly ten more years. Then, at the age of 37, I met Jeanne. She walked into the Queen's Head in Maidstone. She had been to the hairdressers that day and her hairdresser had brought her to my local pub for a drink. She was a local girl although our paths had never crossed before. Tall, slim and remarkably graceful, she instantly caught my eye. Her blonde hair was piled high on her head in the style of the day. She was a strikingly attractive woman and I made it my business to engage her in conversation.

Jeanne was and still is a beautiful woman and the object of many men's desires. I was honoured when she agreed to marry me in March 1955. Alf McDermott, an old chum of mine, agreed to be my best man and we were married that year. Jeanne and I had three children who have now all grown up and left home. I still live in Maidstone, my home town. Why would I live anywhere else? My house is not far from 133 Bower Street which I bought for my sister Lily in 1955 for £250. It remained in our family until she died several years ago.

My parents both lived until their eighties. I never did discuss the war with them. My eldest sister, the wonderfully gifted Elsie, finally found her niche in life. In later years, she became a Justice of the Peace as well as a school governor.

Chem remained a close and dear friend of mine until his death in 1994. He stayed in the RAF and became a wing commander before leaving the service in the late 1970s. He and Eileen had two sons. Then Eileen fell ill with a degenerative disease and Chem nursed her until she died. He was totally devoted to her and when died several years later. I am sure it was of a broken heart.

Owen Hardy, another dear friend from 72 Squadron, now lives in New Zealand and we exchange letters from time to time. Pryth, who was such great company in North Africa and who I pranged on landing at Souk El Chemis, lost his life in June 1943 during the invasion of Sicily. The Spitfire he was flying was hit and he baled out, landing safely in the water, but dear old Pryth couldn't swim and he drowned. Daniels, the red-headed Scotsman, survived the war, as did Bobby Oxspring, the veteran of the Battle of Britain and North Africa, who went on to have a highly successful career with the RAF where he rose to the rank of group captain. He died of cancer a couple of years ago. I believe Chas Charnock ran a successful garage after the war and led a comfortable life. The Souk Al Arba boys met regularly for reunions at the RAF Officers' Club in London for many years. It was an opportunity to discuss the old days and remember those who didn't make it through. There are still a few of us left, but we no longer meet.

Other than Bobby Oxspring, I never saw any of my old friends from 66 Squadron again. I learnt that Johnny Kendal, or 'Durex' as we called him was killed after he baled out of his aircraft in May 1942, shortly after completing his chapter for *Ten Fighter Boys*. He was defending a convoy of British merchant ships on the North Russian route. His last act was to give the position of four German airmen whom he had seen climbing into a dinghy after he had shot down their Ju88. Bogle, the scruffy young man who survived several crash landings and was another contributor to the book, lost his life in a flying accident in February 1942. Athol Forbes came through the war. His tally at the end of the war was seven confirmed kills and one probable. I never found out if Athol realised his writing ambitions. Dizzy Allen, on the other hand, also survived and wrote about his experiences in a book, *Battle for Britain*, published in 1973. Ken Baker, my old school friend, survived his time with Monty in North Africa and returned home to Maidstone.

After the war I thought a lot about those poor men who were little more than boys and whose short lives had ended so violently and so abruptly. But it is now sixty years since the war ended. Much has happened to me in those intervening years and my experiences of combat hold an ever decreasing significance in my life. Maddening as it may sound, the passage of time has not yielded any satisfying answers to some of the questions I sometimes asked myself back then and have sometimes been asked of me.

I don't know how hundreds of us managed to climb into our aeroplanes time after time to fly straight into the face of the enemy, never knowing if it was to be our last day on earth. We just did. I do believe that a few people were exceptionally brave and they took the war to the enemy. But for most of us, the truth was we were prepared to do a job, but we were not as bold as those few. That said, we certainly weren't cowards either. It was just that we didn't like getting hurt. I used to box a bit when I was a schoolboy and I knew what it felt like to get hurt and I didn't like it.

So what was it that got me through? I don't know. In the final analysis, I think it was just luck. I still have that old champagne cork that I picked up at a party in Acklington – somewhere.

APPENDIX

THE AUTHOR'S RAF POSTINGS 1939–45

I WAR COURSE
Burnaston, Derbyshire, 1939–40

14 FTS/14 AFTS
Kinloss, Moray, April 1940
Cranfield, Bedfordshire, June 1940

7 OTU
Hawarden, Cheshire, August 1940

66 SQUADRON
Kenley, Surrey, 28 August 1940

ATTACHED 610 SQUADRON
Acklington, Northumberland,
    10 September 1940

66 SQUADRON
Gravesend, Kent, 24 October 1940
West Malling, Kent, 30 October
    –7 November 1940
Biggin Hill, Kent, 7 November 1940
    –26 February 1941
Exeter, Devon, 26 February–27 April
    1941

Perranporth, Cornwall,
    27 April–September 1941

53 OTU
Llandow, Glamorgan, September 1941

Gibraltar, August 1942

72 SQUADRON
Souk al Arba, 20 November 1942
Souk el Chemis, 15 January 1943
Tunis, May 1943

11 ARMAMENT PRACTICE CAMP (APC)
Fairwood Common, Glamorgan, April
    1944

GUNNERY OFFICER
Culmhead, Devon, June 1944

OC NO 1 FLIGHT, 3 APC
Southend, Essex
Gyro gun sight course

THE AUTHOR'S FLYING LOG BOOK EXTRACT
72 SQUADRON, SOUK AL ARBA, TUNISIA, 1942

1. PILOTS' SCORES, NOVEMBER–DECEMBER 1942

19 Nov	Plt Off Hardy	Me109 confirmed
25 Nov	WO Charnock	Me109 confirmed

	Flg Off Cox	Me109 probable
	Plt Off Robertson	Me109 destroyed
	Plt Off Daniels	Me109 destroyed
	Sqn Ldr Oxspring	Me109 probable
	Plt Off Lowe	Ju88 destroyed
	Flt Lt Krohn ⎫ Sgt Frampton ⎭	Ju88 destroyed
	Flt Lt Krohn	Ju88 damaged
26 Nov	Flg Off Cox	Me109 destroyed
	Sgt Hussey	Me109 destroyed
	Sgt Fowler ⎫ Self ⎭	Me109 destroyed
27 Nov	WO Charnock	Me109 destroyed
		Me109 probable
	Flg Off Cox	Me109 probable
	Sgt Hussey	Me109 probable
	Plt Off Robertson	Ju88 destroyed
29 Nov	Flt Lt Krohn	Ju88 destroyed
	Flg Off Cox	Ju88 destroyed
1 Dec	Plt Off Lewis	M202 damaged
3 Dec	Plt Off Malan ⎫ Plt Off Robertson ⎬ Flg Off Hardy ⎭	Fw190 destroyed
4 Dec	Flg Off Cox	Me109 destroyed
	Plt Off Le Cheminant	Me109 destroyed
	Plt Off Daniels	Me109 destroyed

2. THE AUTHOR'S OWN SCORE

1941

He111 probable
Me109 destroyed

1942

Me109 destroyed (shared with Sgt Fowler)
Me109 probable
Me109 damaged
Fw190 damaged
Me109 damaged

2 petrol lorries, 1 lorry and WT damaged
2 lorries damaged shared with boys

1 MTB type sunk
2 vessels on fire
power barge damaged
2 lorries, approx 10 Germites [sic]
M202 damaged
2 lorries, damaged
1 lorry and trailer

3. SQUADRON CASUALTIES, NOVEMBER 1942–APRIL 1943

1942

27 Nov	Lowe, Flg Off John, killed (Medjez-el-Bab War Cemetery, Tunisia)
1 Dec	Lewis, Plt Off, injured
5 Dec	Browne, Sgt Francis Merer, killed (Beja War Cemetery, Tunisia)
	Mottram, Sgt Alan, killed (Medjez-el-Bab War Cemetery, Tunisia)
	Macdonald, Plt Off John William, RAAF, killed (Malta Memorial)
18 Dec	Charnock, WO, injured
20 Dec	Robertson, Plt Off, injured

1943

5 Jan	Dewar, Sgt, PoW
26 Jan	Stone, Plt Off Gerald Philip MID, killed (Tabarka Ras Rajel War Cemetery, Tunisia)
	Smith, Sgt Arthur Ronald Peter, killed (Tabarka Ras Rajel War Cemetery, Tunisia)
25 Feb	Passmore, Sgt A.E., killed (Medjez-el-Bab War Cemetery, Tunisia)
22 Apr	Hunter, W.O., missing
26 Apr	Malan, Plt Off Francis, killed (Massicault War Cemetery, Tunisia)
28 Apr	Smith, Sgt (Aus), missing

(Extracted from the flying log book of Jimmy Corbin, with additional burial details added by the editor)

INDEX